Chestnut Review

VOLUME 6
2024-2025

Chestnut Review
Ithaca, New York
https://chestnutreview.com

Chestnut Review appears four times a year online, in January, April, July, and October, and once per year in print in July.

ISSN 2688-0350 (online)
ISSN 2688-0342 (print)
ISBN 978-1-965158-17-3

Chestnut Review

CONTENTS

Year Six in Review

Every year at about our anniversary on May 15th, time seems to speed up. We only just closed issue 6:4, the last of year six, but already 7:1 is in the bag, pieces set to go, and we are reading for 7:2 in Autumn. The sensation is one of hardly having a breather between the end of one volume and the beginning—or quickly the half-way point—of another. But that's the task we've set ourselves, and we wouldn't change it for the world, because it lets us live in these moments full of literature and art. Not a bad place to be, especially these days, and one we often cherish as we go about our work.

We returned to the AWP conference in Los Angeles in March and again had an incredible time visiting with friends, contributors, readers, and staff who made the journey. We invited independent literary magazines and presses to join us in the second annual "Literary Scavenger Hunt," which added a few new participating mags and presses and was again a great success. Participants were invited to visit fourteen different booths and/or tables to have their cards marked before entering them for a chance to win one of eight $50 prizes. LA also allowed us to have our first-ever offsite event: partnering with *Muleskinner Journal*, *Black Fork Review*, and Ashland Poetry Press, we packed a room at the historic Central Library with over 60 people and watched as our newest chapbook authors Maya Cheav, Katie Kemple, and Mario Aliberto III gave stellar readings from their works.

Definitely a highlight of our year was the production of our first-ever artbook. We gathered 77 visual artists from our first five years of issues and invited 36 collaborators and friends to create new ekphrastic pieces of writing based on the art. This project was embraced with such joy that the daunting task of assembling all the visual and textual material was a pleasure. The product is a 282-page tome that we intend to repeat at five-year intervals, and stands as a wonderful testament to the creativity of both our visual and written-word artists.

We returned to Mexico for our fourth, and to Riga, Latvia for our fifth international retreats: as ever, weeks of creativity and joy and new faces we now count as friends. Our 2026 schedule is laid in and will see us again retreat in Mexico and returning to Wales, UK, where we traveled in 2023.

On the press side, we opened our new twice-a-year reading periods and were able to select four stunning works this year: Therese Gleason's *Hemicrania*, Mario Aliberto III's *All the Dead We Have Yet to Bury*, Katie Kemple's *Big Man*, and Maya Cheav's *Tan's Donuts*. All are amazing writing by wonderful authors who it has been our privilege to work with.

W e're excited about what year seven will bring, and thank you for joining us on this journey.

Year Six Statistics

5/15/2024-5/14/2025

Submissions received:
11,850

Pieces Published:
73
(20 prose, 20 art, 33 poetry)

Acceptance rate:
.616%

Chestnut Review
VOLUME 6 NUMBER 1 SUMMER 2024
FOR STUBBORN ARTISTS

Ink Flowers

Masking fluid and alcohol inks on Dura-Lar paper
9x12 inches
(Cover Art)

"Ink Flowers" was inspired by projects and techniques from the Inktastic Art Adventures that I host online. It was created on dura-lar paper with masking fluid and alcohol inks. I love the unpredictability and wild nature of inks combined with a resistance technique. Through the creative process, we can experiment, welcome discoveries, and make a marvelous mess while finding a tangible, sensual way to express reverence and wonder. It's an opportunity to explore the mysteries of life, self, feelings and relationships. This piece was also influenced by the synergy in the Born to Bloom Bright book. The book features a bouquet of lovely artists from all over the world. Playful poetic verses were crafted using words from garden catalogs then paired with colorful paintings to create a place for exploration, reflection and reclamation. Both the book and the Inktastic course are about appreciating the natural beauty within and around us.

Chestnut Review

VOLUME 6 NUMBER 1 SUMMER 2024

Chestnut Review LLC, Ithaca, New York
chestnutreview.com

Chestnut Review appears four times a year online, in January, April, July, and October, and once per year in print in July.

ISSN 2688-0350 (online), ISSN 2688-0342 (print)

CONTENTS

SPECIAL THANKS

To our generous Patreon supporters:

Adam Boustead, Judy, Ciel Downing, DrJRad,
Marijean Oldham, Regina McIntosh,
Chris Mikesell, M. Benjamin Thorne

to learn more, go to
https://patreon.com/chestnutreview

Introduction

Our Summer issue marks a turning point—not because spring is done but because we have arrived at a new season at *Chestnut Review*: volume six, year six. While milestones are arbitrary, the last five years feel like whole complete universes with their own inciting events and glorious push towards expansion. Horticulture tells us to plant tulips, rhubarb, and tomatoes in the spring, and they are also plants that—with time and vision—grow in the spring as well. Our Patreon, workshops, retreat program, thriving staff, and magazine all represent seeds that we've planted over the years. Year six is a year for looking at the fruit. It's in our nature to both tend to our sprouts and look forward to new opportunities and offshoots that will help us grow, entrench, and encompass our community in our welcoming branches. While horticulture helps gardeners know what to plan, you, our devoted readers and writers, are the ones who contribute to our garden we cultivate and appreciate every day.

In a dream groping for god[1]

Golden hands in a shower moving horizontally—air crisp in yesterday's
moonlight. I will spend my entire life resisting the shadow of your face
& your breath will still haunt me—cold on a June morning, since events
like these will exist in our world. Our world, now so quiet, eerie—like
watching an entire city atop on a worm moon night. Coyotes hiding
behind a black bush. Perhaps, mutual fear is a kind of love too. & angels
can be sent anywhere. One need only to stop insisting on their wings.[2]
Most times, I only believe some things are real because I fear them.
Tonight, when you sleep, remember you are able to dream anything into
existence—your lover's hands on your tulipped face; the sun facing the
moon, rendering us moonless; stars shining like foam in water, over
which god prepares for a deep, deep dive.

---

[1] Phrase from Lubna Safi's poem, *Shot and Buried with Lorca*

[2] Line from Lucille Clifton's poem, *Unless you Insist on Wings*

A Conversation with Javeria Hasnain, author of *SIN*

JR: Evoking "sin" as a concept is fascinating because it obviously has particular meanings in various religions and sects as well as a generalized Christian sense that often dominates in American discourse. Do you feel the concepts of sin explored in the chapbook speak to a particular understanding of sin? Is it designed to confront that understanding?

JH: I think we have a tendency to descend into more and more extremes, on either side of the scales. Part of it also includes deeming anyone who doesn't believe what we believe in a "sinner." The SIN poems especially came from that space, where I was just hearing a lot of [this] is a sin, and [that] is a sin, and I asked myself, what is a sin? Water is a sin. Smallness is a sin. Sin begins to encompass everything, almost, which simultaneously makes it majestic and redundant, eventually rendering it meaningless. I try to play with that contradiction in my poems.

JR: This is a book that also confronts religion and femininity: you cite Hagar and Eve, for instance. What reactions do you hope to produce in readers of any gender?

JH. Well, I am obsessed with the women figures in religious and mythological texts, for obvious reasons. I remember being fascinated upon hearing their stories as a child. A question I have asked and been asked so many times, why are there no women prophets? I know what I do have, though. The prophets' mothers, wives, comrades. Their names, their stories. I am interested in these women's perspectives and interiority. I try to trace my own matrilineage through evoking them, as I reconcile my own relationship to a patriarchal religion, and god as I still understand Him. I always say I write for my girls. Girls who have grown up where I have, the way I have. If they are able to read this book and feel connected to the speaker, that is the biggest gift to me.

JR: How long did this chapbook take to write? Did any poem feel particularly easy or difficult to write?

JH: I would call SIN a part of my longer book-length project in which I delve into these obsessions, themes, and questions even more. Everything I have written so far has led up to it, so it feels like decades. But more practically, I'd say it took me four years.

I usually write my poems in one sitting. I remember "Water is a Sin" was simultaneously both very easy and difficult to write—I had recently moved to New York City, and Pakistan, where I am from, was flooding. I was thinking about the privilege and guilt associated with "freedom" and about water in its many forms. I wrote it in a haste, maybe within half an hour. Made very slight changes later when I edited.

JR: Several of your poems feature intimate moments of understanding, sexual pleasure, and so on—how difficult is it to be so open in your writing?

JH: I lie in my poems. Which is not to say that I deceive the reader. Rather, poetry is another form of fiction for me. An interplay of imagination and exploration. I cling to fiction to reach something true about myself, or the world.

It is, of course, scary to put vulnerable parts of oneself out for display and consumption. But honestly, I'm only excited by writing that is raw and open, and will always choose that over anything else.

JR: Who are some poets you would recommend to readers who like your poems in SIN?

JH: So many! Sarah Ghazal Ali, Leila Chatti, Ama Codjoe, Mary Ruefle, Linda Gregg, Eileen Myles, Alycia Pirmohammed, Sanna Wani, J. Mae Barizo, Megan Fernandes, Fatimah Asghar, Carl Phillips, Mikko Harvey, Sara Shagufta, Aria Aber. So, so many more. I have an eclectic taste.

Stargazers

Oil on canvas, 30 x 40 inches, 2001

My painting, Stargazers, reflects my interest in astronomy. The diagonals emanate from a point at the center of the canvas, much as the universe, according to current scientific theory, originated at an infinitely dense point or singularity. The painting depicts three stargazers holding telescopes aimed at the cosmos, and planets and the symbols of the planets. My method consists of indirect painting, which involves a series of stages leading to the final effect. Layers of color are placed over a monochrome underpainting. Contrasting elements are juxtaposed: complementary color opposites, darks and lights, biomorphic and geometric forms, etc.

White Christmas

after People v. James (1998)

Mom, the night the mobile house burned,
you were cooking snowflakes in the kitchen.

There was a precise, breathless routine to it:
wafer-thin tablets dissolved in bubbling water,

boiled down, then gassed into something
as solid as a shackle clasped over your wrist.

In the sterile warmth of the microwave, drugs spun round
& round: vinyl voices stretched thin on the turntable.

Firefighters talked afterwards about the radiant color:
green smoke, green flames, even bare dirt flared green

like shoots of phantom grass. You crying & screaming,
My babies. My babies. You burning to the hem

of your bike pants. People running like ghosts
back & forth. Skin dripping off their hands.

My brothers & sister in the house, diapered,
       breathing, breathless.

After they sent you away, the sun turned into
a carved-out wound—a raw, gaping hole in the sky.

Even now, my mouth feels like a raw gaping hole

in my face, thick with sadness & strangeness.

I cannot scrape it off, the guilt that gums the day I said
(seven years old, shaken by death): you'd been cooking

white stuff in the kitchen. They asked, *What white stuff?*
& your life flaked to a snowstorm of ash.

A string of names winds about your throat
like a spiked necklace: meth mother, felony murderer.

I grew up holding this memory clenched in my fist,
a cool, smooth river stone in the blistering heat:

You called for us: *my babies, my babies.*
You spent the days before the fire

collecting money you made from drugs.
You spent almost all of it

on Christmas presents we'd never retrieve.

Our reader describes what it was like to find Esther Ra's "White Christmas"

Ra's opening, directed towards Mom, immediately pulls you into a heartbreaking scene. The opening, while through the eyes of a child, describes the process of cooking down "snowflakes in the kitchen." In a flash of green, a fire consumes the home and two younger siblings. The clashing worlds, from white to green, paint the greed of one Mom and the consumption of an entire family. Each use of imagery unveils another layer of this traumatic Christmas moment. The narrator leaves us in an unfulfilled sadness: no presents, no siblings, no mom, and no home. The writer makes this piece an intriguing read as we spiral down the memory and leaves us with the burn of the fire.

—Reina Garcia

Our reader describes what it was like to find Chidera Ankipe's "Portrait Under the Stairs"

I read "Portrait Under The Stairs" when I needed something to remind me that we all experience heartbreaks. It came at the right time and was a source of solace for me. Each line drifted into another like a spring flowing into itself, taking the reader in and in, showing them all the possibilities in a well-written story. I was hooked by the fantastic opening in the first paragraph—one that a reader would not expect would lead to even more mind-blowing paragraphs as it moves. The characters are endearing and unforgettable, even the ones that were briefly mentioned, like Anwulika's father. These characters pique your interest in their lives, and you feel an urge to know everything about them. The dexterous manner in which the story was woven, and the structure, uncovers the mystery of the protagonist's love life—Solange and her lover, Anwulika. One wonders if her love experience influenced her perspective on Shakespeare's Romeo and Juliet. How the prose uses her teaching encounter with Anozie as a tool that prompted her to seek closure. To discuss and come to terms with the inevitable ending of their love as lesbians in a country and among family that ostracize their kind of love. The irony of Anozie's argument as what gave her the courage to finally send the letter. This is a well-crafted story where the form is closely and cleverly intertwined with a strong narrative. The whole experience of reading it is scintillating, not too devastating, and even comforting in many ways—a balance between all the emotions it evokes.

—Rahma O. Jimoh

Portrait Under the Stairs

Whenever Solange thinks of Anwulika—and she thinks of Anwulika often—she also thinks of sharing a bowl of sweetened garri and milk at their worn dining table; eating plantain chips on the balcony of their apartment in New Brunswick; that day in Princeton when they held each other's hands as they posed before a slightly confused cameraman, who asked with the abiding carefulness of a person who did not want to offend, "Are you sisters?"

She also thinks of the impermanence of home, the feebleness of sanctuaries, and the way a person's laughter can carry into the air, long after they are gone, and sink into your bones until you are wholly consumed by it and them.

In her class, she teaches literature in the Elizabethan era. When she speaks of Shakespeare, she says, "Shakespeare's Romeo and Juliet is an astute example of what not to do when you find yourself edging towards love."

Her students laugh. She enjoys their laughter. It eases something in her.

A student at the back of the class raises his hand and she is, for a moment, reminded of Anwulika. There is something about that action, that small, silent act of asking for permission to speak, that stumps Solange. Her other students—mostly white and Hispanic—do not raise their hands to ask questions.

"Yes, young man in the back."

He rises from his chair, and she is nearly startled by how tall he is, how gleaming black his skin is, darker even than her—she who had been called 'blacky' as a child.

"I'm sorry, ma, but I don't quite agree with your narrative." His voice is a hoarse baritone, a rasping, deep thing that seems too reminiscent of a cold. She wonders about why he has apologized.

"A hopeless romantic, I presume." She hates the small jibe as soon as she says it, and she hates that her other students laugh in response.

A small self-loathing sensation gathers over her skin like sweat, and she wishes that she has the courage to apologize.

He does not seem offended or particularly amused by the trite joke. Only carefully neutral.

"Continue, Mr...."

"Anozie."

"Yes, Mr. Anozie."

She sees it in his face—the color of impression, a gentle thankfulness. She imagines that she is the first person in the school who has pronounced his name correctly.

"I think Romeo and Juliet is a perfect example of what love—true love—should be like."

She cocks her head curiously and watches him speak.

"I know some people think that they both died because they were silly and impatient and dramatic, but I think that their dying was a resounding and final affirmation of their love. What greater show of love is there than 'even death cannot do us part'?"

She likes the subtlety of his accent, the way the Nigerian in him peeks out from underneath his stylish, performative American accent. She wants him to speak as he ordinarily would have. To not feel the need to perform westernization on her behalf.

She thinks of him as she kneads the dough for her pasta dish a week later. *What greater show of love is there than 'even death cannot do us part'?*

Solange wishes that she had said something in rebuttal—even something trite, like another jibe. She wishes that she had not been so rooted to the floor, had not felt so utterly formless in the presence of his words. She sets the dough to rest, and then she walks out into the living room that Anwulika always referred to as 'parlour'.

She reaches the small flight of rickety, wooden stairs and wonders why she has not yet plastered the cream-colored wall with wallpaper. She had always thought it quite drab, but never went through with adding something colorful because even though she would not admit it to anyone—especially to herself—she cared too much about Anwulika's preferences. She notices now the indentations on the wall, the small scattered holes in which nails formerly hung as they held onto cherished frames of pictures. Pictures that Solange had bundled together and burnt along with the rest of Anwulika's things, the day after she left for Nigeria. She regrets it now—the rashness of her anger and grief.

Solange remembers that Anwulika had stood in that same spot, right before the frozen pictures of their life together, and made her into a vagabond.

"I am getting married to a man. It's what my parents want." She had said it so easily, Anwulika, so matter-of-factly, it had made Solange laugh.

"What are you talking about?" But she knew, even as she asked, that the sudden tautness of her skin and the quickening pace of her heartbeat were the premonitions of her impending homelessness.

"I am marrying a man. In December."

It was May 2001. A month before that day, Anwulika held Solange in her arms and cried with her as they watched the Netherlands become the first country in the world to legalize a love like their own. It had been a moment full of hope, joy, and possibility. A bubble of utopia from which they both prayed never to fall out of. But even then, in the starkness of their joy, there had been something else, like an aftertaste in the back of their tongues; a quiet grief in the corners of their minds.

"You can't marry a man." Solange sounded incredulous, unbelieving. After Anwulika had left for Nigeria, Solange would wonder why she had been so surprised by the news. She had always suspected that the thing she shared with Anwulika was fleeting, a beautiful dream from which she would one day have to wake, and yet she had been so petulant in the face of her reality, so utterly unwilling to untangle herself from the fantasy of her life with the woman she loved.

"It is what my parents want," Anwulika said in a voice so cold and monotonous, that Solange allowed herself a moment to believe that the woman before her was not, in fact, Anwulika. Because she knew that Anwulika could be curt and cutting but never cold. Then the moment passed, and the eyes that met her own were the same familiar, warm stones of onyx.

"But…" she did not know what to say. Her objection had lodged itself in her throat, and refused to budge, no matter how hard she tried to push it out. Instead, she crumbled to her knees, discarded her shame, and begged Anwulika to stay.

"I love you, please…don't do this."

She cried and begged, and she knew, even then, that Anwulika would not stay.

Now, before the same flight of stairs where Anwulika had dumped her, she fingers a hole in the wall and makes a mental note to buy new wallpaper whenever she goes grocery shopping.

***

"Nne, you do not look well. O gini mé? What's wrong?" Uchechukwu, Anwulika's mother, owns a voice that belongs in a song. It is sonorous, lilting, and charged with a biding smoothness that reminds Anwulika of pouring liquid milk into a clear glass filled with dark brown coffee.

She musters a smile that does not belong to her, and turns to see her mother decked in an extravagant display of George wrappers, a pristine white lace top, and a red and gold ichafu tied around her head. Uchechukwu's face, usually a dull brown color weathered by years spent in the harsh sunlight of Enugu, is painted a fair yellow with Mary Kay's foundation, and her lips are a sparkling red color that seems almost vulgar on her innocent face. Her face holds this new prettiness with tentative care, as though she does not quite know how to exist in a body that demands attention.

"I am well, mama. All is well." She says the words as cheerfully and convincingly as she can perform.

"Then why are you not smiling? What is wrong? Is your dress too tight?"

Anwulika sits before a stool in the bridal room of the St. Peter's Cathedral in Nsukka and her mother stands behind her with a gentle hand on her shoulder. In the mirror before her, a face as unfamiliar as her mother's stares back at her. Where her skin had always been the smooth brown of glossy chocolate, a new and brighter beige looks back at her. Her eyes have been lined by aquamarine shadow and her cheeks have been coated in rouge, yet she thinks that if she stares hard enough, she can see her real face peek out at her from behind the stranger in the mirror.

"Mama…" she begins, voice steady and assured.

"Yes, nwam."

She waits for the words to come, to take form in her stomach and travel through her throat and out of her lips. She is so sure she can sense the stirrings of those words: *I do not want to marry Livinus. I am in love with someone else. A woman. Her name is Solange. Can you remember? I told you about her in my letters. The one I called 'a roommate' and 'a dear friend'. I love her, mama. I want to be with her.*

"Please make sure the reverend does not talk for too long. These heels are very uncomfortable."

And her mother laughs, long and loud and sonorous, like the melody of a song. Anwulika laughs along with her.

***

Solange and Anwulika met on a snowy day, at the faculty's Christmas carnival. Solange was a tenured professor of Classical English Literature and Anwulika was an assistant lecturer of African mythologies on an MFA scholarship. Solange had noticed her on Campus before; fresh-eyed, curious, and always walking with a hastiness that spoke, not of tardiness, but of a desire to impress. At the party, Anwulika did not look as frazzled as she always did with her oversized sweaters and platform heels. She seemed instead to settle into her skin with a sensual ease. She was clad in a frilly gown that stopped halfway beneath her knees and a pair of furry, brown boots that reached past her ankles. At that moment, she seemed— to Solange—like something almost ethereal; the way she laughed and spoke and held her champagne glass at the rim. Solange was enchanted by her, but only mildly, only curiously.

Solange had always known that she liked girls—from that day in 1982 when she first saw a picture of Marilyn Monroe and felt a stirring in her stomach and a sudden wetness between her thighs. And so her desire for Anwulika did not surprise her. She had been with many women through-out her life; women who experimented with her because they had been curious, women who were convinced that their attractions were only curiosity, women who liked her because she liked them, and women who cried and prayed after orgasming to her touch. Once, she'd kept a lover for seven months, a woman who had looked her in the eye and said, with so much grief packed into her voice, "It would have been easier if you were a man." The moment had left Solange feeling as though she had suddenly become a visitor in her own life. As though, in that moment at least, she could not have been anything other than 'not enough'.

She had witnessed all that she cared to witness and was certain that nothing else could surprise her. Even then, there was a guardedness to her fascination. A tentativeness that underlined her admiration of Anwu-lika.

When Anwulika's eyes caught her own from across the room and she proffered a curious smile in her direction, Solange felt the same things she had felt that day in '82. She knew, too, from the way Anwulika's eyes had squinted, that her desire had been reciprocated, or at least matched with a simmering curiosity. They did not need to speak to understand. As Anwulika sidled out of the atrium where the carnival had been hosted, Solange understood she was expected to follow.

She did not brace herself for the pang of cold that hit her as soon as she walked out the doors. Did not expect to find Anwulika waiting expectantly for her right outside the doors with an impatient hand on her waist, a coy smile on her lips.

"Hi," Solange said, acutely aware of the awkwardness on her part and the sheer lack of it on the other woman's.

"Hi. Nice to meet you. I'm Anwulika." She responded, her accent foreign, her smile still tinged with mischief. She offered her hand to Solange for a shake.

"Hi…again. I'm Solange." They laughed as their fingers met. Anwulika's hand was surprisingly hard, almost brittle, a stark contrast against the supple softness of the rest of her.

"I know who you are."

Solange would think often of that moment in the course of her life. Of those words, *I know who you are.* And whenever she thought of it, she would return from the memory wholly cleansed and newly drenched in affection.

"Let me take you out for drinks?"

"Yes."

***

Anwulika had always suspected that 'love' was nothing more than a verb. An action word. Something that could only exist if it was done. Something that she had to 'do' in order to grasp. And so with Solange, she had always felt an innate desire to perform her affection, to do and to show her love.

The first time Solange told Anwulika she loved her, Anwulika did not respond even though she had wanted to say the words too. She had felt inadequate in the face of the other woman's affection, undeserving of it. And so she said nothing.

"You don't have to say it back. I just want you to know how I feel,"

Solange had said in response to her silence and, feeling guileless and simultaneously unworthy, Anwulika had responded, "I want to know how to do this 'love.' I want to do this love with you. But I just don't know how. I am still learning. I'm sorry."

Now, as she stands before Livinus at the altar of the St. Peter's Cathedral with a priest droning mindlessly in her ear, she imagines that she can one day come to love him if she makes herself do it. She will cook with him, take walks and eat peppered gizzards with him at Ekpe junction, until her love would have no other option than to blossom with him and for him. She knows of his affection for her, sees the way his eyes seem to remain forever trained on her face, the way his aura glimmers whenever she smiles at him. She imagines that if all else fails, she will let him love her into loving him.

All her life, she had watched her mother clamor for her father's love—beg for it, in fact. And all her life she had watched her father regard her mother with something akin to disdainful nonchalance. A blistering kind of apathy.

Her father had never been physically cruel to her mother and yet, for as long as Anwulika could remember, she cried for him, by him, at him. It might have been this, the unattainability of his love, that caused her mother to love him even more. Or it might have been that the more he hurt her with his words, glares, silences, and cheating, the more she wanted to prove—not just to him but also to herself—that she was worthy of his affection.

Anwulika registers that the priest says something about the virtues of keeping a marriage sacred and, for a brief moment, she glances at her father with quiet accusation in her eyes. He is seated in the front pew of the church, a missal clutched in one hand, his other hand placed rather affectionately on her mother's thigh. In that moment, they are a picture of a content and otherwise happy couple. But she catches the tightness in her mother's face as though this—her husband's performance of affection—is something she cannot wholly fathom.

A memory strikes Anwulika. In the memory, her mother—looking vaguely beautiful in a red sequined dress with her ichafu falling loosely over her shoulder and exposing the curls of her newly permed hair—barges through the front door of their parlour and collapses to the floor in a flagrant display of grief. Even as a thirteen-year-old child, Anwulika suspects that there is something about her mother's display that has been colored by melodrama, by theater.

"Your father has been acquired by the devil!"

Uchechukwu screams these words over and over again, lying on the cold tiles and raising her voice with such incisive sharpness, that Anwulika fears that she might succeed in shattering the pristine glass table in the middle of the room. Uchechukwu begins to cry and Anwulika rushes towards her and gathers this newly frail woman into her arms. She rocks her as gently as her awkward flailing posture can allow and whispers, "It's okay, mama. Ndo, sorry. Don't cry. Everything will be alright."

Anwulika wills wellness into the surrounding air, but the wellness does not come. Her mother does not speak for days, wholly enraptured by her grief, rage, and self-pity. Long stretches of fragile silence taint the house. Fela does not play on the gramophone in the evenings, and the silence becomes thick enough to be stifling. Her father does not apologize.

Now, as she stands before the altar and says a breathy, "I do" to the Reverend's questions, Anwulika wonders if—like her parents—Livinus will spend the rest of his life clamoring for her affection. She wonders if she will one day cave.

***

She sees the email on a windy day in February, two months after her marriage to Livinus.

She happens upon it at the computer library in Ekpe where she has gone to print her resumé for the teaching job that Livinus prompts her to apply for.

The week before, with his voice pleading, Livinus said, "It's not like I don't want you to chase your dream of being a writer, but let's face the truth, nne. Being a writer in this day and age is not lucrative. Plus, it's not like you've written a complete novel, sef. I think you should do something more worthwhile…like teaching. You already have experience in that field from your days in America." His voice had been lined by a concern that seemed almost performative and she had bristled in the face of his sly condescension. But she had always known that this day would come, a moment when she would have to fold up her dreams and neatly tuck them in the corners of her mind. She had resented him not only for his haughtiness, but because she had known he was right.

At the computer library, she types in her email address and password and tries to convince herself that she is only checking to see if she has received any new messages from her friends. But she knows, even before the lie can coagulate in her mind, that she is checking for Solange.

She scrolls past ads and scam emails and freezes when she sees an unread email.

The cursor hovers across the mail on the screen, apprehensive, fearfully indecisive. It is dated from three weeks after her wedding ceremony, on the 4th of January 2002.

It reads:

Hi…again. I hope you are well.

I have written and deleted this message seven times now. I pray I have the courage to actually press send on this one. Haha!

I miss you. But you already know that.

There's a boy in my class, Anozie. He is Igbo, like you, and he is so tall, that he has to duck to pass through the doors of the lecture room.

Last month, during one of our classes on Willy Boy (remember this?) He said, "What greater show of love is there than 'even death cannot do us part'?"

Funny, right? I feared we would not be together forever but I still hoped that we would be.

In the end, I guess death did not have to pull us apart. Life was sufficient enough.

I cannot, in good faith, say that I hope you're happy. I know that you are not. But I hope that you will one day be.

It was an honor to do this love with you.

All my heart,

Solange.

PS: I still haven't gotten the wallpaper for the wall under the stairs

Indigo Cats

Acrylic on canvas, 20 x 30 inches
(Next Page)

Over the years a powerful inspiration for my art has been my love of animals — especially cats! I began to paint in acrylics during the mid-1980s producing a series of folk art paintings (among which was Indigo Cats.) which culminated in the publication of a 1993 calendar comprised of 13 of my folk art paintings. I subsequently created an extensive body of art of utilizing the mediums of sculpture, collage and digital technology. All told, more than 200 of my images have been published in magazines, within the format of calendars, note cards and jigsaw puzzles, as well as having been exhibited in both galleries and museums.

Grass Stains

The mosquitoes outnumber us: there seems to be nothing better to do than have a foot race. Space satellites & airplanes alike twinkle approval as we careen down the hill. A sound I've never heard before escapes your mouth: something almost like joy, but not quite. My arm grazes yours as we barrel toward an imaginary finish line. You & I are in a good place these days, I think. To pass the time, we explode like supernovas. We howl just to hear a familiar noise. Legs churning, we trample the dying lawn unloved by summer's heat, grass reluctant to try growing anymore. Half-crumpled hydrangeas line the final stretch of our makeshift course, the blurry moon above us casting a dim spotlight on one last display of teenage self-importance. Your crew socks are stained a murky yellow-green, flecks of mud outlining your Achilles tendons. For as long as I'll know you, they'll never be fully white again. I beat you to the fence by a half-step—an instant, & you're next to me. *It was a tie!* I say to nobody in particular, & collapse into the grass. The world is quiet except for the sound of us: breathing the same warm air, squinting at the same tired stars.

Crossing

As we approach the Atlantic's western shore
America's outstretched arm rises from the ocean—
Long Island's palm either
open to us in welcome,
or a warning to come no further.

My ancestors' kin made this passage
in the leaking bowels of ships
tracking the hypotenuse
of a trade route.

We make ours at 43,000 feet above sea level.

The currents, up here, while stronger,
are not nearly as turbulent
and we count the cost of our crossing
in hours,
instead of months.

We left Nairobi in darkness
and chased west after the night.
Now New York unfolds before us,
the rising sun red
on the wings of this Dreamliner.

My ancestors' kin made this passage as cargo
in the holds of American vessels.
Today we approach her shore as pilots
sitting at the helm.

Girlhood Gothic

2001 / American malls are booming, department store sales reaching an all-time high at $19.9B. There are malls with rollercoasters, aquariums, wedding chapels. Cars pack parking lots, people pack stores, and clothes pack bags, bulging against paper seams.

At eleven, Laura's mom let us go by ourselves for the first time. Stay together, be careful, she said from the sunken depths of their purple couch, smoke coiling from her mouth like a wonderland caterpillar. In our southern, suburban backwater—a highway exit turned almost-town— every street that didn't end in a cul-de-sac led to the mall.

We held hands as we entered, the doors breathing open at our approach. Open sesame, we said. And the mall unfolded before us, a treasure trove of possibilities.

Ahead a fountain glittered, dewy and musical. Teens lolled around its edges, midriffs exposed as they leaned, leaned towards the water, sucking on white plastic cups of soda with one hand, tapping at Nokia phones with the other. Beads and feathers and colored clip-ins rippled in their hair when they moved. As hard and sleek and immortal as the mall's marble concourses.

This was the place to be. And here we were.

"Where should we go first?" I asked Laura.

Still clutching my hand, she dragged me towards the Nordstrom wing. We ducked beneath spritzed samples of Paris Hilton's new perfume, dodged snapping mouths of CHI hair straighteners. Come try. Come try. Come buy. Come buy.

Hollister yawned like a cave, its thick, cologned clime washing over us as we entered the darkness. The whole store pulsed with a deep backbeat, rail-thin associates modeling thinner shirts, mini cargo skirts, UGG boots.

Laura held up a hot pink classic tee, cut in deep v. "What do you think, Lizzie?"

"So cute," I said.

She picked up a second one, pressing it into my palm. "We should match."

The fabric was soft and supple. I wanted to drink it. "I don't have enough money."

Laura stuck her tongue out at me. "Lame."

I continued to hold the shirt while she checked out. I did have just enough money. But my mom would never let me wear something like this. What she didn't have in time, she made up for in worries—and rules. I wished she was more like Laura's mom. Laura's mom said Laura's dad had been a real Mussolini: charming, Italian, dictatorial. Now that they'd gotten out from under his thumb she didn't believe in rules.

"Actually, I found another five," I said, sliding my shirt onto the counter after Laura's. Pins pricked my cheeks. I glanced behind me, expecting to see my mom. But there was only a pimpled boy, arms full of jeans.

We changed in the same bathroom stall. Something shifted and shuddered as I slipped the shirt over my shoulders. Laura peed before putting her shirt back on—just sat on the toilet, jean shorts around her ankles, shirtless.

"You look like a nudist," I said, giggling.

Laura snorted, covering her mouth. "You know, my mom actually knows some nudists."

We went to Victoria's Secret, peaked nipples pressing through paper-thin polyester shirts, breasts still too small to fill even the 32AA bra. My mom also wouldn't let me go in here. The Angels stared down at us from on high, the muscles in their matchstick thighs sharp as glass. I envied their wings, their breasts. I spritzed *Heavenly* on the insides of my wrists, rubbing them together, wishing.

We walked the long concourses, possibilities packaged like presents in each window. Here was Hot Topic. We could be like that, if we wanted. Slouched and nose-ringed and glowering. Here was Lucky Brand. We could be like her, if we wanted. Flowers in our hair, neck heavy with chattering beads. We stopped in front of Abercrombie. One day, we could be like them. The beautiful couple, gazing into each other's eyes, perfect bodies pressed together in perfect jeans.

In the food court, we shared a Cinnabon pretzel and large Diet Coke. Our fingertips shone with icing and cinnamon sugar. I licked my finger, leaned across the table to suck the last of the Diet Coke from the cup.

"I think they're looking at us," Laura said.

I glanced up, across the field of tables, just as Laura hissed, "Don't look."

A cluster of boys, hair long, jean hems hanging heavy to the lolling tongues of worn sneakers. Piercings winked from cocked eyebrows. High schoolers.

"They're not looking at us," I said, returning to our pretzel.

"Maybe," said Laura.

Maybe. Anything was possible at the mall.

2007 / The Great Recession begins. Malls are hit hard. But the change isn't obvious right away. Like a wolf in the woods, we can feel it behind us, smell its hot, fetid breath. But we don't turn around, don't want to acknowledge what is coming.

The gift card slashed through the card reader, plastic on plastic. The cashier's nails clacked across the keys.

"You've got six bucks left."

Laura accepted the card with French-tipped fingers, sliding her other hand through the shopping bag's pink strings.

I pulled at the elastic band of my own Hanes t-shirt bra. Laura's older sisters had given her a Victoria's Secret gift card for her sixteenth birthday last week, and she'd bought the bombshell bra in pink, with red wings of butterfly lace. She'd even had enough for the five for twenty-five under-wear deal. I envied Laura her sisters. They seemed part twenty-something part fairy godmother, sprinkling Laura in edgy hand-me-downs, boy advice, and, occasionally, sparkling pink baggies of drugs, which we gummed, tongued, or sniffed in the handicap stall until the mall dripped and shimmered all around us.

"Don't look so gloomy, little Lizzie," she teased, poking my shoulder. "One of the pairs is for you."

"Really?"

"Of course. It's Christmas."

I beamed at her, taking her hand, and letting our arms swing as we strolled down the concourse. Christmas at the mall. Carols tinkled from tinny speakers, echoing off marble. The parking lots and garages were packed, but we took our bikes, tinsel wound through the baskets. The adults were harried, crumpled lists clutched in sweaty fists. But school was out. We had nowhere to be but here. And here we were.

Toddlers shrieked and parents cajoled as Santa hemmed and hawed. Lines snaked along aisles, out of doors. Samples were jasmine, frankincense, myrrh, and Frasier fir. Signs advertised Ho Ho Holiday Savings at Brookstone, and the Apple store now had silver and black iPod Classics. Laura had asked for a silver one for Christmas. I didn't bother. Mom was more stressed than usual. She did remote customer service for a bank and she said they had been laying people off, that Christmas might be smaller than usual this year.

Laura and I stopped in front of the mall's biggest Christmas tree, stretching twenty-five feet to touch the top of the domed ceiling at the main entrance. I passed Laura a chunk of our warm TollHouse cocoa cookie.

"It's beautiful, isn't it?" she breathed, taking a bite of the cookie, her dark eyes reflecting the dazzle of red and gold.

"Yeah. I love Christmas."

"What do you want this year?"

I saw us reflected in a big, silver Christmas ball, bobbing from a branch in the central air. It distorted us, making us huge.

"I want everything."

Later, over a plate of Panda Express in the food court, Laura said, "Don't look up. Don't turn around."

Orange chicken dangled from my fork. "What. Why."

"I think they're coming over here."

They slid into the seats around us. The boys that haunted the fountain looked so similar to the ones we'd fantasized about as pre-teens. Those high-school boys, we'd whispered to each other behind pudgy palms. Of course, now I knew they weren't in high school anymore.

"Hey," said Laura.

"We've seen you two around," one said, black hair slashing forward as he leaned in close, top teeth tugging at the skin of his bottom lip.

The second nudged Laura's shopping bag, "What'dja get."

She smirked at them. "What's it to you?"

I took a bite of orange chicken, felt it stick in my throat, took a sip of water, coughed.

"You seen us around?" The third asked, looking at me. My eyes found the hollows under his cheekbones, the muscle that ran from the base of his ear down, beneath the collar of his shirt.

"Maybe," I said, as Laura said, "No."

They laughed, seats screeching across the laminate as they dragged them in closer.

"We're having a party tonight. We'd love if y'all could come."

"Okay," said Laura.

"But we don't have a car," I said.

They stood, shoving hands deep in jacket pockets. "We'll take you."

They led us through the warren of parking decks, twisting round bollards and Hondas as we moved deeper into the underground labyrinth beneath the mall. I watched them walk, the loping swing of their hips, the lazy way they checked over their shoulders to make sure we were keeping up. The one nearest me scratched his lower back, lifting the hem of his black t-shirt. I wanted to touch the slice of skin there, just above the waist of his jeans, press my finger into it until it left a divot—like the thumbprint cookies Mom always made this time of year.

In their car, a lifted truck littered with oily fast food wrappers and bags stomped flat, I sat in the back with the boy I'd walked closest to, Peter. Laura sat on Zac's lap in the passenger seat. Paul drove. Laura asked for Christmas music. Paul turned on "Holiday" by Green Day. The rear speaker thumped against my calf. Peter sat halfway into the middle seat, his knee bumping against mine each time we hit a speed bump.

Over the whine of the electric guitar, he said, "You're really beautiful."

I blushed, trying to think of something to say. "Thanks."

"No, seriously," he said. "There are so many girls in the mall, but we noticed you two. Seriously. Really pretty."

I swelled. "I like this song," I said. I wasn't lying. It wasn't what I normally listened to, but the grind of the singer's voice, the wild desperation. I loved it.

"Do you," he said, scooting closer. "Turn it up, Paul."

Paul pushed his finger against the dial. The song filled the car. Peter rolled down all the windows. Laura whooped, letting her head fall back, hair whipping in the winter wind.

I put an arm out of the window, my fingers dipping and dancing in the air, the cold slicing spots of red into my cheeks. The lights of the mall and hundreds of other cars, white then red, sped past. Zac wailed along with the song, his voice rough and pleading. I pressed my thigh into Peter's, feeling a zap of adrenaline snake from the place where my leggings met his jeans. I whooped into the passing traffic, and Laura's laugh was a shriek in the night. When we got out of the car, my fingers were numb in Peter's hand.

"You guys live here?" Laura asked. The house was a sloping heap of a bungalow. Christmas lights hung from the porch rafters, their twinkle lending a fairy tale quality.

"Us and a few other guys," said Paul.

I tried to catch Laura's eye. How old were these boys? But she was already through the front door.

Inside, it wasn't so much a party as a hang-out. A few other guys languished on couches, settled deep into the folds of splitting leather or pilling polyester. A coffee table sat in the middle, glass-topped and glinting with the reflected light of a slowly spinning disco ball. My Chemical Romance thumped from two standing speakers by the bathroom: "Welcome to the Black Parade."

"Welcome to our castle," said Zac, giggling, as he pulled Laura down beside him on the couch.

"Yes," said Paul, in a British accent. "May we offer you some of our treasure." At this, he opened a drawer in the coffee table, shaking a twisted white baggie at them.

Laura slid from the couch onto her knees in front of the table, offering Paul her credit card. "Why, thank you, sir."

"Of course, milady," he said, doing an awkward curtsy that sent the rest of them into fits.

I hovered, standing over the table, Peter's body pressed against my back.

"Wanna sit?" he said.

I sank onto the couch, watching Laura lean over the table, press a finger to one nostril, and drag the other along the line of white powder, inhaling sharply. I'd only ever snorted off the tip of her finger. Little hits. Just the two of us. Maybe her sisters had shown her how to do it like this.

When she looked up at me, her eyes were damp pools, full and bright. Her nostrils fluttered like a deer's. I don't know why I thought that.

"Come on little Lizzie," she said. "I'll show you."

And she did.

They turned up the music, and we were on the coffee table, dancing. Laura pressed her body against mine. I could feel her bombshell bra against my chest, soft and firm. When had she changed? I looked at the guys, wondered if they were watching. Laura's hand was at my chin, turning my face towards hers. Her mouth was at my neck, whispering, trust me, they're watching. And she was grinding down my body, our fingers tangled above us, the glass sticky beneath our feet, crusted with a dusting of cocaine. The disco rushed over our face, shadows and light. I could smell her perfume.

"I love you Lizzie," she said.

Her hands were at my waist, pressing my shirt up towards my ribs so her palms could rest against the flat of my stomach, the place where my hips jutted.

"I love you too," I said. And I did. I loved her so much. The boys cheered, and we grinned, turning to face them.

They stood up, and pulled us down from the coffee table, joining the dancing, spinning us, crushing us against them. Their bodies were hard in a way Laura's wasn't, their arms strong. They felt like the boys in the Abercrombie ads. I tried to be like the girls.

At the end of the night, Peter dropped Laura off first. When he parked in front of my house, he turned to me, pupils wide and dark and earnest, and asked, "Can I kiss you?"

I leaned in and pressed my lips to his, blazing and confident—bright as the star the wise men followed all those years ago—bright as a mall lit up at night.

2008 / The Great Recession sees retail sales drop to 35-year lows. Malls struggle. Vacancy rates climb. But we hear they are opening a 2.3 billion dollar mall somewhere in New Jersey called Xanadu. A utopia, a pleasure dome. We prevaricate. Things can't be that bad. We dig our nails into the promise of permanence.

We moved through the mall now not as a pair, but as a crew. A shambling, stumbling, shrieking bunch, the kind that made store managers step out from behind the cash wrap, eyes squinted and wary. It was Laura and Zac, me and Peter, at the core of the crowd. Sometimes Paul was there, sometimes other boys.

In Lids, Peter tried to see how many snap-backs he could try on at once. When they finally toppled to the floor, there were twenty-six in all. The manager growled, and Peter scooped me up, slinging my arms around his neck as he whisked me, piggy-back, down the concourse, Zac and Laura trotting behind, laughter ricocheting between kiosks.

In Claire's, Peter paid for me to get a second and third piercing. Cubic zirconium, white gold plated. The nice stuff.

He said, "I always take care of you baby. You don't need nobody but me."

"You and Laura," I whispered into his ear, laughing, biting his lobe.

Zac bought Laura more underwear from Victoria's Secret. We didn't have to split meals at Panda Express anymore. They always paid. We fed them fried rice from plastic forks as their hands slid up our legs beneath the tables, fingers sliding beneath panties until we were both giggling too hard to keep going.

There were fewer stores open at the mall. The Sears at the South entrance had shuttered, leaving a big empty shell in its place. But we didn't care. This is where the boys wanted us to be. So here we were.

We sat on their laps by the fountain, swirling lazy fingers through the water, poking at pennies. They bought us phones, LG Chocolates. That way we could always be in touch, they could always know where we were. When we got bored of the mall, we went driving. Or back to their place, Laura and I splitting into separate rooms before reconvening an hour later on the common couch, wearing our boyfriends' sweatshirts, smelling of sex, cuddling together to watch Lost. Sometimes we skipped school when they asked us to. They didn't like being away from us, didn't like not knowing what we were up to. They loved us so much.

It was one of those afternoons when Peter said, "We're having a party tonight."

"A real party?" asked Laura, eyebrows arched.

"A real party," said Zac, sliding his hands up her sweatshirt.

Laura and I got ready at her place. We filched her sister's Urban Decay palette, painting our lids a phosphorescent, shining black. Under our jean shorts, we wore fishnet tights. With scissors, we slashed band tees to the bone, widening the necks, shortening the hems. We were Avril Lavigne, without the pink-blonde hair. We took a while getting ready, dancing around in various states of half-dress, cycling through eight different lipstick shades until we landed on the one. I thumbed Laura's bottom lip, leaning in close. That's perfect, I said. She made kissy lips at me, tugging her shirt off. Another outfit change. We did a couple key bumps while we jumped around Laura's room—courtesy of the boys, as always.

By the time we showed up, the party was in full swing. We walked in slowly, holding hands as usual. We paused in the threshold. Look at us.

Zac loomed out of the pulse of bodies, his hand closing around Laura's upper arm.

"Where the fuck have you been?"

"What! Zac—we were getting ready!"

"And you don't answer your phone?"

Peter stalked up next, pulling me towards him by my belt loop.

"No, I left it here—it's in your room," I heard Laura say, as Peter growled in my ear, "You embarrassed me. I told people you would be here."

"We both did," said Zac.

"Sorry," Laura and I said. "We can meet your friends now."

They seemed to relax, glancing between each other, the hard lines of their jaws unclenching. We relaxed too, sliding our hands in their pockets, under their shirts.

"Sorry, baby, come on. Sorry we're late." They could get like this when they did too much blow. Wild and intense. No one could calm them but us.

In their room, we did a few more lines, giggling at the white powder hanging from Paul's long nose hair. "Brooooo," Zac moaned. They passed us vodka sodas. We tipped them back. Fire in our stomachs, in our eyes, our hearts. We danced on the couch, staggering back and forth across the sagging cushions. Peter and Zac introduced us to two of their friends from out of town. In the kitchen, I sucked a wobbling line of Bombay Sapphire off Peter's friend's chest. He grabbed my ass as I leaned over his body. I glanced at Peter, worried. But he winked at me and smiled. So understanding.

Then the six of us were dancing beneath the disco ball, the coffee table pushed to the side. We were all pressed against one another, sweat slicking limbs, dripping from chins, sliding between breasts. Peter was behind me, his crotch pressed into my back. His friend danced in front, hand sliding down my neck, skimming the side of my breast, coming to rest on my hips.

"Baby," Peter whispered into my neck, "Baby you would do anything for me."

"Yes," I breathed, eyes wavering on his friend's hand.

"I think you're beautiful, you know that."

I nodded backwards into his chest, lifting my arms so they framed his face above me. I felt his jaw move against my upper arm as he whispered, "My friend thinks you're beautiful too. Why don't you guys go into my room. He really wants to. Would you, baby. For me."

My arms fell to my sides. The floorboards throbbed beneath me, my eyeballs pulsing with each buckle. Peter's sweat was like battery acid when I licked it from my lips.

I turned to face him, "You're joking, right… baby?" My voice was a high whine, like a kid at the mall begging for something they couldn't have.

"It's not a big deal, baby," he said, running his thick thumb along my jaw.

People thrashed around me like wild things. Waifs. Ghosts. Goblins. Demented in the swinging light of the disco ball. Shadow then light. I shook my head, and he took a step away from me, his face closing, darkening. I reached for him, fingers stretched across the space between us, but Peter turned, and disappeared into the bodies, my heart clutched in his fist.

My eyes wouldn't close, and it was all so bright, and glittery, and endless. Hands pulled me back as I waded towards the front door. They knotted in my hair, clawed at my waist. And then they were gone as the chill December air blasted me, cooled me. I stepped into the night, ready to run. Then I remembered.

"Laura," I called back into the shape-shifting mayhem.

And she heard me, and she turned, locking eyes with me, just before the bedroom clicked closed. Before Zac's friend nodded at me and closed it behind the two of them. Before I ran home, grateful for the colorlessness of my mother's house. The clean, gray laminate floors. Grateful I had this place to run to, that my mom would find me here in the morning.

2009 / There are dozens of malls around the country so empty, so abandoned that people call them "ghost malls" or "dead malls." Solitary shoppers shamble from store to store, searching for signs of life. We watch metal grates fall across the entrances of our favorite shops, never to be opened again. We rattle the bars. Let us back in.

I wandered the mall like a zombie, looking for Laura. I wore one of my mom's Irish fisherman sweaters, champion sweats, a ball cap. I hoped no one would recognize me.

More stores were shuttered, finally giving up hope after the holidays, leftover decorations hanging limp from stripped window displays. A blow-up snowman slumped against the window of a closed Build-a-Bear workshop. His nose was deflated, coal eyes downcast.

A group of elderly people speed-shuffled past, sneakered and sweat-suited for their morning workout. There were more of them now than ever. They loved the open concourses, the air conditioning.

It'd been a week since the party. Peter had deactivated my phone. I'd tried calling Laura from my mom's landline, but she never picked up. Probably didn't recognize the number. Or else Peter had told her not to. Or else she didn't want to talk to me.

When my mom found me on the floor, she asked me three questions: what happened, was I ok, was Laura. I buried my throbbing head in her sensible khakis. "I don't know," I gurgled into her thigh. When I closed my eyes, I saw Laura, glitter streaming from her eyes like tears, the door closing between us. I wished I'd had the strength to turn back, to turn the knob.

I shuffled into Hollister, the cologne and music buffeting me, harsh in a way it had never been before. Victoria's Secret was messy, underwear strewn over tables in the post-holiday chaos. There were no smalls left anywhere. Urban Outfitters didn't have anything good either.

Finally I went to the food court. A third pretzel couldn't hurt. It's not like I was seeing anyone. And there she was—hunched over a plastic table in front of Chick-fil-A.

"Laura," I said, speed-walking to her as fast as my UGGs allowed.

She flinched at my voice, giving me a feeble sort of a half-wave.

I wrapped my arms around her shoulders. "Laura, I'm sorry. I should've never left you at that party. But I panicked. I mean I really panicked. Peter went completely insane. And I've been trying to call you. Have you been getting my calls? Where've you been?"

"Jesus, Lizzie, slow down."

I retracted my arms, crossing them across my chest. "Sorry. Sorry. Didn't mean to spaz out."

I sat down across from her, biting back my questions, more apologies, waiting for her to talk. She looked way better than I did. Makeup done. Cute new outfit—cable-knit UGGs, low-rise Abercrombies, True Religion puffer coat.

"Lizzie. Peter is really upset with you."

"Peter? You've been talking to Peter?"

Laura rolled her eyes at me. "Of course. He lives with Zac."

"You're still with Zac?"

"Duh. I'm picking up his lunch right now."

"Laura. Are you ok? What happened with Zac's friend?"

Laura took a long sip from her soda. Her lips pursed in a thin line when she swallowed. "That's what happens when you leave early, girlie. You miss things."

I stared at her, stomach clenching, face burning. "I'm sorry."

Laura laughed, rolling her eyes again as she shook the pellet ice loose. "Lizzie. Honestly you need to stop being so dramatic. It's not a big deal."

I remembered Peter's words. "What's not?"

She didn't answer. A child spilled a milkshake and started to shriek. She took a long draw of soda, stared at me, dared me to ask.

"Laura, let's go back to your house. Hang out with your sisters? Watch a movie? We could even go back to my place, if you want."

"I don't see why you can't just apologize to Peter."

The unsaid thing, our eyes meeting in the swinging sliver of that closing door, hung in the air between us like shitty perfume.

"Laura!" someone called, and I jumped, thinking for a second it might be Zac, or Peter. But it was only a red-faced teen behind the counter at Chick-fil-A.

"Laura," he asked again, looking hopefully at the two of us, bag outstretched.

She stood up. I grabbed her wrist. "Laura," I said.

She shook herself free. "I've got to get the food back to the guys. Come if you want."

"I'm not going back there."

"I'm not coming with you."

I watched her leave, watched her wade away from me through the sea of chairs, beneath the giant, vaulted galleria ceiling, surrounded by fluttering banners advertising stores long-since-closed. She looked so small, even in her big puffy coat.

2017 / 7,000 mall retailers—many of them department stores—have closed their doors. In desperation, communities begin to repurpose their malls. They pick at the corpses of these dead leviathans, scavenging, salvaging. We are determined to find something of value in the wreckage.

I turn off the exit, blinker clicking like film in a teacher's old projector. Click. There's the McDonalds where I used to get breakfast. Click. There's my old bus stop. Click. There's the turn-off to my old neighborhood. Click. In the distance, I see it coming.

I'm back in town for the first time in years. Couldn't avoid it. My mom's remarrying. I'm happy for her, but I don't like being back here. Too much is the same. Too much has changed.

The mall rises up like a ruin in the driver's side window. I slow to a stop at the red light, drumming my nails against the wheel. The parking lots are empty, plastic grocery bags windmilling like tumbleweeds over faded lines. The Sears sign has been taken down, but not away. Busted out and faded, it leans over padlocked glass doors.

The light turns green. I press the gas. The mall slips past, hollow and howling. Like a crumbling castle, a haunted house on a hill. Ghosts walk its marble concourses, charm bracelets clattering like chains, moaning. Come try. Come try. Come buy. Come by.

20-02-2024

for Suleiman Auwal

i watched you die, my good friend. i stood
there, helpless—like anything before fire.

blind and armless, like water. what use
are arms if they can't save me from myself?

i stood, poetry in my one hand, the shahada
in the other, as if to push them down your

throat and say *these are the only things i've got.*
as if language could buy you more breaths.

Auwal, at your janazah, the imam said nothing
bad comes from God. i cannot help but think

this was what he meant: the beauty in how
God watches the air in your lungs rusts in your

mouth, how it whitens as it bleeds through
the gap in your teeth like a cursed wind. how

after you died, we buried you like a tender
seed and how the ground swallowed you

as if you were the first sporadic rainfall. tell it
anywhere: the world's ugliest thing is silence.

dear friend, i know every grave closes its mouth
eventually, but there is enough blankness

to be buried where your emptiness stops. enough
absence to feel holy. a man, in a bid to console me,

said God's biggest blessing could be absence. if to
be blessed implies wearing your lifelessness like a

skin, i plead to be glorified in my ruin.

Almaty, Kazakhstan

Digital photo
Outskirts of Almaty, Kazakhstan
2017
(Next Page)

Kazakhstan is emblematic of humanity's ever-continuing insertion into once-'natural' spaces. It is a low-density Central Asian country that has changed considerably since its most recent independence, with remnants of the Soviet era mixing with hyper-modern projects and swaths of natural space that continue to be impinged upon long after the Aral Sea began disappearing in the 1960s. This human insertion is never far from my mind and affects how I see and compose photographs of the world.

It was night when you died

for J.L.

Clean white sheets strung across the dusty road and us just down the hill, at the bayou, baptizing ourselves in each other's names. Me trippin round the tree stumps and your summer smile, all peanut butter skies and patchy hair, still smellin like smoke from our trip past the silos, the fire too big but full of the same splendor as your hands. After the sun set we rolled in grass and lit lighthouses on our heads. Soon your mind swelled balloon and nothin to relieve the pressure, you decide you're done with soil stains and take to the sky. You choose to go. I can't pick what is fact but I can decide what is true. Your eyes shed their light. I sat beside myself, waited for my feathers, a chance to go, too.

Arrival

"I have murdered the lovely and the helpless; I have strangled the innocent as they slept, and grasped to death his throat who never..." —*Mary Shelley*, Frankenstein

This is a story about hands: how I
am always searching for things to bury. I have
only this blue body, this terrible body, this murdered
self. A face blue like overripe stars, like pigeons. I want the
ending to be bright. Inside a forest, a place so green, so lovely
it burns. This is a story about burning &
being burned. I will give you bellflower root, mugwort, the
sour skin of my throat, my tongue still helpless,
noiseless against the rain. Here is my body & here is what I
can give you. I am only what I sing, stretched shirt, stale half
of a bread roll. Just a little music as the birds unfurl, strangled
into song. What can I give that will make you stay? The
song looped over, the other half. Innocent,
soft. Something that has known warmth & swallowed it. The body as
a measure of everything but itself. The birds as they
continue to sing. A beat of quiet for flickering rain, for ruin slipped
under pillowcases. This is a story about hands &
everything they cannot touch. The only ending I know: grasped
mouths & blue palms & a forest burning to
silence. Here is what's left. Here is my body, death
-less & waiting & so cold. All I have is this:
a face nothing like yours, your voice still scratching at my throat.
Here is my body & the way it has forgotten who
-leness. Here is my body. A story about how it never—

Cōnfessiōnem

"If only I could want something simpler." –Kanika Ahuja

Nothing is more certain than my wound.
Everyday, I watch the same fire

burn me a little more. I say *never again*
with this addiction; still I fall back

into the wound. I am hollowed out. I sit
with guilt, my confidence ship-

wrecking. Elsewhere, someone I love is
torn open to make room for a syringe.

I'm five cities away, yet like floodwater,
I gather filth. I remember the origin

of my addiction. How she had called to
say *Chiwenite, your brother's bleeding.*

How, two weeks later, she called again
& this time it was my father who

had collapsed with a stroke. I howl
& I scratch & I leave the whole room

slippery with blood. Hypothesis or law,
I'm willing to bend, to break if it means

starting afresh. O, mercy. O, relic.
O, whatever little laughter's lodged

beneath my throat. The addicted—
I have realized—never know how deep

the blade. Look at my body, at the flame
that thaws it from the inside out.

Look how someone I love lies motionless,
mistaking *survival* for *safe*.

Yet the world blooms. When all this
is over, it's my hope that there will be

this poem to show how, sometimes,
we can be so stubborn

we make water out of our wound, & float.

Belle Epoque

Doctors are such idiots. The thing is, they don't know they're idiots.

Take the guy who had me out for drinks last night in Back Bay. Five minutes of back-and-forth on the dating app assured that he would pay for everything, as long as I played the dumb, interested college boy. A know-it-all that wouldn't believe me if I told him that chasing the bug was the best way for a nineteen-year-old gay runaway like me to get healthcare. I had friends who'd taken the government up on the offer, but I won't tell him about that. I won't tell him that my name is Jasha or that Boston is the second east coast city I've made my own—fifth overall if you don't count my parents' place outside of Detroit, which I don't because I bailed when I was thirteen, when their hearts and minds were still in Poland anyway.

The doctor took a long drag of his Macallan and leaned into the middle of the table. He was at least twenty years older than me, his polo and khakis tailored into a second skin that underscored his time in the gym. "I can tell you're having a good time by the way your pupils are dilated," he said, and sighed gasoline. He worked at Mass General and said he'd seen me on the Common. The trees hadn't quite bloomed yet, and the worst heat didn't linger past sunset. "That's amazing," I said. Anyone able to enter another person's headspace for a fraction of a second would have seen through my act.

The good doctor smirked and his big head bobbled to one side. The low lights and mahogany walls really enhanced the effect. He'd said discreet in his profile, but was willing to meet in a public space. A tangled, perfect mess.

I smirked too, like we were in on some big secret, and twisted in my seat. "What else?"

Our waiter asked if we needed anything and I looked at the doctor— let him take over. That's what I give, and sex. He gives drinks and breakfast, and a couple of small items from his place that he won't even miss. My first year out, before I'd wised up to the system, a social worker called it survival sex. I was thinner then, if you can believe it. I sleep better now, and my clothes fit. She meant well. All the helpers do.

The doctor ran his tongue along his teeth. "You think you've got it all figured out," he said, and chuckled. "A real know-it-all. Hell, I was too at your age."

The vodka in my Sprite burned my throat. Poured out from a nip in my pocket when only the doctor was looking. Man did his eyes light up.

"I know a lot of things," I said, and realized I was drunk.

His foot slithered up my leg under the table and I giggled to counter-act my squirm. "Such as?" he said.

"Your pupils are dilated too." What bullshit, but I'm pretty sure they were. His lips melted out like putty and his eyes closed like Venus flytraps poked with a stick. I'd found a bed for the night.

***

Most days I wander the Common and set up dates, and haunt the bagel shops around the edge for loose bags. So far only other people in my situation have noticed. The other day at Café Ecru on Tremont, I spotted a girl of about thirteen toss her bright pink backpack onto a chair at an empty table. When you've been alone long enough, you can just tell when someone else is. She cased the entire shop with a steady, careful eye that kids with parents just don't have unless they're looking for escape or they're with the wrong kind of foster. Let me tell you, some of those people who smile and open their doors are the worst people in the world.

The girl shifted in her seat toward a shiny leather satchel at the next table with an unyielding seriousness. Some finance bro had thrown it down before making his way to the counter, shouting into an earbud the whole time. An easy mark, but she wasn't taking in the bigger picture, seemed to me. Better to wait for a rush of customers and work with the commotion. Kids who get caught either end up back where they came from or in the system.

I turned to tap her shoulder but she spun around on me first, eyes wide as donuts. A cherubic unicorn embossed the front of her shirt, and her hair was pulled back by hair ties with orange cats waving one paw. The illusion of innocence and an overprotective parent nearby.

"My mom's waiting for me outside," she said. "I just came in to use the bathroom."

"It's right back there," I said.

The girl just stared at me for a moment. If she saw past the disheveled college student, the greasy hair, she didn't let on. At her age, I wouldn't have trusted anyone either, and that absence still would have scared me. She grabbed her pink bag and was out of there. I dropped into her seat and scrolled for dates. Sometimes you let the scene play out, sometimes you give it a nudge. We all learn, one way or another.

***

After drinks, the doctor had invited me into one of the slick new glass towers in the Seaport. He gushed facts about the building—no street noise at or above the horizon terrace, nearly half of the owners bought their residences cash down, sight unseen, and lived overseas. Over three hundred feet high. On-site pet salon and daycare. On and on. I spit some facts back at him: over four-thousand unhoused in Boston; average wait time of four years for housing choice vouchers. The doctor booped my nose with his index finger and we entered his energy-efficient, geometric two-bedroom. The gray doors, tucked kitchenette, and wall of glass all reminded me of a hotel. The best place to trick because nothing suggested permanence. Half those buildings had hotels at the base anyway, and the whole neighborhood split between them and trendy restaurants. All so busy and slick and empty, an extension of Logan just across the water where everyone's on their way to somewhere else.

The only potential problem with a place like this is the lack of toys. A few books, Waterford glassware, a little gold clock, all spread out on some shelves. No easy media catches either—any video games, music, or films either downloaded or floating in the cloud. The crafty architect had billed the oversized closet as second bedroom, where the doctor's aluminum laptop rested on a small metal desk. Above it hung various diplomas and photographs, one that showcased a younger, more vibrant version of the doctor. He and a crew of about twenty other volunteers struck various poses in bright green shirts that read "The Home for Little Wanderers." The recoil I felt earlier crawled back up my leg as I realized that he was a product of the system. Enough bad experiences at an impressionable age forced the certainty that some hidden danger lurked in him, because no one made it through unscathed.

As I turned to leave the room, he pressed his hand gently in the middle of my back and I froze. "There's a long story behind that one," he said.

"I bet," I said. "It's getting late."

"I came up through foster care," he said. "It's more complicated than the caricatures in the movies. That's all most people know." He'd practiced this speech before. "I was lucky, for the most part, compared to some other people I know."

"And you're a doctor," I said. Either he'd grown up in Disney Land or he was Superman, from where I was standing.

"A lot of hard work and a lot of help." He dropped his hand from my back and lifted it in front of his face like he'd never seen it before. "As a kid, I never wanted to be touched. A lot of shame. Watched families out in the world and didn't understand how they did it." He placed the hand on my shoulder and squeezed. "Still feels like a square peg, to be honest," he said, and chuckled. "Probably why I'm not attached."

"Me either," I said, almost without thinking. I was a college kid to him. It was like facing another iteration of myself, a little further down life's road, if only a couple run-ins with the system had gone the other way or I'd held on tighter when it tried to throw me off. The disgust I felt at his touch in the restaurant softened into a compassion for his self-awareness. With so many trophies on the wall to envy, at least I knew how to be intimate with someone. Sometimes I even enjoyed it. "Is that why you're discreet?" I said.

His sigh fell flat onto the cold metal desk. "Hard to say. A lot of FBOs, sorry, faith-based organizations, have their hands in shelter and foster care. Most of those people aren't trained in social work or child care, and since they volunteer, they only answer to the Lord."

"Clear enough," I said. I guess we all learned that on our own.

He stepped back and folded his hands on his hips. "I really admire you. Your generation. As hard as you all have it in some ways, you know exactly who you are and what you want. No one can stop you." His eyes flashed with all the life of the younger man from the photo, just for a moment. His shoulders hunched more toward the ground, and sadness pinched the edges of his mouth. Altogether not uncute. I kissed him and asked to use his shower.

***

The next morning, the doctor made us coffee and a bitter green shake from the Vitamix that he swore cured cancer or something. I never eat the day of a date so the shake didn't cut it, but he had to be out just as the sun came up and had the good sense to make sure I headed out with him. The gold clock hid in my jacket, all tucked under one arm. If he texted me to meet again, I'd wait a few days, then agree. But insist on pancakes or an omelet, and toast. If he asked about the clock, I'd deny, then ghost. When I was younger, this part of the dance always grated a bit—better survivors than me got tripped up for less. The helpers tossed them back into whatever part of the system God or the daily horoscope whispered to whatever robed clown sat behind the bench. Point is, I've seen human beings thrown every which way for the pimped-up transgression of doing their best with a bad situation.

I make sure never to overstay my welcome. Claiming a souvenir is a kind of insurance policy to that effect. There are a number of pawn shops around Boston, and on the rare occasion anyone starts a search, they keep to the ones closest to them. Always sell on the other side of town. My heart used to drop whenever I'd pass a guy who looked at me funny, especially when I carried my jacket, but that's just how some people watch the world go by.

EZ Pawn and Diamonds lurked at the garden level of a row of student apartments along the B Line in Allston. The proprietors were old-fashioned businessmen who knew their products and asked few questions. The clock caused quite a stir with the stocky fence behind the register, who betrayed his excitement by pulling his mustache like a mannequin just come to life.

"Four hundred," he said, still as a puddle.

"I think I'll check around a bit more," I said.

He frowned and I waited for him to roll out the spiel about how I wouldn't find a better price in all New England. Instead, he leaned into the clock so close that his breath fogged the glass.

"That piece is worth at least five," I said. "A family heirloom." The possibilities that really came to mind included a corporate retirement gift or country club golf prize, maybe worth two. The certainty with which the doctor threw his opinions around at drinks echoed a well-off foster parent with appropriate ties.

The proprietor raised a fuzzy eyebrow and coughed. "Family heirloom," he repeated. "Ok, five." He never agreed to my first price. This thing needed a proper appraisal. I scrolled through the dating app as I puzzled out next steps. Blocked a couple of guys who opened with nudes and responded to a more aimable "hi handsome." Five-foot-nine, one-hundred sixty-five pounds, smooth with a decent smile, said he was visiting in Beacon Hill. House-sitters were ideal; no real ties to the home and once removed from the owner. A star icon for the future prospect. Nothing from the doctor, so I texted, "Had a great time last night xx." Leave it there for now.

"I really shouldn't," I said. "Nana would be crushed." I glanced up vaguely at the suspended ceiling and decided on some research at the library. The barrel vault ceiling of Bates Hall stretched fifty feet. A good price for the clock would get me a sublet on Craigslist, maybe with on-site laundry.

At Café Ecru, I spotted that same girl with the pink backpack as I ordered an everything bagel with the works. Near the entrance, a dusty trio of two men and one woman I knew from the street, all wild-haired and puffy from fast food, argued grievances with enough volume and animation to make the tourists and workadays rush through their coffees. Maggie always entered with shoulders back and chest out, which signaled to everyone inside that she and the two men, Allan and Dinger Dog, would hold court. Bracelets of various makes and colors clacked and rattled as she announced all the local goings-on that the papers didn't cover. Allan hunched over his coffee in a thick, sooty coat as though he just stepped in from a blizzard. Some days Dinger Dog reeked of meth, a combination of urine and rotten eggs that just about peeled the beige off the walls, but not today.

The girl nibbled at her donut and sipped her orange juice like an anthropologist who'd drawn her conclusions with weeks left in the field. Somehow she'd hacked the chair discomfort code. That she was still there at all surprised me. It usually took the staff or a beat cop a few days to spot these kids and contact their parents or the doctor's Home for Little Wanderers. I mean, what the fuck in the Charles Dickens. A lifetime of blending in and fading back became a superpower years before most of us got thrown out or ran away. Most kids who got caught were green, or on something, and who could blame them.

"Thanks for saving me a seat," I said and sat down across from her. A yellow stain ran across the unicorn on her shirt, and the cat ties in her hair had loosened so that they stuck out at odd angles. Her fiery almond eyes saw the worst about you first. The trio glanced over from their corner, silent, but they recognized me well enough.

"My mom's coming back any minute," she said. "I'm just waiting while she's out on some interviews." Her upper lip stiffened and her gaze didn't leave mine. Either she was older than I'd guessed or set on her own earlier than I had. The trio would act up if I pressed her too much; some of our souls still bled from long ago run-ins with predators, and the more wounded or compelled of us boxed any shadow that suggested a recurrence.

"Ok, sis," I said, then let my tone float like a feather on the air. "You staying somewhere?"

She winced at my bluntness, and I braced for a kick or a scream. She composed herself enough to nod, with more grace and grit than an adult three times her age.

"Good," I said. The trio had fallen silent again. I winked at her and spun up on them in a squall of bluster. "Don't let this crew give you any trouble," I said. My arms hung off Maggie and Allan as I inhaled the fullness of this buttery, burnt coffee life. They laughed and said I was the one to watch out for. Maggie poked at my coat and I shrugged and decided to head out.

***

The grandeur of the Bates Hall always unnerved me a bit. The main reading room for the third largest public library in the country, originally named "a palace for the people," and projecting that Boston Brahmin paradox of appearing exclusive while proclaiming universal welcome. The pay-to-play Atheneum was just a mile away. Even as a kid I'd loved books, especially ones that reflected the dogged ignorance and violence of the world I knew. A little hope, sure, but not without leveling with me first. Both of my parents cited Bible verses from memory, and thought most novels perversive. They didn't know any better. Every winter now, I spread out at one of the long tables or slipped into one of the open conference rooms. A friend or two often shared the same mindset, and we helped each other pass the time when imaginary humans didn't cut it.

As a frequent visitor, I had no trouble signing out one of the public use laptops. The clock remained bundled in my jacket, in my lap. Folding back the fabric revealed the sterile gold cube within. Little clawed feet extended out of the base, and a small empty cup or urn topped it off. The clock itself was dead; no way I would have carried a ticking jacket out of the doctor's home, or around the city for that matter. The closest matches online suggested a nineteenth century French officer's clocks worth three, four thousand dollars. *Known as The Belle Epoque, a "golden age" between the Napoleonic Wars and WWI, marked by optimism, prosperity, and innovation.* My laughter barked through the grand columned hall and ruffled a few patrons bent over the glowing green reading lights. At the other end of the long table, a young man with harvest wheat field hair and a stained crimson H T-shirt coughed over a stack of law books. On another day I would have asked what drew him across the river, but, to be honest, I wanted to crawl into a stack and disappear. No need to stay longer anyway. Learning the streets didn't mean forgetting how to read a room, at least not yet.

***

The Common was wide and green and mostly empty. That weekday lull between lunch and rush hour. Smatterings of tourists strolled along the hilly paths and students played frisbee or took the sun on the cool grass. The late night and early morning with the doctor began to press its weight. My favorite bench tucked beneath a sycamore that played in the breeze not far from the State House. Any trouble and I was just a student in between classes. Usually somewhere accessible and non-threatening to potential dates, like Northeastern or BU. Across the street, the trio at Ecru had moved on, but the bright pink backpack rested unattended at a table. Not my business, but I decided to go and wait until the girl returned.

Ten minutes in, I pointed at the backpack and asked the cashier if he'd seen my sister. A new guy with a birdlike posture and a glazed expression, he shrugged and shifted his attention to a customer about to order. I scanned the sidewalk and the green beyond and startled as the doctor, in blue scrubs and white sneakers, crossed the street to the café entrance. I dumped the clock from my coat into the backpack and zipped it back up. As the doctor walked in, the girl turned around the corner that led to the bathrooms. She carried a little black cosmetics bag. Her face glowed and her hair shone with new attention. Thick eyeliner caked the edges of her eyes, which held everyone who had failed us both, just as I would fail her. There was no way around it.

The doctor squinted between us and studied the girl for a beat too long. No way they knew each other—another shock of my past overtaking the present. Transference transference transference. Maybe not the right term for the situation, but close enough, and the rhythm of the words brought me back.

"Hey!" I said, smiling. I introduced the doctor to my sister, up for a visit, and the girl to my friend who I went out with last night. Her sour expression fit her role, and I flinched in a quick entreaty for her to play along.

The doctor nodded like a mug and asked the girl what she thought of Northeastern. Only someone who rejected his past wouldn't recognize the two of us reliving it in front of him. The clock became a gaudy trinket of his denial. I would've felt guiltier if it had been some cheap sentimental token after all.

"Fine," she said. She opened her backpack to return the cosmetics bag and stared up at me after noting what else was inside.

"I've been a lame brother," I said. "She waited here like a champ while I caught up with some friends on the Common."

The doctor chuckled and stepped up to order. He asked if we wanted anything, and when we both shook our heads, he asked me to join him anyway. "Strange question," he said. "Did you happen to notice a small gold clock at my place, near the flatscreen?"

I pretended to think it over, visualizing his little hotel suite a few feet at a time. I glanced back at the girl and nearly shouted as the golden claw feet stood atop the sticky table, as ing and out-of-place as they had been on the doctor's steel shelves. The girl smirked and narrowed her dark eyes. She stuffed it back down just as the doctor turned to see what had gripped my attention.

Laughter shot through me like a hemorrhage, as flattened by the vinyl ceiling as it had lifted into the library's great dome. I coughed and straightened myself. "I do, I think," I said. "Yes."

"What's so funny?" the doctor said.

"It's stopped," I said. Intrigue rushed into his face. "Not funny, exactly. Just accurate."

The years of scamming and being scammed—this is your home now, your family; that camp will make you right; your body isn't yours—had conditioned me to a revolving door of misdirection. "Oh no," I said, eyes wide. My ruse crumbled in his dark eyes but I pressed on. "I was the last one out. Maybe I didn't shut the door right." Don't deny or hide the guilt, a friend in San Fran had said. Use it.

The doctor squeezed my shoulder and an old impulse rose up in me to punch him right in his face and run. But I knew better. Real gentleness, a surgeon's hands at that, so studied and attentive the previous night after I'd stepped out of the shower and into his bed. By the end he knew my body so well that I barely had to be there.

"It's ok," he said.

I just couldn't help myself. "No," I said. "It looked really nice." The girl had unzipped the bag again and pretended to rummage around while her attention remained fixed. "Let me replace it for you."

It was his turn to laugh. "It's an antique," he said, and mentioned nineteenth century France, its pricelessness, the Belle Epoque, all of my library research nearly word-for-word.

"Where'd you find a piece like that?" I said. He fidgeted the coffee and cruller the cashier handed him as though searching through stories, untangling my guilt until it dropped away. He wouldn't say, not really; he was too attached to his new life, and something about that clock drew him back into the one he'd left. Like the life I'd escaped in Michigan, when my mother found a men's magazine under my bed and my father hit me hard enough that my jaw still clicked when I chewed gum. A nurse and a civil engineer nurtured in the fear and disgust of the Catholic Church and Poland before its baptism. "Odmieniec!" my mother yelled, weeping. Changeling. The life that had only just stretched out its hand to the girl.

The doctor described an older friend of his family, or a neighbor, he didn't remember. An estate sale, anyway, he said. I decided that five, ten percent of the pawned price would go to the girl. More than I ever fell into at that age without being cheated right out of it again.

But she wasn't at the table. Outside, tourists and students passed by on the sidewalk. Across Park Street by the fountain, a man sold Boston hats and t-shirts from a wheeled cart. People rushed in and out of the glass-roofed cement cube that led down to the T. Maggie and Allan entered the café and set up court by the door. Mid-argument, Maggie studied me and sucked her tongue, but then resumed. I sped around to the bathrooms. An older woman called out "occupied" from one while the other was empty.

I turned to the doctor and the cashier. "Did you see my sister leave?"

"That girl's your sister the second y'all's mother steps in from her interview," Maggie said. She and Allan laughed.

"You kids. Playing games," he said.

The doctor only looked at me, with that painful remove that felt like home, now with the added fastidiousness of a surgeon who'd fought his way out of it. I almost said I was sorry, almost asked him for every detail of his life so that we might both feel less alone in these silent depths, so that he might toss me a rope to climb out of them. Instead, I ran out onto the sidewalk while Maggie and Allan cheered me on. A bright blue, steel-plated duck boat blocked the path across as the tour guide's history of the Park Street Church shouted from the loudspeakers. I glanced back, expecting to find the doctor behind me in a rage. His face greyed to that same stiff mask the girl had worn on our first meeting, and he seemed to mouth the words, "keep it."

***

All afternoon I searched for the girl, down Tremont into the theater district, back across Charles and past the Garden to Beacon Hill. That backpack would jump out at anyone from a mile off. About an hour after dark, I doubled back to the café. She was smart or scared enough to stay away, but she would be back. We all returned to our patterns; maybe we worked through them toward something else, but that took more than one night, and wouldn't erase them altogether.

I returned to my bench in the Common as shadows breezed up and down the walkways in bits of conversation and laughter. Shoes hit the pavement in the constant rhythm of a ticking clock that's framed the edge of every silence since.

Identicals

The night was strung together
like paper cutouts, those faceless identicals,
body after body after body joined
where hands would be but are not.

In this morning light, my eyes gather multiplicities—

glasses of bedside water, two lamps,
grandfather slippers on the floor.

French doors widening to the rain,
dogs asleep near the blowing curtains.

In your dream, there were three of you in a speeding car—
you driving you, you angry at you,
you slapping you
in the back of the head.

I'm not sure which one to hold.
You're not sure
which one to wake to—
and which one to forget.

Words are spoken—
good morning
my love
marry me—

We lean our bodies into one another.
We look for the warmth of two.

But there are only these paper-thin replicas of us
fluttering in the morning wind,

their edges, inexact and unsettling.
This is how it begins.

For God so loved the world, He left it burning

after the ten commandments

for God so loved the world, He left it burning
for God so loved the world, He left it burning
for God so loved the world, He left it burning
for God so loved the world, He left it burning
for God so loved the world, He left it burning
for God so loved the world, He left it burning
for God so loved the world, He left it burning

Tadpoles

Brother, in over-sized rubber boots, snow pants with holes in the knees, traces the cracks in the ice with his fingertips. With every clunking step of my boots, I test the limits of the ice's shattering, imagining my fate sinking to the bottom of the pond. Do you think they're still fighting? Brother asks. He looks back at the house looming behind us; its shadow cast along the shimmer of the ice. I listen quietly for sounds of my mother's sobbing, the booming echo of my father's exasperated snarls. Their commotion creates a crackling in the distance, a TV station playing static without a remote to change the channel. Instead, I focus on the ice, on the creatures that wriggle beneath in their own frozen kingdom.

Brother says come here, watch the tadpoles with me. He likes their resilience in the face of the freezing, the way their bodies form despite the suspension of time. In my own desperation to be cocooned, I make myself a cave out of the mounds of snow left by the snowplows. Breaking through the shards of hardened ice to form my own womb, I ignore the shaking of my hands, the frost that stiffens my mittens despite the resistance of my fingers. Come here, Brother says again. Really, Sister, you ought to see. Look at how the cold doesn't faze them. Do you think it's lonely down there away from the rest of the world? He looks up at me with reddened cheeks. His hair sticks up in clumps of unkempt yellows. Mama told him to wear his beanie, but he has torn it off and discarded it in the driveway, where the snow seeks to bury it. I leave my mittens in my cave, unafraid of the bite of winter, and I join Brother on the ice. He leans his face close to the ground, to hear for the rush of running water, watching the tadpoles in their explorations. Do you think they feel alone, the only ones in the whole universe? He asks, and his question echoes through the darkening street.

Years later, he will tell me, The cold raised us. This landscape of New England evergreen, up to our shoulder blades in snow, our hardened snow angels like gravestones in the lawns of the neighbors' houses. We think that this water that is no match for the tadpoles must, just the same, be no match for us. It gives us an escape from the harder things in life, the sort of cold mittens and gloves can't ward away.

The snow flurries down around us in big wet globs, sticking to our cheeks, to the tips of our noses. For a moment, there is no sound. There is no movement. It is Brother and I in a world free from the world. I reach my hand out to catch the falling snow, trying to hold it tight in my hand like a treasure from a discarded world, the ruin of a universe that belongs only to me, but it melts into water in my palm. Soon, Mama will call for us to come inside, and the snowplow will drive over my makeshift womb, rolling over my mittens in the dirt with it. Soon spring will come, and the breaking ice will reveal only shallow water beneath. Flowers will bloom, as they always do, and the tadpoles, which fought the cold and won, will wake up one day as frogs.

Melding Buildings, New York City

Archival Digital Photograph
20 x 30 inches
2012

Documentary photography, also known as street photography, has a long history that most often focuses on images of people. I am more interested in the little thing, some object or scene that might offer some insight into the place I am photographing, perhaps offering an epiphany. I am drawn to what the French call a flaneur, someone who "takes advantage of a wanderer's paradise: the streets of the city, filled with charming shops, stirring landmarks and ephemeral encounters."

J. L. BERMÚDEZ

Quadriptych of an Open Relationship

I.

_____ is the first man. I know he wants me the first day we meet in philosophy class. Something in the way he spreads his legs as I shed my coat full of wintry morning, or maybe the slant of his look, or the tenor of his jokes, or his questions about my philosophy of friendship. The way he asks me if I am really bi after I share my sexuality. How he thought I was a lesbian. His interest in my open relationship. How eager he is to share his poetry.

I have been pining after another classmate, a girl with dark hair and dark eyes who is named for an oracle, and I decide that she has become my muse. I want her in a way that ties a knot in my tongue and I spend pages of my time writing poems for an Archer, from Taurus. I am sure that she is straight, so I resolve to never tell her how I feel. Instead I go home every night and share my crushes with my girlfriend, who pays all our

II.

_____ is the second man. We meet in poetry class, and later I will learn that he is friends with _____, who was the first. My girlfriend and I stumble upon him on a drunken Saturday night in spring, deep in his cups at an Irish bar and willing to buy us ours. He is desperately in love with his best friend, a boy, and my girlfriend and I know this without him saying so. He wears his best friend's Vans proudly.

He showers my girlfriend with attention all night. He compliments her afro and when I step away, he tries to kiss her. He is surprised to find me feminine, in red-lipped warpaint and a cat eye, because I often present masc. When my girlfriend and I are alone in the bathroom, I ask, "are we doing this?" and she says "yes," so when we go back to him, I let him kiss me like the afterthought that I know I am.

III.

______ is the third man, but it's his friend who starts the conversation in line at the arcade. Something in the friend's smile tells me that we are both used to playing second fiddle, so I let him hook his hand around my waist while my girlfriend flirts with ______. We all smoke with a man who pulls pristinely rolled joints from the brown leather of his trench coat and shows off the stash in his cracked, metal briefcase, and my girlfriend laughs in that way that turns her all squints. We make friendships that last for only a summer, and we do not tell them that we are girlfriends.

I stumble upon the girl who I have made my muse on a thirsty Thursday evening, and as we take the T together, I invite her to get drinks at a bar in Allston. I tell her that my girlfriend wants us to meet up with our new friends, so on our way we talk about what it means to be bisexual, and she makes it clear that

IV.

____ is the last. We meet up for a drink after classes have ended on a cool night in fall. I shave everything despite telling myself that we're just friends, even though I like the gap in their teeth when they smile, their sandy wave of hair, their poems in our workshop, the way they smoke their Marlboro Reds. The gentleness in their voice. The way they move their hands.

I buy our drinks with my girlfriend's credit card, and after flirting in the chill, I say, "Just kiss me already," and their tongue lifts the words directly from my lips. So I tell myself that I will ask my girlfriend for permission. Because I like ____ too much. Because I want to do whatever this is right.

I go home and wait and write a sonnet about the ocean, about how I am torn apart by an undertow. Maelstrom, I call ____. Whitecap in my chest.

bills and puts me through school and cares for my dog, who loves me, who stays in the closet and does not desire to make love to me.

My girlfriend has been pining after a classmate of her own, a boy with dark hair and dark eyes who is named for a wolf. She tells me that I'm ____'s muse, and I preen at the idea of so much power over a man. My girlfriend tells me to pursue this if I want, reminds me that I do not need to ask her for permission, that we've finally decided it's okay to be open. So when he invites me to a party three days shy of twenty-one, I tell him yes, knowing exactly where it will lead.

Half a bottle of tequila later, he asks me if I'm flirting with him, and I tell him that I'm like literature: open to interpretation. So he kisses me on a stranger's balcony and buys me tacos that I don't touch before we Uber to his apartment in the heart of Cambridge. I tell him he's the first, and he tells me to use less teeth.

All is well until tequila wells in my throat and I'm on my knees in front of his toilet texting my girlfriend that I can't stop vomiting, calling for an ambulance be-

Everything about him is sharp and pale: his eyes, his hair, his milky white chest. He likes to put on lipstick and skirts in the bathroom of his apartment. We kiss him rosy in the stillness of his blue-black bedroom, and in the darkness his pet cat watches as my girlfriend's hands blur into ink blots against the creamy canvas of ____'s breast. He is pink in his cheeks and pink at his tip and pink in his hand when he slaps my girlfriend hard enough to make me hurt. He takes off the condom without letting us know and when I notice, we decide to keep going anyway. He is so drunk and nervous that he can't keep it up. He turns soft when I hold him in the cradle of my mouth.

He is my girlfriend's very first man.

We meet again, but this time at The Tam. He introduces us to a black-bearded bartender and buys us shots until we're smeared at the edges.

"I'm kind of an alcoholic," ____ jokes over his whiskey, "I've been in and out of rehab a couple of times." I laugh because he seems so young and I am only twenty-one and I haven't lived enough to learn what a cry for help sounds like.

she is straight and will only be my friend, and still I spend the night mapping my future in her words. I walk behind the group with her while my girlfriend teases ______, and I grind my teeth when he drapes his arm around the girl who is not my girl on the brown-banistered balcony, and I say nothing.

A week or two later, my girlfriend texts ______ and his friends to come get a drink with us. To her immense relief, it's only ______ who can meet us, and although she buys the drinks, we spend hours orbiting the tension like a three-person tango, flirting with the possibility of going back to ______'s place. While we play darts, I watch my girlfriend admire the tight cords of his arms, and I lament that my arms will never be strong enough to hold her tight to me in the throes of lovemaking I so desperately desire.

When we finally head to his house, we giggle and take pictures against the backdrop of a mural at the end of his block, and then we play what has to be the world's worst game of strip poker: taking off bracelets and socks and rings and a single t-shirt. I am tired of waiting, so when my girlfriend leaves the room to grab a glass of water, I use my

I do not show my girlfriend the love poem that isn't for her.

And when I am given permission, my throat pythons around the truth and I do not tell her: that I am craving the massage oil, the orange-candled sex: that every inch of me has become an ode to a fling with a poet: that I feel like a line break / my breath an enjambment // that leaps across a stanza. I tell myself that hiding this will preserve my girlfriend's feelings, and when I'm awoken by the gasp of her going through my texts and seeing all of the longing that I have kept for myself, I pretend I do not see the tremble of her lips. I remind myself that I have chosen this commitment. That I have indebted myself to loving her.

___'s girlfriend does not like me. Maybe this is because I have misgendered ___ for the first few months of our friendship, or maybe this is because I do not understand what it means to be poly and have entertained the idea of competing for the spot of the primary lover. I ask my girlfriend if she would try polyamory with me and she asks me why I like cause I'm feeling too faint and I can't believe that this is how she's meeting ____, helping me out of his apartment, refusing the ambulance because it will cost us far too much, taking an Advil even though I can't keep any water down and somehow I make it back to our apartment in one piece but something is unquenched, something disappoints me, and I'm reminding myself that first times are often disappointments, remembering our first time and how she flinched at the sight of me, accepting that I'm only attracted to how much ____ craves me, grappling with the idea that I can wield my sex like the edge of a sword, learning that I can seduce someone with one long look, filling the void that I attribute to my girlfriend's unwillingness to touch me and my unwillingness to leave her—because she is my first, because she must be the last, depending on her and the all the security she gifts me. I tell myself that I must stay with her, that in accepting her money I have cuffed myself to her ankles and must learn to love the taste of dust kicked in my mouth.

I fall asleep in her arms and am grateful that she takes care of me.

In the sweat of his apartment, he asks me to leave because he's having trouble staying hard with both of us there. My girlfriend doesn't mind, so I step out of the room, and in the doorway, I record them to remember that she never sang as sweetly for me. His cat curls up next to me on the little sofa and together we wait. He ends the night with an apology and calls an Uber for all the trouble.

My girlfriend texts ____ again, but he never responds. We assume that he's embarrassed. She laments the potential for a friendship with him and I don't tell her that I am festering on the inside when she won't fuck me the same way she fucked him. I am embittered by the fact that I knew him first, that her curls and her hands and the soft dimple of her lips should have been mine. I listen to the video in the lowest hours of the night.

When I visit The Tam for the first time in months, the bartender recognizes me as a friend of ____'s.

"Did you hear?" he asks as he serves my whiskey sour. "____ died a couple months ago. Asphyxiated at a party."

hands to say what she is so afraid of and break the dam of his desire.

When my girlfriend flies out to visit family for a week, _______ comes over with a weak excuse to see me. I ask if I can taste him and we fuck before he leaves, and although it should be permissible, I'm afraid to tell my girlfriend. She responds how I expected she would: why would I have sex with him, without her, if I knew she wanted him first?

I don't have the courage to see _______ again, to give him a proper goodbye, to treat him like the friend I so desperately need. When he moves to NYC a couple of weeks later, I do what I do best: I delete his number, his social media, his name.

doing what is most convenient for myself at any given time.

I ingratiate myself to ____'s beautiful mother, and I learn that ____ comes from music, money, and a happy family not afraid to love their child, who welcomes a handful of twenty-somethings onto their Airbnb balcony to smoke pot and pet their dog named for a pie. I imagine a life with ____ where we listen to Simon and Garfunkel with their father, where their money is not like Damocles' sword, where their love is not like my own mother's: holding onto the hope that I will outgrow my bisexuality and marry a nice man. I do not consider what would happen with my girlfriend, and I cling to this foolishness like an oasis after the desert.

Our last date that is not a date is a failed seduction. We smoke behind their apartment and although we kiss, I am the initiator. When I am with my girlfriend, I am always the initiator. A mutual friend texts them and they ask if I want to hang out together. I imply that I would like to have sex and they tell me that they're not feeling it. When they don't look at me, I realize that the fling is already over. It was never, not for a moment, a

I think of ____ often. His
crooked nose, his blonde shock
of hair. I wonder who will feed
Batman, his little black cat.

I finally stop watching the video
of a dead man with my woman.

competition with their girlfriend—
I wasn't ever in the running.

The last time I see ___, they help
me with a project on Bisexual Era-
sure because although they aren't
interested in me, they are still kind.
I wish I could smooth the tangle
of their tawny hair, but my girl-
friend is with me that day taking
pictures on the Common. I ask
them to write down the most hurt-
ful thing that someone has told
them about their sexuality, and
their sign reads "___, 22, 'You flit
around when you're young, but
eventually you have to pick…'"

I take a portrait of them hold-
ing this sign, and I smile even
though I know I will never see
them again. I long for the choice
to leave, for the luxury of not hav-
ing to pick someone over myself.

I do not sleep with anyone in our
relationship again. I love her, I re-
mind myself as I go home with
my girlfriend. There is a part of
me that knows this to be true.

CONTRIBUTORS

Adamu Yahuza Abdullahi, THE PLOB, TPC V, is a poet from Kwara state, Nigeria. He is a pioneer resident of Muktar Aliyu Art Residency, Minna, Niger state, Nigeria. He is a Best of the Net Nominee, and second place winner of both the first edition of Hassan Sulaiman Gimba Esq Poetry Prize and the Bill Ward Poetry Prize for Emerging Writers 2023. His works are published in *Lolwe, Strange Horizons, A Long House, The temz review*, and other places. He is on X / Twitter: @yahuza_theplob and Instagram as @Official_yahuzeey.

Iyanuoluwa Adenle (she/her) is a poet and essayist from Nigeria. She is curious about how memory, time and place work, and how we navigate life with language as a witness. Her works make a conscious attempt to explore the human conditions based on grief, loss, and love. Her writings have appeared or are forthcoming in *Agbowo, Banshee Lit, Maroko, Peppercoast Lit, Blue Earth Review, 20.35 Africa, Olongo, Kissing Dynamite, Lolwe, Empty Mirror*, and elsewhere.

Anselmo J. Alliegro is a visual artist and writer. Alliegro attended the Pennsylvania Academy of the Fine Arts and worked with some of the best artists in the country. At the academy he took courses in drawing, painting, printmaking, lithography, and others. Alliegro worked as Monitor of Models and Props assisting artists such as Vincent Desiderio. He gained a scholarship to Parsons School of Design in New York City. Alliegro has exhibited in galleries and benefits in the US and internationally. His art and writings have been published in various journals.

Chidera Solomon Anikpe (he/him) is a queer, Igbo storyteller with a flair for the dramatic. When he is not writing—which is more often than you would expect of a self-proclaimed 'writer'—Chidera spends his days binge watching an unhealthy ton of Korean dramas, listening to garish pop music and fighting senseless Twitter wars. He can be reached via email at chideraanikpe@gmail.com or on Twitter @ Dera_Writes.

Beth Anstandig holds an MFA in poetry from Arizona State University. Her work has appeared in *Caesura, Clackamas Literary Review, Flint*

Hills Review, Yale Anglers' Journal, Louisiana Literature, Phoenix New Times, and *Hayden's Ferry Review, Big Muddy, BODY*, and *El Portal*, among others. She is the author of *The Garden of Forking Paths* (Prentice Hall/Pearson) and *The Human Herd: Awakening Our Natural Leadership* (Morgan James Publishing). She has received a Pushcart Prize Nomination, Willamette Award in Poetry, The Clackamas Literary Review Poetry Prize, The Atlanta Review International Merit Award in Poetry, and three-time finalist standing for her first poetry collection.

J. L. Bermúdez is a queer Nicaraguan-American from sunny South Florida. She received her MFA from Florida Atlantic University and has served in the past as the Editor in Chief of *Swamp Ape Review*. Her short fiction has been published in *New Delta Review, Quarter After Eight, LEON Literary Review*, and is forthcoming in *Clockhouse*. Her nonfiction is forthcoming in *Passages North*. When she isn't writing, she loves going to the beach and playing fetch with her Boston Terrier, Odysseus.

Caroline Beuley is an alumni of the Breadloaf Writers' Conference and the Oxford Advanced Creative Writing Seminars and is currently pursuing an MFA in Fiction Writing at the University of North Carolina, Wilmington where she works as a publication assistant for Lookout Books. Her writing is published or forthcoming in *Chestnut Review, Cleaver, Fractured, F(r)iction*, and *Ghost Parachute*, among others. In her free time she loves to take her dachshund, Dumbledore, on walks and throw bits of paper around for her cat, Eloise. She is currently working on a short story collection and a young adult fantasy novel.

Charles Byrne is a photographer and writer with other photos forthcoming or recently published in *The Black Fork Review, F-Stop Review*, and *The Sun*.

Roger Camp is the author of three photography books including the award winning *Butterflies in Flight*, Thames & Hudson, 2002 and *Heat*, Charta, Milano, 2008. His work has appeared in numerous journals including *The New England Review, Witness* and the *New York Quarterly*. Represented by the Robin Rice Gallery, NYC, more of his work may be seen on Luminous-Lint.com.

Audrey-Anna Gamache is a writer based in Maine, who has been passionate about storytelling since she was young. This is her first publication.

Javeria Hasnain is a poet, translator, and educator from Karachi. She is an MFA Poetry candidate and a Fulbright scholar at The New School. Her poems and prose have been published in several journals and anthologies, including *Pleiades*, *Poet Lore*, *Mascara Literary Review*, *The Brazenhead Review*, and *Isele*, and nominated for Best of the Net and Best Microfiction. She has worked with Cave Canem Foundation, Teachers & Writers Collaborative, Tupelo Press, and Alice James Books. *SIN* is her debut poetry chapbook.

Alvin Kathembe (he/him) is a writer from Nairobi, Kenya. His poetry has been featured in *Dust Poetry Magazine*, *The Lumiere Review*, *Old Love Skin: Voices From Contemporary Africa*, and other publications. He co-edited down river road's third issue—"Asphyxia." His short stories have been published in *Jalada*, *Omenana*, *Brittlepaper* and *Equipoise*, available on Kindle. Find him on Twitter @SofaPhilosopher.

Elane Kim is a Korean American writer attending Harvard College. The editor-in-chief of *Gaia Lit*, she is the recipient of the 2024 Roger Conant Hatch Prize for Lyric Poetry, the winner of the 2021 Columbia Journal Winter Poetry Contest, and a Davidson Fellow in Literature. Her writing can be found in *Poetry*, *Narrative Magazine*, *One Teen Story*, and more. She is the author of *Postcards* (Bull City Press, 2022).

Andrew Nickerson (he/him) is a writer from Massachusetts. His fiction has appeared in *Waxwing Magazine*, *Stoneboat Journal*, *Guesthouse*, and elsewhere. He likes to read on his porch when the weather is nice and received an MFA from Emerson College.

Chiwenite Onyekwelu's debut poetry chapbook, *EXILED*, is forthcoming in Red Bird Chapbooks. His poems appear in *Cincinnati Review*, *Adroit Journal*, *Hudson Review*, *ONLY POEMS*, *Frontier*, *Palette*, *Chestnut Review*, and elsewhere. He was shortlisted for the 2024 Isele Magazine Poetry Prize. In 2023, he won the *Hudson Review's* Frederick Morgan Poetry Prize, and was a finalist for the Alpine Fellowship Prize, as well as the Writivism Poetry Prize. Chiwenite served as chief editor at The School of Pharmacy, Nnamdi Azikiwe University, where he recently completed his undergraduate studies. He's on Twitter as (@chiwenite9).

Jules Ostara is an eclectic artist and writer. She greets a blank surface as both playground and temple. Jules thought she wasn't good enough and pursued a practical degree resisting the attraction to art supplies for too long. She's since learned to embrace the beauty of imperfections, trust the process, and play with possibility. She also loves encouraging others to do the same through creative courses. There may be obstacles, such as limited supplies or physical conditions, let's make art anyway! That's what being a stubborn artist means to her. At ThriveTrue.com you can see her books and other offerings.

Esther Ra is a bilingual writer who alternates between California and Seoul, South Korea. She is the author of *A Glossary of Light and Shadow* (Diode Editions, 2023) and *book of untranslatable things* (Grayson Books, 2018). Her work has been published in *American Literary Review*, *Boulevard*, *The Florida Review*, *Rattle*, *The Rumpus*, *Bellingham Review*, *PBQ*, and *Korea Times*, among others. She has been the recipient of numerous awards, including the Pushcart Prize, 49th Parallel Award for Poetry, and Sweet Lit Poetry Award. Esther is currently a J.D. candidate at Stanford Law School. (estherra.com).

David Sheskin is a self-taught artist who has been published extensively over the years. Among the magazines his work has recently appeared are *Palooka*, *Cleaver Magazine*, *Shenandoah*, *Quarterly West*, *Superstition Review* and *Pacific Review*. You can view more of his art on the website sheskinart.my.canva.site.

Em Townsend (they/she) is an emerging writer from the Washington, D.C. area and a student at Kenyon College in Gambier, OH. Their work is published or forthcoming in *Chestnut Review*, *Shō Poetry Journal*, *West Trade Review*, *Frozen Sea*, *Unbroken Journal*, *Rough Cut Press*, and elsewhere. Read more at https://townsend31.wixsite.com/em-townsendportfolio.

Nikki Ummel is a queer artist and editor living in New Orleans. Nikki has been published with *Gulf Coast*, *The Georgia Review*, *Black Law-*

rence Press, and others. She is the 2022 recipient of the Leslie Mc-Grath Poetry Prize and 2023 recipient of the Juxtaprose Poetry Award for her manuscript, Bloom. Nikki is the co-founder of LMNL, an arts organization focused on readings, workshops, and residencies. She has two poetry chapbooks, *Hush* (Belle Point Press, 2022) and *Bayou Sonata* (NOLA DNA, 2023), funded by the New Orleans' Jazz and Heritage Foundation. You can find her on the web at www.nikkiummel.com.

Chestnut Review
VOLUME 6   NUMBER 2   AUTUMN 2024
FOR STUBBORN ARTISTS

Roses12

alcohol inks, acrylic and watercolors on yupo paper.
12x12 inches, 2024
(Cover Art)

I primarily use acrylic paint, latex paints, inks, papers and charcoal. My images contain many diverse layers of meaning, from the universal to the specific and personal. Many of my works are abstract. I am frequently interested in pattern and/or creating a rich sensual surface by making layer upon layer of marks. There is often an unseen history within these layers as images are obscured and revealed.

During our Covid times I worked on a series of colourful abstract and floral prints in both black and white and vibrant colors. At times my work speaks to issues of social justice, revelation and connection. My work frequently gives reference to my experience with nature. My images can provide occasions for contemplating the unity that underlies things which at first may seem disparate.

Chestnut Review

VOLUME 6 NUMBER 2 AUTUMN 2024

Chestnut Review LLC, Ithaca, New York
chestnutreview.com

Chestnut Review appears four times a year online, in January, April, July, and October, and once per year in print in July.

ISSN 2688-0350 (online), ISSN 2688-0342 (print)

CONTENTS

SPECIAL THANKS

To our generous Patreon supporters:

Adam Boustead, Allan Ebert, Ciel Downing, John Fredericks,
Buddfred Levi, Marijean Oldham, Benjamin Thorne,
Regina McIntosh, and Cynthia Wolley

to learn more, go to
https://patreon.com/chestnutreview

Introduction

Autumn has arrived, and with it a fresh new wind. We look to the turning of the year with enthusiasm, with this being the last issue before the calendar year changes to 2025. We are looking ahead to new initiatives such as an art book that represents the last five years' worth of art, with artistic responses by our community, and a new retreat next year in Riga, Latvia.

We are pleased to publish our nominees for Best of the Net and the Pushcart Prize on the site. Many congratulations to those writers and artists: Lena Zycinsky, Vincenzo Cohen, Richard Lingo, Tamara Panici, Quinn Rennerfeldt, Claire Zhou, Daniel Brennan, Michael Imossan, and Maryhilda Obasiota Ibe, Sara Graybeal, Nicole Hazan, Caitlyn Hunter, and Shauna Friesen. Claire and Michael have since joined our staff and are doing great work behind the scenes for us.

Our hearts go out to those affected by Hurricane Helene and other climate disasters this year. We hope that you are proof against ill winds and that you may follow kind currents where they lead.

Annunciation

Always the gray dawn
when the pain angel appears:
strange bells ring in my ears,
tinkling up and down my limbs.
I dissipate into the bruised
half-moons under my eyes.
The sun's white light glares
on the horizon—it must be almost five.

On the bathroom floor,
I think of Mary, who said *Behold:*
I am the handmaid of the Lord,
let it be done to me…
but I would pass this chalice if I could—
and I have, to my daughters.
My mother to me, her mother
to her: a trinity of Marys,
none of us unscathed.

Agony makes me crave
meaning, not just relief.
I want to commune with martyrs,
sweat blood, trade in miracles
or a little holiness, at least.
But even with my head
exploding, I know the truth:
I'm no more chosen than I'm god
forsaken.

A Conversation with Therese Gleason, author of *Hemicrania*

MSP: Hello everyone! I'm here with Therese Gleason, the author of *Hemicrania*. Throughout this process Therese has become a dear friend. My first comment in Submittable on this chapbook was that it was "inventive and weird in all the right ways." However, it goes beyond weird for the sake of weird and into Therese's specific, unique blend of witchcraft and natural remedies, medical disability and contemporary healthcare, historical takes on the health and hysteria of women, and elements of Catholic religion and, if I may say so, culture.

Therese, from the very beginning this chapbook struck our staff with its voice, experimentation and variation in having found poems, hermit crabs, and visual poems, and outlook. How did you develop the unique recipe when formulating this project?

TG: Thank you so much, Maria! 'Weird in all the right ways' is high praise and I'm beyond grateful to you and the team at *Chestnut Review* for believing in this project and helping me develop and refine it. It's been a joy finding in you not only an astute and sensitive editor but also a kindred spirit and lovely friend.

Hemicrania emerged over the last few years in an organic way during a period when my headaches, which I have had since childhood, became much more severe and frequent—crossing the threshold from episodic to chronic migraine. Finding effective treatment was a long process, as it is for many migraine patients, since accessing newer therapies requires a healthcare provider who not only acknowledges and validates your symptoms, but is also savvy about navigating the labyrinthine hoops required by the medical industrial complex: basically, you have to try and "fail" older and less effective, often off-label drugs with unpleasant if not intolerable side effects before insurance (if you are lucky enough to have it/have a decent policy) will cover the cost of treatments. Not only is this infuriating, but it is also inequitable: un- or under-insured, economically disadvantaged and historically marginalized groups such as BIPOC patients face steeper barriers to accessing migraine treatment, and are more likely to have their pain minimized or discounted when they do. It's no surprise, then, that outcomes are far worse for these migraine patients.

During the worst of this migraine stretch, I found myself struggling to function with near daily pain lasting weeks at a time, ranging from mild to severe, and often hovering at a frustrating level that was tolerable (i.e., I wasn't vomiting or unable to see straight from the pain) but bad enough that I wanted to lie down in a dark, quiet room. I also began experiencing more intense migraines more frequently, with intractable headaches and nausea that sometimes required IV medication to break them since I couldn't keep anything down. I write about one such experience in my hybrid piece, "In My Head (He Said, She Said)," in which I was initially denied care in part due to the strains on the healthcare system wrought by Covid. The encounter I describe left me physically and emotionally drained, demoralized—and angry.

In response to this and my increasing helplessness and frustration with my worsening headaches, I wrote a long, initially rant-like essay describing what had occurred, and began reading about the history of migraine and its treatments. I sought out poems, essays, and memoirs by others who have struggled with this disease, seeking validation and solace. I started compiling notes on the weird lore I dug up, adding them to my essay. While I struggled to put my experience into poems because of my migraine symptoms—not only headache but the attendant brain fog, fatigue, and visual (i.e., computer screens) and sensory sensitivity—I experimented by arranging and rearranging the words of other migraineurs along with a mix of migraine remedies spanning centuries, cutting them out and pasting them, finding this tactile work with language strangely soothing and satisfying. I began making collages using pictures of my migraineur great-grandmother, Eva, and the ads and medical ephemera I found or was referred to in the books I was reading. I sent out the long essay, which was growing unwieldy, a few times, but it wasn't picked up, and gradually I decided to try breaking it up into pieces. I threw in a couple of poems I had already written about migraine between and around these found poems, and began writing into the gaps that remained with my own experiences. Over time, this accrued into a (hybrid) collection.

MSP: Part of the interplay of the chapbook is the long history that extends to the present—which is true of the Catholic Church, the gender inequity that extends to the present day, the marginalization and undermining of women's bodies, and the intergenerational inheritance of migraines themselves. How do you see your work responding to this in poems like "Remedia" and "On the Heredity of Migraine," which use found text from historical authors?

TG: Migraine goes back at least five generations in my family that I know of, and probably further, given how heritable, and prevalent, the condition is. Migraine has been documented in medical treatises all over the world for literally millennia. For instance, Bald's *Leechbook* is from the 10th century, and the epigraph for "Revenant" is from an incantation against headache found on tablets at the royal library at Nineveh from the 7th century BCE.

Nearly all the women on my matrilineal line (and a few men) from my great-grandmother to my children, get migraines. According to my great aunt, my great-grandmother may have had hemiplegic migraine: one side of her body would temporarily become numb/paralyzed during attacks. I can't imagine what she must have gone through at the time, sharecropping with my great-grandfather on a farm with no electricity or running water, caring for three little children and scraping by during the Depression when she had little more than caffeine, aspirin, and "nerve tonics" like the one described in "Maiden, Mother, Crone." Apparently, she drank copious amounts of coffee, all day long, probably to self-medicate her headaches, and often complained of feeling nervous. No wonder!

I started searching for newspaper articles on headache and advertisements for migraine remedies in Indiana and Iowa (on newspapers.com) during the time she was alive (1896-1961) which yielded some of the found language in "On the Heredity of Migraine:" ill-informed male "experts" and doctors expounding on the moral failings and weaknesses of the "female sex," blaming women (not to mention mentally ill, epileptic, and gay people, for that matter) for their own migraines. I felt compelled to use some of the horrid language from the medical columnist Dr. William Brady (who was, to be fair, regarded as a quack, but still published widely) and doctors such as Harold Wolff and Walter C. Alvarez because despite the absurdity of their claims, they are resoundingly similar to the attitudes still espoused by some in the healthcare profession (and sometimes even well-meaning friends and family) today.

I included the language from the *Leechbook* and other ancient sources with migraine remedies partly because I love the obscure herbal references, diction and sound of these texts, but also because in a way, they serve as vindication that migraine (i.e., "ache of half the head") is a certifiable, recognizable (we now know, brain-based, neurological) illness that has affected people all over the world since time immemorial—no matter what any doctor past or present might suggest to the contrary. But my overarching goal was not to vilify (male) healthcare practitioners, or any particular medical provider, but to raise awareness so what happened to me won't happen to someone else.

In fact, one of the (uncomfortable) realizations I gleaned from writing this collection was that I had internalized much of this "medical gaslighting:" I told myself for years and years that my headaches weren't that bad, that it wasn't worth seeing a neurologist again (when I first sought help for my migraines fifteen years ago, I was not offered preventive treatment, in part because it was not yet available, and in part because my migraines were more episodic than chronic at that point). My hope is that the pieces in this collection raise awareness about migraine and validate others living with chronic headache and other pain disorders.

I should also point out that I have also received timely and compassionate care for my migraines at other times, both at the same urgent care clinic referenced in my piece, and at the emergency room. It just shouldn't depend on the luck of the draw to be able to get relief in the throes of a severe migraine episode. Nor should the color of someone's skin, class, sexuality, gender orientation or income limit their ability to access effective preventive and acute treatments. The reality is that there is no cure for migraine, but there is hope for managing the pain and symptoms of the condition. And a whole community of others who understand you, believe you, and want to support you. I wouldn't choose, or wish it upon anyone, to be in the migraineurs' club, but I have found many supportive friends.

MSP: Much has been written about the Church and the modern day crises it faces, especially the recent blowback regarding what is perceived as increased openness to LGBTQ+ Catholics, female priests, and other modernizations of the church. How is it possible to write into religion as a reclamation, an affirmation of identity, and a rebuke? What advice do you have for others who are struggling to integrate their religious heritage with their artistic practice and beliefs, no matter what religion?

TG: Because I was raised in a devout, southern (Kentucky) Catholic family, and attended Catholic school from grades K-12, I suspect I'll be disentangling aspects of my identity, religious upbringing, and innate spirituality and beliefs for the rest of my life. There are no easy answers or roadmaps, but I do think over the years I have become more comfortable with ambiguity, with acknowledging two conflicting feelings or truths at once. That is, I can oppose the Church's doctrine that women can't be priests and that marriage must be a union of a (cis-gendered) man and woman, but I can also appreciate the beauty of the Psalms, the faith and courage of the saints, the wisdom and compassion of Jesus's teachings, and the glorious tradition of sacred music, art, and architecture. After all, the Church was my first introduction to poetry: the language of the Bible readings, the music of the psalms, the hymns and songs of my youth. I can decry the repression of the divine feminine, body, and sexuality while also acknowledging that I find the rituals, relics, and mystical elements of Catholicism compelling and meaningful. I can acknowledge that, despite the ways I have had to extricate my own will and voice from a pattern of self-effacement and 'martyrdom,' particularly among the women in my family, I have also had many models of genuine love, strength, and faith.

I love the rituals (communion, confession, funeral rites, Ash Wednesday, the washing of feet, Palm Sunday) of the Catholic religion. Over the years, I have come to imbue them with my own interpretations. And too, as a white American whose ancestors immigrated to the country several generations ago, my Catholicism has served as a kind of cultural identity for me in a vacuum of sorts, and has provided the gift of communion and community. I am grateful to have inherited rituals and holidays to mark important occasions, and to share with my own children. I can seek out the female saints and mystics, revere the example of Mary and the Magdalene, and imagine myself into the stories of the women of the early church and beyond whose voices and actions, while not always recorded, were nevertheless formative. For me, spirituality is now less about how I define myself in terms of organized religion, and more a practice of trying to be open, grateful, kind, and alert to grace. I also believe writing can be a kind of spiritual and contemplative practice, though it doesn't have to be.

MSP: In your poetry, you invoke St. Teresa of Ávila, your namesake and the subject of a very sensationalized episode in Catholic sainthood. What is your personal connection to her and her story?

TG: I grew up reading the "Lives of the Saints," little books my grandmother would get us from the Catholic store. I was fascinated by the often gory portrayals of the martyrs, especially the beautiful and virginal female saints who chose God in lieu of male suitors, even if it meant death by spiked wheel, burning, or beheading. There are two "Therese" namesake saints in the Catholic Church: St. Therese of Lisieux, the "Little Flower," known for her small acts of kindness and devotion to Jesus, and the passionate (and sexualized) Teresa of Ávila—take a look at Bernini's sculpture of "St. Teresa in Ecstasy" and you'll see what I mean. I chose Therese for my Confirmation saint in 8th grade, but I remained fascinated by Teresa of Ávila, whom I came to know more about when I lived in Madrid, Spain for two years, and visited her birthplace in Ávila.

I learned along the way that Teresa of Ávila is the patron saint of headaches and migraines. A reformer, mystic, and intellectual, there is speculation that Saint Teresa was also lesbian. She founded the (both male and female) Order of the Discalced Carmelites, and is one of only three female saints to be named a "Doctor of the Church," a title reserved for

(37) saints who have made significant theological and doctrinal contributions. Incidentally, Hildegard of Bingen, another female Catholic mystic and Abbess featured in this collection, is also Doctor of the Church, leaving behind not only many theological and spiritual treatises but also medical manuscripts such as *Causae et Curae*, which described physical ailments and remedies. All three of these saints (Therese, Teresa, and Hildegarde) also lived with chronic (often migraine-esque) illness including headaches, bodily pains and weakness, often depicted as part of their visions and mystical experiences. In fact, some believe that the drawings and writings of Hildegard reflect migraine aura although historian Katherine Foxhall disputes this. For me, Therese and Teresa reflect at times dueling but also dual aspects of female identity: on the one hand, the pure (virginal) woman revered for her acts of self-abnegation as much as kindness; and on the other, the fierce and fearless woman who embodies and steps into her power, sexuality, and intelligence. I find in both of them, and Hildegard, saints to venerate and emulate.

MSP: I love that the form and content of *Hemicrania* reflect each other, as migraines often have auras, sensitivity to light and sound (and scents!), nausea, and other changes in physical perception and mental acuity. "Photophobia," to me, is a standout poem that captures this, lauding the "fish [gliding] through the Mystic" with "finned tongues, pink-white, eye-/less." There's a sense in the chapbook of any port in a storm—any remedy or relief from a migraine, whether natural, medicinal, prayerful, or the cool dark cave from "Postdrome," with its " waking dream that unfurls/in cerulean, gold and green." How much does the arc of these poems reflect your own journey as a migraineur?

TG: Yes, there are many ways in which migraine leads to a kind of sensory synesthesia, and I did try to invoke this in playing with the form of the poems—and I appreciated your encouragement to lean into and explore the visual and concrete elements of the poems. Some reflect my experience of a severe migraine episode quite literally, and viscerally (e.g., "Migraineur," and "Our Lady of the Burning Bush"). I was also inspired to evoke the experiences of other migraineurs who experience visual auras and other strange symptoms. While I don't experience a visual aura, just extreme sensitivity to light, and sometimes blurry vision, I do experience a sensory aura at the beginning of a very bad attack: tingling and numbness in my face, lips, and arms, and hot and cold flashes and prickling up and down my body.

Now that I have been on preventive treatment (monthly injections and Botox for migraine every three months) for the last three years, my headaches have improved in terms of frequency and severity. I haven't had to go to urgent care or the ER (knock on wood) and my symptoms are easier to get under control, even during a more intense attack. It's rarer now for me to get to the point of vomiting or having to call out of work, but it still happens occasionally. Lately, I'm experiencing more neck pain and vestibular symptoms (dizziness) which might be benign positional vertigo, which is also associated with migraines, so I'm currently getting physical therapy for that. I still have to take my Nurtec rescue medicine several times a month when a bad headache is coming on, and I sometimes still have days at a time of headache or rough weeks or months, but in general the pain and symptoms are muted, more manageable. I'm so grateful for this, and hope it continues. I currently hold a full-time job as a public school educator, teaching ESL to multilingual learners in grades K and 1 in an inner-city school. I love my job—but there is no way I could do it without my migraine prevention treatments in place.

MSP: Would you mind telling us a bit about what's next for your writing career? Are you working on other projects and/or thinking about extending this chapbook into a full-length manuscript?

TG: I've been sending out my first full-length manuscript, *Driveway*, about the reverberating impact of grief, anxiety, and parenting. It's an elegy for my father, who died suddenly at my childhood home in Kentucky when my mother was the same age as I am now, and my brothers were the same age as my teenage children. It's placed as a finalist a few times, but hasn't found a home yet. Some of the poems in it were written over 20 years ago, while some are new. I am continuing to refine it, and am practicing patience and perseverance, essential requirements for being a writer/artist.
I'm also working on a second full-length manuscript which will meld some of the poems and themes of my chapbook, *Matrilineal* (Finishing

Line, 2021), with *Hemicrania*. My great-grandmother Eva figures promi-
nently in *Matrilineal* as well. She was an adoptee whose mother (Faley)
was also adopted, and the origins of her birth parents were a mystery
until my great-aunt unearthed a remarkable story through her painstaking
research, and did us all the favor of writing it down. I'm excited to delve
into this project more fully in the future.

MSP: Thank you for responding to my questions. It's been a pleasure
working with you and helping this chapbook come into the world. All,
please look for Hemicrania on our site and Amazon page, which will be
out later this month!

TG: I can't thank you and the team at *Chestnut Review* enough, for every-
thing: giving me feedback on an earlier draft of my chap (I resubmitted
when it wasn't accepted the first time around), for the transparent and
organized process for publication, for connecting me with CR contribu-
tor Sheila Gomes, who created the most gorgeous cover with pictures
of my brain, and most of all, for your generosity, support, and brilliant
input. It's been a dream come true!

Hemicrania will be available soon in print and
ebook!

See the next page for the beautiful cover by
Chestnut Review artist Shee Gomes

HEMICRANIA

Poems

Therese Gleason

Sonata for Pain

Sonata: A musical structure consisting of three main sections: exposition, development, and recapitulation. The first movement of Beethoven's Fifth Symphony, for example, is written in sonata form.

Da-da-da-dummmm. "It's Fate knocking at the door," Beethoven supposedly said of the opening to his Fifth Symphony.

"Death is coming for you," the notes seem to say. "It is here." The fate motif hovers throughout the entire first movement like a fog, condensing, solidifying, gathering strength, gliding closer, sometimes backing off but never far away. You inhale its mist. You learn its bitter taste.

The fermatas above the fourth and eighth notes means the sound is held in the conductor's fist for as long as they choose. Beethoven gives no directions on this. You are gripped, immobile, forced to endure the existential terror "until," as he later wrote, "it pleases the inexorable Parcae to break the thread."

I imagine sticky, white tendons wrenching themselves off my bones, dying their wretched death in despair. While I don't have an official diagnosis, this seems, from my internet sleuthing and several misdiagnoses, like a form of tendinopathy. My husband, who is Greek, tells me that *tendono* (τεντώνω) literally means "I am stretching."

Yes, I suppose I am.

I think of David Foster Wallace: "…sometimes human beings have to just sit in one place and, like, hurt."

Except that I can't sit.

I lie face down on the floor and stare at clumps of dust under the TV stand. I turn the other way and watch the tiny stitches of white fabric in the sofa. I come to know them intimately. My thread friends.

⌢

Stretch: to adapt or extend the scope (of something) in a way that exceeds a reasonable or acceptable limit.
My days:

~~Breakfasts with my mother, her laughing so hard I worry for the state of her blood vessels~~
~~Evenings with my husband, teasing each other, prying open emotional doors~~
~~Walks with my dog, watching her come alive in the fresh morning air~~
~~Voyages to psychological depths with my therapy clients~~
~~Dawn writing hours, bent over the paper like a hook~~
~~Talks with friends along elm-lined streets~~
~~Meandering through novels and poetry~~
~~Restorative guided meditations~~
~~Dishes, laundry, yoga~~
~~Thought~~
~~Hope~~
Pain.

My life: swept off the table by the cruel swipe of a cosmic hand, which now grips my bones, twists and wrenches them into contortions of pain.

⌢

I hit play on the podcast Apple has selected for me and lower myself into CBD-infused bathwater. If I let the back of my legs touch the surface of the basin, my skin and muscle tissue feels like it is being crushed in a carpenter's vice, so I use my hands to try to keep myself afloat. I try to focus on the story of a wild-haired, unkempt man, a man who emerges from suicidal despair and into a life of severe pain. A man who chose to live in agony, but to do so for his art. A man whose music, I hope, exists as a kind of blueprint, as a map from despair to whatever exists on the other side of it. As I learn about Beethoven, as I learn about his anguished Fifth Symphony, I feel the grip of obsession. A distraction from my pain and, possibly, a way through it.

⌢

A solitary oboe rises above the rest of the orchestra in the Fifth Symphony's first movement. It's a slight parting of clouds amid an existential storm. Suddenly alone, no strings, no woodwinds, no timpani, it plays a sad little solo and fades away. The march of dread resumes its progression. How long did it last? Maybe fifteen seconds? Fifteen seconds of freedom, of life, of a tender human song, of a voice saying it doesn't want to die, it just wants to sing a bit longer, a pleading voice, a dissolving voice, a voice dissolving too soon because of course it must, because of course everything must. I play the first movement again and again, clinging to the fleeting voice of the oboe, then grieving its inevitable loss.

⌢

I tuck a small list of questions into my phone case. Could this be gluteal tendinopathy? Should I try to exercise? What movements should I avoid? It is written on tiny yellow flip-pad paper, about six items. Like many women I know, I am working to undo years of social conditioning that has warped my true voice into an excessively placating and polite one. I want to advocate for myself, but I want to be a "good" patient. I want him to *want* to help me.

I emerge with a sticky note on which the scribbled name *Brad* is underlined twice. "This is my guy," the physician had said, referring to a young athletic therapist at his clinic. It was only after I pressed him to give me some—any—advice that he wrote the name. No physical exam was done and no questions were asked about my pain, there was only a shrug and the word "weird," and then he nearly ran out of the room. Back in my car, hunched behind the steering wheel, I put the two pieces of paper next to each other and for a brief second between sobs, snorted with laughter.

The first movement begins in the stormy key of C-minor, briefly tries to struggle its way into C-major, fails, and ends up in the same tempestuous key in which it began, with the same dreaded four-note motif.

Da-da-da-dummmmm.

2

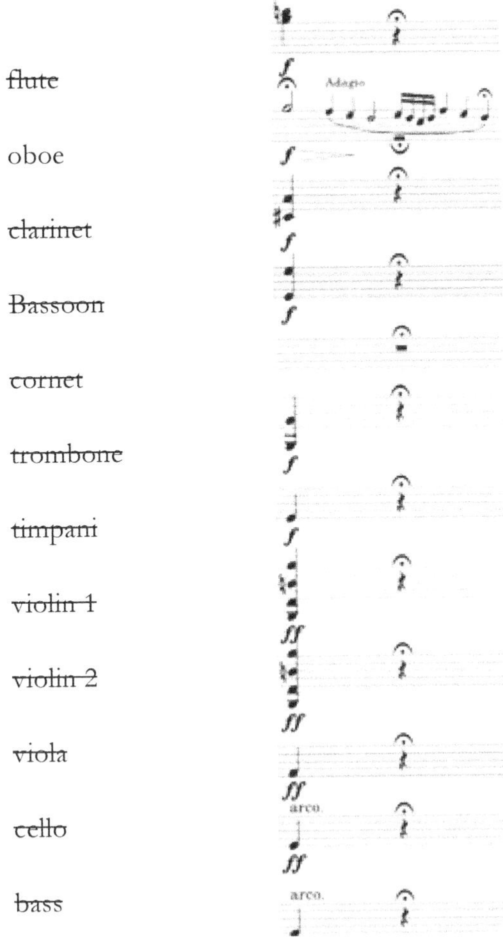

This illness is a dress rehearsal for death. I find myself saying good-
bye to all the things that used to fill my days, grieving them one at a time.
Loss isn't mentioned in the medical research papers I'm reading, nor is
it on any internet list of symptoms or treatments or potential complica-
tions, nor is it in the conversations I'm having in doctors' offices. Yet
grief for my former life shadows me everywhere.

I watch the same BBC documentary on Beethoven over and over.
I listen as conductors discuss the Fifth Symphony, longing for their
interpretations, longing to understand my own pain through Beethoven's
notes, to see how he made sense of his anguish, how he lived with and

through it. Conductor Iván Fischer is unblinking and harsh when he says the Fifth Symphony is our medicine, the pill we absolutely must swallow. "You have to," he says with a terrifying certainty, his eyes bulging. He points at me through the computer screen. The Fifth is the triumph of light over darkness, he says, beginning in the depths of C-minor and fighting its way into the bright glory of C-major. "Beethoven invented the journey from hell to heaven," he says. I listen for that transition, longing to feel it deep in my bones, willing it to seep into my writhing tendons.

⌢

The oboe. The orchestra is silent while it vibrates unsteadily on muted air currents, fluttering with strange and soulful beauty, like an improvisation, a rustle of grass in winter, a loon haunting the darkening sky, a curl of smoke lifting into air. As the aching voice disappears, your heart, in longing, tries to go with it, and now you sit with a heart torn in half, bleeding, knowing once again the deep pain of all your losses.

⌢

I have to miss my writing workshop, and ask another member to send the Zoom link. Nancy, one of the group, writes back and says "Life is sometimes/oftimes horrible with pain. It makes an ogre of me." Ogre is the *exact* right word. The fist loosens just a little. Makes room for Nancy, for her word, now ours.

⌢

Beethoven, I learn, was an ogre much of his life. He was at his most ogre-like when he isolated himself, which he did at first to hide his increasing deafness and finally in an attempt to cure it in a countryside retreat. After four months away, forced to confront the continued and often painful loss of his hearing, he wrote to his brothers: "…that fond hope—which I brought here with me, to be cured to a degree at least— this I must now wholly abandon. As the leaves of autumn fall and are withered—so likewise has my hope been blighted."

The cosmic hand had come for him too.

⋅

"Chronic pain isn't just pain that doesn't stop," Julia Buckley writes, "it puts your entire body into a chrysalis and morphs you into a monster." When I read this line in The Guardian I join a new family of ogres and monsters. I am learning that words can stretch down far enough to find you wherever you are, can reach even into the unreachable depths of pain.

⋅

"There is little holding me back from ending my own life," Beethoven wrote in that same letter to his brothers. "It is only art that is keeping me going."

I see another doctor and admit that I've noticed suicidal thoughts. "Well if it gets worse," he says, "you know what to do." I am perplexed so he says, "Go to the Emergency Room." I crack a smile thinking it's a joke but it isn't. Nine hours in the ER for an assessment and a discharge? I can't even sit in a chair for nine minutes without crushing pain. But, the fact that he gives me space and silence in which to look down at the floor and cry, that he doesn't rush me, or, like so many other doctors, keep asking me to sit down, to take a seat, to pull up a chair, just that alone puts me in mind of Mary Oliver: "No one has yet made a list of places where the extraordinary may happen and where it may not."

⋅

After months in emotional turmoil and physical agony, Beethoven accepted that his hearing would not improve, that he would become completely deaf, that he was helpless against this fate, that he would live with screeching tinnitus and intolerable blasts of noise, and he created his best, most penetrating work on the other side of this acceptance. He decided he would live for and through his art.

"I will take fate by the throat," he said. "It will never completely bend me to its will."

Stretch: cause (someone) to make maximum use of their talents or abilities.

Toward the end of the development section, the woodwinds and strings alternate, each playing a single note for eight bars in a call-and-response pattern. Next to each other, their strange and silky voices create an atmosphere of mystery and tension. You wonder: What new synthesis might they develop together? The answer: both are snuffed by the four-note fate motif.

The recapitulation begins with the most terrifying version of the fate motif yet. It shakes your blood cells and bone marrow. You know it is coming and yet are not ready for it. As the theme continues, the oboe begins a new countermelody and then it is suddenly alone, singing its small, sweet song, asking, perhaps, what it means to be without the luxury of becoming.

Even as it fades away, like a voice trailing off, a perfect cue for others to pick up the conversational slack, no other instrument speaks. Not until well after it whispers its final note, a note that merges with air and is wafted away, do the strings add their sinewy voices, tentative at first, picking up speed and volume and then the awful grip of fate is back. Why did nothing interrupt that little voice? Was it too powerful, somehow, even for fate? Or is the message that even with such beauty, fate will find you? I note that woodwinds, including the oboe, need breath. Strings do not.

The chrysalis, I am learning, is a suffocating place of death and a horrible struggle toward life, a lonely world between worlds, belonging to none. But I feel its transformative power. I feel it reshaping me in ways beyond my control. I sense there are gifts—humility, gratitude—coming from this time. Gifts I would love to return. If I could, I would slice through this slimy membrane and burst out, breathe again.

I am not consoled by Beethoven's greatness. I don't care that he created works of utter genius in the midst of suffering. I care that he created anything at all in the midst of suffering. That humans are capable of such feats of spirit and strength. That we are able to stretch outside of our pain and find—what?—beyond its borders.

But this is a lie. I know that there is a threshold of pain beyond which creativity, even thought, is impossible. The fog must first diminish, just a little, to let in some ribbons of colour, some raw material with which to work.

Tonic: 1) A medicinal substance taken to give a feeling of vigour or well-being. 2) The first note in a scale which, in conventional harmony, provides the keynote of a piece of music. Tonic comes from "tone" which comes from the Greek ténōn (τένων) meaning "to stretch."

My husband talks to a doctor friend who says this sounds like something she had once, a common condition for active women in their forties. She says she'll book me an appointment with her husband, a physician at the minor injury clinic. She texts me later: "Don't worry, we'll get this figured out." I sob on and off the whole day, understanding now that "we" must be the most powerful word in the English language.

The oboe is the true tonic, I argue to my husband that evening. It isn't the key of C Major at the end of the symphony. We don't have such things as the "triumph of life over death" or "light over darkness" or a "journey from hell into heaven." In life, we have a beautiful, tiny sliver of hope here and there, amidst oppressive pain, amidst our approaching fate, amidst tragedy and death, and we must content ourselves with this. I have my snort of laughter, I have words like "ogre" and "we." That these things exist at all is worthy of our gratitude and astonishment.

I sense my husband has been waiting to say something while I'm speaking. "But what if the writing of that symphony at all," he says, "IS the triumph of life over death?"

Of course, he is right.

Maybe we both are.

I see the doctor at the minor injury clinic who is kind but unable to help. I see seven doctors in total, plus three physiotherapists, one chiropractor and one athletic stretching specialist. ("Doctors know little," Beethoven complained, "one tires of them.") A friend recommends osteopathy. Another sends energy healing from her home. Well-meaning people drop off tools: a TENS machine, a massage gun, an acupressure mat. I have an MRI scan which shows nothing. I eat painkillers like candy and the painkillers eat through my stomach lining. And then, after months in agony, for reasons I still don't understand, the pain begins to ease, just a little each day, a droplet of rain onto burning flesh. I am skeptical of lasting change, but as the fist loosens its grip, I allow little things to repopulate my life: a line in my journal, the reading of a poem, a short walk, a phone call. I don't resume my previous strict schedule, I just let the world wedge me open bit by bit.

⌣

Emerging from the chrysalis, I find myself humbled and it hurts. But I do not want to go back to life as I lived it before this pain. I want it to change and extend me, I want to live stretched, expanded. I now know the depths of human suffering, can be the "we" for someone else. I know there are further depths to which I have not yet been.

⌣

The end of the first movement is a tutti, meaning the entire orchestra plays all together, everyone, oboe, timpani, strings, trombone. They play variations on the fate motif and then end with three short, sharp notes. The notes, this time, have spaces between them. A small mercy.

⌣

Stretch: to be capable of being made longer or wider without tearing or breaking.

Editor's note: This essay contains images of sheet music originally composed by Ludwig van Beethoven. The images were sourced from The Mutopia Project, a website which provides free sheet music by classical composers to the public. The creators of these images have dedicated their work to the public domain. All definitions are taken from the *Oxford Languages Dictionary*.

Our reader describes what it was like to find Jennifer Robinson's "Sonata for Pain"

I had the pleasure of being the first reader of Jennifer Robinson's "Sonata for Pain." What first struck me about the piece was the author's knowledge of her material—the theory, composition, and biographical context of Beethoven's Fifth Symphony—and her skillful handling of this information. The piece educates the reader so beautifully: gently, but without condescension. It assumes that its reader is intelligent and curious enough to absorb complex ideas about music, ideas not often encountered outside of a classroom. At the same time, it explains things clearly and simply, with an understanding that many readers (like me) won't be arriving to the piece with a background in the subject matter.

This educational instinct would have been enough to make for an exceptional work, but as the piece went on, it became clear that the second component of the piece, the author's account of physical pain and medical trauma, was written with honesty, vulnerability, and tremendous lucidity. I was impressed by her generosity of spirit, both in letting us, the readers, into this intimate and moving experience, and in her recognition of moments of grace: moments of connection with friends, moments where pain lightens and beauty can be seen. These moments made the piece a true delight, a multi-faceted and real reckoning with the human experience.

You might not be able to imagine how these two parts—Beethoven's Fifth and the reality of pain—marry to form a whole, but after reading Jennifer Robinson's essay, you will be impressed, as I was, by her ability to interweave them so skillfully that it becomes clear they were always linked.

—Charlotte Kidd

Our editor describes what it was like to find Callan's Latham's "Intimacies"

Callan Latham's "Intimacies" is a sweet, secretive glimpse into a quiet longing to desire and to be desired. The mundane is painted as curious (When I take the bus, it's my own / admission of intimacy") and the obscure is laced throughout as an unsettling balm ("The you, having lost / its shape. I own a dictionary, / but it's all in German").

Latham's control of language and narrative in "Intimacies" is what set this poem apart for our editors. The symbol of the pear tree is established early, wrapped up in nostalgia and longing. We follow the speaker along their thread of desire and remembrance, returning to the pear tree, reinforcing the longing central to the poem. Latham does not give too much away—this poet's diction is held taut, guiding readers to a satisfying resolution.

My favorite line is, "Spring, the rippling / of asphalt." In this key moment, the speaker leaves their apartment and its "stale / air," fully experiencing the pear trees—intimacy—for themselves. It is not simply the trees, but the embrace of spring, that is available in abundance to the speaker. This experience is a "confession"—a confession of desire the speaker can now fully realize on their own terms.

—Courtney Heidorn

Intimacies

The man I've been watching
from across the street tries to

convince me that pear trees
are the only method of intimacy.

I often find myself talking
to an empty room. *This is how*

I make my tea. This is
the painting that reminds me

of you. The you, having lost
its shape. I own a dictionary,

but it's all in German.
When I take the bus, it's my own

admission of intimacy.
I wish I could tell the pear man,

I'll buy all your trees. I took
the bus because of you. Leaving

the apartment in its stale
air. Spring, the rippling

of asphalt. The bus
driver laughs when she stops

too early: my body through
the other bodies. The pear

trees, their tang yet
another confession.

Atsikana!

Atata reappeared on a cool Saturday morning wearing his favourite dark blue safari suit, carrying in his right hand a big, red plaid suitcase.

We stumbled into each other at the kitchen door. Him, hand poised to knock. Me, rounding the corner with an empty washing basket, my heart still cartwheeling from kissing Justin over the unfinished fence demarcating our backyards.

Atata and I stared at each other.

Around us, the breeze stirred the leaves of our avocado tree and filled the air with the smell of dirt.

A shy smile tugged at the corners of my father's thin lips.

"Lumbiwe." He said my name, but it sounded like a question.

Three years he'd been gone. Three years that had receded and greyed his hairline, and shrunk him a little.

I was no longer the twelve-year-old girl he'd left behind. Three years had stretched me up to his eye level, widened my hips and peaked my breasts.

"I'll get Amama," I said, scooting in front of Atata to let myself into the house.

"Wait—" Atata was still speaking, but I closed the door in his face.

I dumped the washing basket on the linoleum floor and rushed to Amama's room where I found her making the bed.

"Nichani?" she asked, wide-eyed.

I paused in the doorway.

I had learned to interpret the fear in Amama's eyes and voice. "Salome is fine," I said even though I didn't know this for certain.

My big sister Salome slept out most nights, and until she resurfaced in the morning, Amama was jumpy. It had taken a while to get to this point, but Amama's concern for Salome's safety now superseded the humiliating fact that the whole Kabwata would be awake to see her nineteen-year-old glide out of different vehicles.

"Atata is here," I said, shifting from foot to foot.

Amama gasped. "Here? Kuti?"

"Outside."

She froze. Then a strange laugh escaped her lips. "Mulungu uyu," she said, pointing upwards.

I glanced up, saw nothing but white ceiling whereas my mother's eyes shone as if God's face truly was painted upon it. Her reaction confused me and had me doubting my decision to leave Atata standing out there.

"Should I let him in?" I asked.

"No," Amama said sharply.

She took off her floral nightdress, wrapped a chitenge round her body, and disappeared into the bathroom at the end of the corridor. When I heard her humming, I knew she was brushing her teeth.

I went into the bedroom I shared with Salome and sat on our unmade double bed. The kiss with Justin—my first kiss—sat giddy on my tongue.

Atata was back.

Amama, who had spent the last three years mourning him as if he were dead, was now carrying on with her morning routine.

And Salome, the only person I could talk to about all this—except about the kiss because she didn't approve of Justin—was God knows where.

I caught a glimpse of my reflection in the full mirror on the wardrobe door. The old pair of tights that once belonged to Amama was still on my head, doing its nightly duty of protecting my mukule from unravelling. My grey robe looked like an old discoloured dish rag. And yet, Justin—tall and handsome—had watched me over the fence as I hung the washing and asked me to kiss him.

Justin and I had been through some phases. From running around barefoot and pushing wire cars, to playing Tetris in his sitting room, to not talking to each other because his first girlfriend didn't want him hanging out with me anymore. These days, Justin spent time in his backyard listening to Busta Rhymes and lifting the rusty crankshaft he used as a weight to bulk up.

My eyes shifted to the chest of drawers in the corner and settled on the fake flower amongst Salome's growing collection of body lotions, sprays and makeup kits.

"Let me tell you something mufana," Salome said when she noticed me looking at the flower last week.

There was nothing small about me. My physique—sturdy like Atata— made me and Salome look like peers. She only called me mufana when she was about to tell me something she knew I wouldn't like.

"You don't have time for plastic flowers. Find someone who can help when we're running low on groceries, not a boy who is focused on building muscles."

I turned to leave the room, but Salome must have seen the disgusted look on my face.

"Being smart doesn't guarantee you a university bursary," she said just as my hand touched the door handle. "You know how things work in this country. Start thinking ahead. What would you do if I moved out?"

I spun around. "You're moving out?"

"I'm thinking about it," Salome said, removing the lid off a pretty pink bottle of perfume I'd never seen before and sniffed it. "Amama doesn't know yet."

I was fifteen and in grade eleven because I'd skipped a few grades in primary school, but what if Salome was right and I didn't get a bursary? And what would Amama and I do without her?

Though, at the moment, my biggest worry was what Salome would do if she found Atata outside.

*

Atata sat on the doorstep with his back against the door. Every so often he alternated between resting his elbows on his knees, and stretching his long legs in front of him and crossing them at the ankles.

I peeked at him from the corner of the lace curtain covering the kitchen window. The black kettle-shaped wall clock behind me said half past eight.

He had been out there for two and a half hours.

Now dressed in a loose fitting chitenge dress, Amama scooped hot maize meal and pounded groundnut porridge into two bowls. Normally, I'd be asking her to put a little extra in mine but that morning, I wondered if the sweet aroma was making Atata hungry, and if the sounds coming from the house he'd once called home made him sad.

I had no business worrying about him. He was the one who had left us, barely a week after his pension cheque cleared. Atata had walked out of the house that morning in the same blue safari suit, his black leather compendium tucked under his arm as if he still worked for Earnest Insurance Corporation. He had even returned Amama's wave before climbing into his white Golf CTI, and proceeded to drop me and Salome off at school.

"Be good. Okay?" he'd said. That should have been a sign. He always said, "See you later, atsikana anga."

Oh, how those words filled me with warmth.

We were *his* girls.

"Lumbiwe, come and eat." Amama's voice yanked me away from the window.

I joined my mother at the table. The sound of our spoons hitting the sides of the bowl echoed through the house, but when I got up to turn the little radio on, Amama shook her head as if reading my mind. She looked too bright. Yellow doek tied expertly around her head, purple earrings dangling from her earlobes. She hadn't looked this nice in ages.

With willpower, I finished my breakfast. We never wasted food. If Salome so much as saw a morsel of nshima in the bin, she'd rant about the price of mealie meal.

At that instant, I heard her voice. "Excuse me, I'd like to pass."

I jumped to my feet and scuttled to the window.

Salome stood in front of Atata in a short, red sequined dress and high-heeled silver sandals. A black handbag hung from her right shoulder.

"Is that how you greet your father? And why are you dressed like that?" Atata motioned with his hand.

Salome rested her left hand on her slim waist and cocked her head to the side.

Amama stood besides me, her breathing rapid and audible. I knew she wouldn't intervene but still, Amama's inertia never ceased to astonish me.

When Justin's mother Bana Mwila bustled into our home to inform Amama that Atata was shacking up with a twenty-something year old woman in Villa, Amama laid in bed like an invalid. Bana Mwila said she was visiting her business partner, who lived four doors down from Atata's girlfriend, when she saw them shamelessly walking hand in hand to his car. Amama didn't move a muscle. It was Salome, sixteen at the time, who'd gone to ferret Atata out of that flat.

Seeing my sister now, it is hard to believe she was the same girl who'd returned wailing because Atata had told her to go back home. That she had no right to involve herself in his affairs.

Now, Salome looked ready to box him out of her way. Atata must have sensed her rage because when Salome pushed past him, he did not retaliate.

She slammed the door so hard the windows rattled.

*

I followed Salome into the bedroom.

She flung her handbag onto the bed. "This man! I swear to God!"

I sat at the foot of the bed, watching her march around our room.

"If Amama lets him in, I swear to God, I'm leaving this house for good!" Salome said.

"Don't say that," I pleaded. "She hasn't even seen him or spoken to him at all. He has been out there since six."

"You know what she's like," Salome said, finally locking eyes with me.

But Amama wasn't always like this. And neither were you.

Salome bent down to unbuckle her sandals. When she rose, she gave me her back. "Unzip me."

She smelled sweet and smoky like a cigarette. I'd never seen this dress before. That's how it was with her. Things just appeared. A pink bottle of perfume. A new pair of shoes on the wooden rack. An expensive looking dress.

"Try to come home earlier," I said as the zip peeled apart. "Amama worries about you being out all night."

Salome's shoulders tensed but I placed my hands on them gently.

Our skin, dark brown like our father's. Blemish free like our mother's.

My sister and I didn't hug or touch much. Gone were the days when we held hands in crowded places, when we slapped each other and kissed it better. These days, the only time our skin came into contact was when one of us encroached onto the other's side of the bed in our sleep.

Salome stepped away and opened a drawer

"There's something different about you," she said, squinting at me.

"What?" I asked.

Salome pulled an army green T-shirt dress over her head and shuffled closer.

Then I remembered I had kissed Justin and for a second, I wanted to tell her, but she wouldn't understand how much the kiss meant to me. I dropped my gaze to my socked feet.

"Atata is back," I said.

Salome frowned. "So?"

I hugged my elbows.

"Don't be soft mufana," Salome said, walking towards the door, "or you'll end up like Amama."

*

Salome sprawled out on the sofa with her arm draped over her face, shielding her eyes from the daylight. She liked to relax before going to bed for the day but when I saw how she kept flexing her red painted toenails, I knew her mind wasn't winding down.

In the adjacent armchair, Amama absentmindedly chewed the lid of a blue BIC pen. Splayed open on her lap was her battered Good News Bible with the orange sunrise cover, and a small notepad. On the TV in front of her, an American pastor with a cropped bob haircut paced around on a podium, preaching about turning the other cheek.

I roamed from the kitchen table where I had my Biology exercise book open, then to the window where I could spy on Atata, and back to the sitting room where the looming tension wet my armpits with sweat. The fear that Salome might cause a scene while I was in the shower kept me from washing my body or changing out of my bed clothes.

As soon as the credits started rolling, Salome sat upright and faced Amama. "You know he's only here because that woman won't have him now that he is broke."

"I know," Amama said, scanning the notes she'd jotted down during the sermon.

"He can't just show up here empty-handed, expecting us to welcome him back. Like we're fools."

"I know."

"He bought her a house, pumped money into her new restaurant," Salome said, gripping her hands together. "He is a finished man now. He doesn't even have a car. She sucked him dry!"

Of course, we knew all these things, courtesy of Bana Mwila. As Salome impressed upon our mother the ways Atata had failed us, Amama rested her chin on her hand. She looked directly at Salome but said nothing.

"Don't let him in," Salome said. After a while, she curled up on the sofa with her back to us. Perhaps it was the relief of having had an uninterrupted rant or fatigue from being out all night, but Salome was snoring in a matter of minutes.

Amama stood up, took the maroon fleece blanket from the small stool beside her chair and draped it over Salome.

*

In the past, whenever Amama hinted that she wanted to join Bana Mwila and a group of other women who did cross-border trading, Atata coaxed her into rethinking that proposition.

"What for? Don't we have enough? Don't I give you money for grocery shopping? Plus a little extra for your womanly things?"

"Yes, but you said I can work again after the girls are grown. I'm tired of being a housewife."

"You're *my* housewife," Atata said in that sweet, sweet voice that caused Amama to swat him playfully on the arm. "You don't *have* to work. Don't let the likes of divorced women like Bana Mwila plant silly ideas in your head. Everyone knows the shameful things these so-called businesswomen do when they cross those borders. You, *my* virtuous woman, are better than them. Trust me, I have a plan for our future."

Atata's plan was fool-proof. We were to continue living modestly in this rented two-bedroom house until he retired. Then, he'd buy us a nice house with a big yard for gardening and still have space leftover to extend the small servants' quarters in the back into a rental.

He was also going to help Amama set up a catering business. "Better than the shabby one run by the old lady you worked for when I met you," he told Amama many times.

"And for you, atsikana," he'd turn to me and Salome, "bedrooms with wardrobes so big you won't fight about which side belongs to who." At this, Salome's eyes would sparkle with excitement.

"And a study room with shelves for all your books because you," Atata would wink at me, "are the future leaders of this country. The *Sylvia Masebos* and *Margaret Mwanakatwes* of your generation."

I'd wink back, chuffed that my father thought I was smart enough to be a minister or a bank executive. Those women spoke with such confidence on TV.

It was with this blind faith that when Atata took us for drives after church, we rolled down our windows to marvel at beautiful houses in Roma and Rhodespark and Woodlands, believing he'd make good on his promise.

After he ran off, that faith we'd had in Atata curdled. It left Amama
so stunned she took to bed, and impelled me into a part time caregiver, a
role I wasn't prepared for. But Salome, she went through a metamorpho-
sis.

*

Atata had left his suitcase on the doorstep.

He was crouched near the avocado tree, pulling weeds that engulfed
the little garden bed that used to grow rosemary and hot chillies.

The more I watched him working, the angrier I grew. Who did he
think he was fooling? Weeding with his bare hands and realigning bricks.

My anger stopped me from concealing myself behind the curtain.
I stood there with my elbows resting on the windowsill, staring at him.
Where was he when we were running low on food and Bana Mwila,
growing frustrated with having to feed us as well as her family of five,
advised us to ask the church for help? Where was he when Salome turned
to family because the only thing Pastor and his wife had to offer was
prayer? Both the maternal and paternal sides pitched in here and there,
but only for a while. They too had children, obligations to take care of.
That's when Salome started hanging out at Kabwata market after school.
Where was Atata then?

Behind me, Amama sang along to music playing on the little radio
tuned into Radio Christian Voice.

Once more, Atata had tipped our world over. He had robbed me of
relishing in the warm glow of my first kiss. A kiss I had wanted badly
since Justin started talking to me as a girl, not a childhood friend. Because
of Atata, Salome was asleep on the sofa, not in our bed, for fear that
Amama would let him in. And our mother had remembered God again.

*

As far back as I could remember, the church was Amama's second
home. Every Sunday, she ushered congregants to their seats, passed
around offering baskets. After service, she welcomed new members and
visitors with plastic cups of orange juice and cream biscuits. She ran er-
rands when Pastor and his wife requested, and attended bible study every
Wednesday evening. The day Bana Mwila told her of Atata's whereabouts,

Amama was in bed because she had been up all night, begging the Lord to help the police find her husband in one piece. Even after reporting him missing for three days, it hadn't occurred to Amama that Atata could be safely tucked away in the arms of another woman.

"Ni shock," Bana Mwila explained to Salome and me over the fence when we told her that our mother remained confined to her bed. "Give her time."

Days became weeks. Amama complained of a headache that no amount of panadol could cure. Her eyes became so puffy from crying that my heart shattered looking at her.

"Amama wants to fade away, disappear into the mattress while Atata is out there enjoying his new life," Salome said when I expressed my worry.

Salome started bringing home beef pies. Some days she brought packets of chicken giblets, which Amama ate with tears dripping down her sunken cheeks because the little fried hearts reminded her of Atata.

I had my questions about how Salome could afford to feed us, but I kept them to myself. She was so angry and irritated those days, leaving me with the responsibility of forcing our mother to eat, to brush her teeth, to wash her own body.

One day, a group of women from church led by Pastor's wife stopped by to visit. It soon became clear that the reason they were here wasn't because Amama's presence was missed.

"Sister, the devil's hand is upon your household. First your husband, now your daughter," they said.

They had come to let Amama know that the pies we had been eating were courtesy of the greasy-faced man known for ogling schoolgirls from behind his food stand in the market. The giblets, courtesy of the butcher. Both grown, married men. One of the women said she'd also seen Salome in our landlord's car on more than one occasion.

After the women left, my mother, who had exiled herself to the bedroom, got up and sat on the doorstep, waiting for my sister to return from the market. The second Salome was inside the house, Amama covered her with loud slaps. I waited for Salome to deny the rumours, to defend her reputation but after the sixth slap, she seized Amama by the wrists and said, "you're too weak to go and bring Atata back, but you have strength to beat me? Beat me Amama, beat me if that's what you need to feel better."

When Salome let go, Amama slapped her some more until I thrust myself between them. Amama took a step back, her arms hanging limply on her sides. Salome walked off to the bedroom, dry-eyed, leaving me to pick up the bag of food she had brought with her from the floor.

The next morning, Amama entered our room with a hot cup of black tea, and gave it to Salome.

Those were strange times for my family. Amama never laid her hands on Salome again, but she rebuked her for coming home late, and for the shame she was causing. Still, Salome saw to it that we never went hungry, didn't get evicted or sent away from school for falling behind with payments. While I studied harder than before, convinced it would pay off in the future, Amama read her Bible less and less until it disappeared altogether. Eventually, we figured out how to live with each other, just us three.

*

At twelve hours, I opened the door and sidestepped Atata's suitcase. I walked around to the back of the house, holding the washing basket against my hip. My heart leaped into my mouth at the sight of Atata talking to Justin over the half-fence.

Justin was topless and glistening with sweat. The work he had been putting into transforming his body was beginning to show, especially around the abdomen.

I considered running back into the house. What if Atata took one look at Justin and me and knew we liked each other? That we chatted and flirted in the very spot he was standing? That, hours ago, we had kissed?

"I can't believe how big this young man is now," Atata said, smiling at me.

I ignored him, busied myself by touching my white school shirts and grey skirts to see if they were dry.

Little mounds of twigs and dried grass had mushroomed out here too, evidence that Atata was still at it with his clean up. It would take many months to restore this yard.

"Stay out of trouble," Atata said to Justin and came to stand beside me at the washing line.

I almost rolled my eyes. *Trouble?* The only trouble around here was Atata showing up where he was no longer wanted.

"And greet your father for me when you see him," Atata said.

"Okay," Justin said.

I knew the greeting wouldn't reach Justin's father's ears because although Justin saw him at family weddings and funerals, they weren't on speaking terms. Justin's father had run off long before mine and left them with a half-finished fence which Atata had vowed to finish when he collected his pension. One time, Justin joked that the best thing to come out of our fathers' desertion was the fence as it allowed us to see each other.

"I named you after my mother," Atata said softly. "That woman had a big heart I tell you. Our home was open to everyone."

I had heard this story a million times.

"You have her hands."

I looked up at my hands, swiftly moving from peg to peg.

When I finished plucking my things from the line, I didn't pick up the washing basket from the ground. I stood face to face with my father, waiting for him to tell me something new. Like how he had managed to go three years without phoning or visiting. Or why he had sent Salome away when she followed him to that woman's flat. The hate I felt for him descended upon me like a heatwave.

Atata couldn't hold my gaze. "Let me help you with that," he said, reaching for the washing basket, but I grabbed it quickly.

"You're not going to use me to enter the house," I said.

I braced myself for Atata to reprimand me about my sharp tone. I had never spoken to him like that before.

He gave me a nervous smile and whispered, "So, what is your Amama saying in there?" He tilted his head towards the house.

"About what?" I asked loudly.

Atata gaped at me. Twelve-year-old Lumbiwe would have whispered back, lapping up the opportunity to be on his side. But I wasn't that girl anymore and the man in front of me wasn't the father I adored and respected.

Before I walked back to the front of the house, I glanced over my shoulder. Justin was gone.

Atata was right behind me when I reached the door and this time, he wedged his foot in to prevent me from closing it.

"Maida," he said Amama's name.

Amama stopped stirring the pot on the stove and blinked at him, confused.

"Won't you invite me in?" Atata asked.

It was so comical I almost laughed, but I pressed back against the door so he couldn't enter.

Amama raised her eyebrows. "Do you need an invitation to enter your own home? What's stopping you from walking in the same way you walked out?"

Salome rushed into the kitchen, eyes bloodshot and permed hair disheveled from sleep. "Mufuna chani kansi? There's nothing for you in this house."

"Everything in this house is mine!" Atata growled.

"Everything in this house is Amama's! She deserves more than that woman who left you with nothing!" Salome growled back.

I felt Atata's force before I saw it. The door pushed me back against the wall and he flew across the kitchen, grabbing my sister by the collar. I don't know the exact moment I dropped the washing basket or when my mother zoomed from the stove, but we weren't going to let him attack Salome. All our bodies collided, and our screaming voices cut the air. Salome and I hauled Atata back towards the door, but he spread his arms out in the door frame and held on for dear life.

"I'm still the head of this house," he panted. A big vein bulged on his forehead and his body trembled.

"Leave him." Amama tapped me and Salome on the arms until we released Atata's suit from our clenched fists. We didn't move though, we stood firm in front of our father like a wall. Our mother at our backs like we were her bodyguards.

"These aren't the same atsikana you left," Amama cautioned him.

Atata smoothed his now ruffled suit. He looked old and tired. Pitiful.

"I can fix it," he said.

"Something is burning," I said.

Amama scampered to the stove.

"I can fix this," Atata's eyes darted desperately from my face to Salome's.

I turned away and picked up my uniforms and the washing basket.

"I'm going to bed," Salome said, walking away.

"I can fix this," Atata said, louder this time.

No one answered.

Inner Child 2

Digital illustration, 2024

Reconnecting with your inner child is like finding a sanctuary within yourself—a safe haven where you're free to grow, flourish, and embrace the purest essence of who you are. It's in this sacred space that you build the foundational pillars of your being, shaping the authentic blueprint of your existence.

Yes, Virginia, There is a Santa Claus

My husband wants to try a different position. I ask him what he's been watching, then climb aboard, knowing already the outcome of this adventure. We are old, after all.

My lovely friend cries over coffee. Her husband left her for someone else. *I was not prepared*, she says. I assume she's referring to the betrayal. She leans in, whispers *I am not ready for a life without sex*. Her tears pool, spill over. *That's not up to him*, I tell her. *It's up to you*. In her eyes, I see equal parts hope and doubt.

Another friend shows me pictures of the men she matches with on *SilverSingles*. Most have decided to put their best nose forward, with selfies angled up their nostrils. We laugh until we cry. She perseveres and finds one who knows how to hold the camera straight on. Kind eyes. He's even smiling. They are dating now. I'm obnoxious, so I ask about the sex. With a grin, she says, *The gift is under the tree, but we haven't opened it yet.*

Distance Running Dreamscape

Country roads at dusk: packed dirt shoulder, gravel. I am
alone until a passing pickup truck coughs smoke like a man
choking on a cigarette. Dragging on by, passing me slowly,
the driver's gaze lingers in the rearview. I feel it creeping
down my bare back like a bead of sweat. Across the fence:
a pasture of pairs, mares newly foaled. Haze billows white
like tailpipe smoke in tall grass, the horses stir. Nostrils flaring,
marble eyes swallowing the scene of me, the truck, the flat road
to nowhere, the mist. They kip into motion and then the herd
is running too, along the fence, tossing muscled necks
and wind whipped manes. I strain to match their stride,
chest tight, imaginary hand at my throat squeezing breath
from my lungs. The horses go ahead, I am outrun.
The truck drives on. I am alone in the mist once more.
A mile down the way, I hear the pickup caterwaul into a stop,
brake pads so worn through they cry out against the rotor
press. It sounds like a woman, screaming herself awake.

A Language for Boys

On the second day of practice, Coach tells me my first sparring match will be against Jack Fisher, another junior in my same weight class with freckles like sunspots. The only time we've talked was on our freshmen field trip when he tapped me on the shoulder because he confused me for the other boy in our class with arms as scrawny as mine.

Jack catches me by the drinking fountain outside the gym, my lips half-wet. "Your dad was a wrestler, right?"

I don't think we've been alone together before this moment. My first thought is that he must be making fun of me. Most of the other boys only bring up my dad as they pull up his most embarrassing promos on their phones to shove in my face. His early days are a special target, the red of his spandex more fitting of a tomato than a hell-fiend.

I deepen my voice. "Why?"

"My dad used to watch yours on TV. He still says your dad retiring was the worst thing that's ever happened."

Jack brushes past me to fill a water bottle at the fountain. I can hear all the other boys howling inside the gym, so they can't be listening at the door, waiting for me to spill something about my dad worth a laugh. No hidden camera, no mean joke.

I blurt the first thing that comes to mind, an image of bright lights and a man teasing me with a finger. "Some of the other wrestlers held me as a baby when he brought me to tapings."

"Really? What were they like?"

"I don't know. I was a baby."

Jack laughs—an honest laugh, like I'm meant to join in—and it's my first time hearing it. His left eye, slightly larger than the right, bulges out as if trying to leap from its socket. I can't think of anything else to say, so I head back into the gym and hope the yellow lighting will mask the red embarrassment pooling in my cheeks.

*

Jack lunges at my midsection.

We tangle only for a flash before he ends up on top of me. He isn't just taller than me, but meatier too, a lion to my gazelle.

My shoulders hit the floor, and pain rises through me. Even though the match just started, Jack's about to have me. His stomach is hot against mine. He ripples through the singlet.

Dad's ultimatum to be the best or nothing seemed reasonable when he said it, but I now see how impossible it is for a kid with rib-shapes instead of abs. The camera flash painting Dad's wicked smile fluorescent, the total knockouts, the biceps of unrivaled power—forever out of my reach from this moment on. A pathetic smallness churns inside me, but I remember how Dad tried out four times before someone at WWE would take him seriously, and the feeling ignites into fury, the kind invented by a man with red and orange slathered all over his boots.

My left arm slips off at the elbow.

It's like twisting a ring off after years of soap, a splinter sliding free. My arm slides off the humerus and onto the floor, its fingers—still mine, still connected to my brain—clenching and releasing. This is my first time realizing this trick, yet it feels like my body has been developing the skill for a lifetime.

Jack's eyes go wide at the separation, at my arm on the floor, and he lets up for a fraction of a moment. That gasp is enough for my disembodied limb to launch at his neck. With Dad's old war cry blistering in my mind, the signature sound he refined for years as AJ Shiro, I dive forward and press one of Jack's shoulders to the ground. My nerves send signals through empty space to command my unhitched arm to pin Jack's other shoulder. A count begins, and Jack can only gape.

From the gym bleachers, a girl cheers. I turn to see Patti Levenson on the top row hollering my name through cupped hands. Everyone knows that two seniors asked her to prom last year and she went with one and took the other to the Sadie Hawkins dance. She must think the world of me right now, just like those screaming women on TV who wore AJ Shiro T-shirts to every one of his matches. I'm getting what every boy wants: Patti Levenson thinking the world of him.

Jack taps my shoulder when the match ends. The trails of sweat rolling down his cheeks make him look like he's weeping. With each breath, his broad chest struggles against his singlet. Dad would hate me for the loss Jack took, but he wears it well, nearly glowing with it.

"Cool trick," he says. "You're good."

"Thanks. You, too."

"Did your dad teach you to do that?"

I don't know where the trick came from, but not him. This must be what art feels like: adding something new to the world, all on your own. "I think I taught myself."

Jack laughs. His eye bulges again. That's twice now—him laughing when I try to answer his questions, him acting like we know each other well enough to trade jokes invisibly. He picks my arm off the ground by taking it in a handshake, and it reattaches to its stub with a nudge, my body taking back its own. We keep shaking, and when Jack squeezes tight, I squeeze back even tighter. The moment goes so long I think we might start fighting again just to give the pressure somewhere to go.

*

Dad and I are sometimes like twins. At parent-teacher conferences, my teachers always tell us how much we would look alike if I put on some extra weight, and I never believed them until the start of this school year when I fell asleep in my homeroom watching one of Dad's reruns on my phone and dreamed that it was actually me vaulting off the top rope.

I try to pinpoint my face in his as we sit across from each other in a booth at The Nicollet Diner, one of the only places in the city that serves food this late. Dad and I both order the hangover combo off the twenty-four-hour breakfast menu and tackle it the same way: first the over-medium eggs, then the crispy hash browns with extra salt, then the pancakes. This time, Dad spears all the pancakes off my plate before I can reach for the maple syrup.

"Lay off the sugar. Otherwise, you'll add some pounds, but you still won't have any muscle."

"You got strong by never eating pancakes?"

"You bet. Backstage, they called me Godzilla. *Stand clear, Godzilla's coming through.* You want to be a monster, don't you?"

I imagine Dad levitating up and down the ramps, crew members scrambling out of his path and begging not to be stepped on. Cheerleaders swooning, jocks flattening themselves against lockers.

"Of course, Dad."

"Then you can't eat like a pig."

A familiar sound echoes from the TV playing across from our booth. Nobody but us look up to see the WWE logo and AJ Shiro standing on the ropes, the Heel from Hell mean-mugging an anonymous audience and receiving venom in return, boos that echo until they sound like praying. Dad barely blinks when these reruns come up in public. As the camera zooms in on AJ Shiro's upper half, I watch his elbows for any seams that might have been passed down to me, any rust signaling kneecaps that moonlight as hinges.

Our waitress comes to deliver the bill. As she gathers our dishes, Dad's eyes dart toward me, then to her and back again. Even though his body has softened over the years, nothing can dim those eyes. In one pre-filmed bit, he lit a referee's shirt on fire just by staring hard enough, and it might be happening to me now.

These days, that red-hot look is the silent code Dad uses when he wants me to be his wingman—not that he's shown any interest in dating since Mom died, but he still likes it when women notice the fighter he was before eroding into a middle-aged man with a beer gut at a twenty-four-hour diner.

I knew he would want me to say something to this waitress. She has Mom's smile, unbroken white save for a gap between her upper front teeth.

"That's my Dad on the TV."

The waitress swivels in time to catch AJ Shiro putting an opponent into a camel clutch, one of his fingers slipping into the smaller man's mouth and pulling the gum-flesh into a shape that doesn't belong on a body. I think I catch AJ licking his lips before a bar of static drowns out everything but his hands feeling the space behind teeth. I feel Dad buzz with pride across from me.

"Big guy in the boots? Must be proud of him," the waitress says. She focuses on me instead of Dad; he won't like that.

"I watch his matches all the time."

"Are you going to learn to fight like him?"

"I just joined my school's wrestling team. It was my idea. Someday, I'll be up there on the TV." I still remember the first match I watched, AJ Shiro standing on top of a cage and sending every climber flailing back to the floor. A roar of awe, a victory pose slick with sweat. From then on, I spent the weekends watching ladder matches instead of cartoons. I tried to teach myself how to perform a suplex by making a GI Joe and

Ken doll do it to each other under my bed, then on the kitchen floor and underwater in the bathtub.

Dad leans over the table and slaps me on the shoulder just hard enough to sting. "As long as you're good enough for them to see a heel in you."

When the waitress leaves, I notice two men at a booth across the room, one with an eyebrow piercing and one who looks just like Dad, the version on the TV—it's his brick-wall body and the thunderbolt eyebrows. The two have their fingers clamped, palms kissing. They're locked in a round of arm wrestling, and since those tank tops don't cover anything, their paired biceps are on full display. As his veins pop, the Dad-copy starts to giggle. All ten fingers tighten, like one set of five will absorb the other. I want to go up and join, beat them or be beaten by them. I know I should prefer one result over the other, but I don't think I'd mind this time. Just get my fingers in there; I'll put my whole arm up as collateral. Just let me mark the table with my sweat too.

"See those two?" Dad barely looks up from the tip he's trying to calculate. "I could beat those girls any day of the week."

My gaze snaps to my hands under the table, where my pinkies have just severed their connections to my palms and fallen into my lap. It happened without a moment of thought. Dad asks me if fifteen percent is too much, and the rest of my fingers follow suit: ring, middle, index, thumb. I try to reattach them soundlessly, but they break off as fast as I can tack them back on.

*

I divide myself at the ankles to beat Gabe Santos. There's no way for him to see it coming: my feet separating from the rest of me and stepping on his toes, his body carrying the rest of him forward onto the ground. For Jesse Elrod, I shed the outer layer of my neck when he grabs for it. The boys can grapple me, get on top of me, but they can't keep my wrists from twisting off or my waist from unlocking my body into clean halves.

Since Jack, I've refined my control to the smallest possible pieces of myself. I get better under my bed covers. I'm like a kid staying up past my bedtime again, but instead of watching YouTube videos, I listen to myself taxonomize in the dark. One quiet night, I think I even separate a fingerprint from the pad.

Coach tells me this strategy will be legal at tournaments as long as my heart stays behind my ribs and my shoulders stay connected to my torso. Dad wouldn't understand any of it. I can hear him hissing at me, telling me that there's no sense in winning by making myself small. But I win, and I feel nothing but joy every time those boys try to wrap around me and I come apart at their touch, twist and shuffle until I'm on top and also beneath.

Patti Levenson keeps coming to practices, keeps cheering my wins from the bleachers. She'll throw the other winning boys a compliment or two, but she saves the loudest of them for me. After another string of wins, she finds me at the school entrance. "You looked Roman. Like we were at the Colosseum."

We make plans to hang out over the weekend. I don't even remember how it happened, just that I ended up staring at my bedroom ceiling with her number saved in my phone. When I order chicken breast at the restaurant because I think that's what wrestlers are supposed to eat, Patti gets a stack of waffles, and I would give up the entire date or whatever this is just to take a lick of the powdered sugar. I drive Patti back to her house, and she asks if we can sit in her driveway for a while.

A passed-down deja vu hits me as the engine dies. Dad met Mom on a night like this. Even though she rejected him the first few times he asked her out, they finally ended up in his car together, and he kissed her in a McDonald's parking lot. At her funeral, Dad said that there was no better time in his life than when he was wearing down his late-night love.

In the moonlight, Patti could pass for a ruby. Dark red fills out her cheeks, and being this close to a girl's face is so new to me that I can't tell if this is the color of blood or blush. Patti glances at me, then her frilled sleeves, and I know I'm supposed to start the conversation engine.

"Why did you start showing up to practice?" I ask.

"My brother's a wrestler. He's jealous of you, actually."

Strange to imagine anyone wanting something I have. But I must have beaten him; I've beaten all the boys on the team. "Would you be into it if your brother wasn't there?"

"I like watching you. That thing you do…it's so cool. You could beat anybody. But wrestling's too ugly for girls."

But wrestling makes me feel more beautiful than the fucking sun. The jaguar in me wants to tackle her right then and there, just to show her the handsome feeling that only comes from straight adrenaline. I want to show her my family tree, point to every man on every branch and explain how the only thing that turns these leaves perfect autumn-gold is the sheen of the heavyweight belts hanging off their waists.

Patti takes my silence as an invitation. A strand of hair coming loose from behind her ear, she leans in. This is what every boy wants, but all I taste is bile. I try to force myself through; this is my one chance at this.

Her lips smear against mine with the taste of rotten fruit. I remember to close my eyes. After a few seconds have passed, I think I might be able to get away with breaking loose, but she pushes deeper, her tongue slithering past my boundary of teeth. I wonder how much farther she'll take this, if she'll push so far that she ends up in my brain.

This isn't how I thought a first kiss would go. I thought the sensation took you to another place, but I'm more in my body than ever, remembering to coordinate my lips and tongue and jaw and hands in the way I know from movies. The mechanics take so much focus that I forget about the pleasure part. I try to take a little control, push back harder against her lips with mine. Isn't that usually how pleasure happens?

Patti screams.

She throws herself against the passenger door and spits something fleshy onto the floor. Her shrieks saturate the car like blood through water, and I speed through the errors I could have committed—too wet, too dry, too pushy, too limp. I try to ask what's wrong, but my mouth finds hollow space where it expects letters. It's only when I spot the tongue glistening with saliva on the passenger seat floor that I realize what is missing from inside me. I want to apologize for letting the muscle-mass slip into Patti's mouth, but I still can't make the sounds, and she has already found the door handle and is speeding into her garage.

On my way home, I stare at my hands on the wheel and practice popping each knuckle into my lap. But those pesky horrors keep washing back up: Patti's face of disgust, her lips parting to allow my tongue to spill out. For two stoplights I try to conduct an autopsy in my head, understand exactly how I can fix myself for next time—if anybody ever gives me a next time. When that gets too hard, I go back to the knuckles.

*

Some of the other boys start calling me a monster when they think I'm not listening. I try not to show how much it means to me. At our first tournament, I win and win again, a horde all on my own.

In his way, Dad congratulates me for all of it. It's a miracle that I've kept him from seeing me in action for so long. A lucky work conflict here, a lie about competition dates there: it's like I'm playing two sports instead of one.

He tells me how he called the school and Coach confirmed my wins.

"Didn't think you had it in you. Good job."

"Thanks, Dad."

"I'm not sure how you do it. Did you go to the gym today? I saw your workout clothes in the dryer."

"I'll go tomorrow."

Dad nods slowly, like he's processing my sentences one word at a time. "Whatever works for you."

He knows how to cut me down better than anyone; it's a superpower. I don't know why I thought winning would be good enough, especially when I need to keep my strategy a secret. It's not like Dad's word is sacred. If he knows the tactics that I use, how I've turned his sport into a kind of dance, he might call the school to pull me off the team no matter my track record, and I'll never be king the way I am in that gym, never on the floor with my utter victory of skin again.

We put on another one of Dad's reruns while we eat our paired TV meals, the bread-flaked fish undercooked and the mac and cheese burnt. It's the rare match I haven't seen before.

"This was one of my first ones," Dad says. "Luke and I rehearsed the backbreaker a thousand times before the day. I wonder how he's doing now."

AJ's opponent is a little larger than he is, blue boots and gold details, but that never deterred the Heel from Hell. The two lock up, and I don't speak, only watch the outlines of both men's muscles. If I want to be up there too, I'll need that same definition. Knowing the goal has never been my problem; the curse has always been getting there. Lifting weights, taking over the treadmill—always hitting it harder, faster, but for some reason I'm still left at the end of the day with whispers instead of muscle.

On the TV, AJ puts his opponent into the backbreaker. Hours were put into that single move. I lean forward on the couch. The opponent's screams are some of the best I've heard, a perfect performance of pain. The camera captures his agony before panning down to AJ's face, then down his bare chest and down his stomach.

The frame reaches his trunks. AJ Shiro is aroused.

I blink as if the image will go away if I reload it, but the outline under his trunks doesn't leave the screen. AJ turns in a large circle to show off his conquest overhead, and the audience goes crazy. Every time his bottom half is in frame for the rest of the match, his arousal is impossible to ignore.

Dad doesn't move in the edge of my vision. I can't look at him; I might explode, or he might strangle me for breaking the silence. We sit in our frozen spots for the rest of the match. I don't dare to finish my meal, since even lifting the fork might remind Dad that I exist.

The moment AJ pins his opponent and is declared the victor, Dad pauses the TV. "Go to sleep early for once. That's how winners do it."

In the shower, one feature at a time, I take off my face. I grab the edges of my lips and pull off the mouth opening whole, followed by my nose. All sound leaves my head with my ears. I pluck off my left eye, then the right—in total, a treasure of senses caught between my hands. Weeks of fighting catch up with me, and muscles sigh across my body, the signals all rushing to the same dark cavity.

My thoughts become readable in oblivion. There was a point in that awful silence at the TV when I wanted to tell Dad about myself, but I don't even know what the words would have been. I go through my catalog of Dad, try to come to the conclusion that if I start the confession, he'll finish it for me, accept it for me. There is more to a body than power. He has to understand; it seems AJ Shiro did. But I keep returning to the few things I know about Dad's childhood.

"When I was your age," he told me after one of the boys in my elementary school started biting me, "some kids could tell that I couldn't afford a lot of new clothes. They sang this stupid song whenever one of them spotted a hole in my sock. Then I kicked their asses, and they stopped bothering me."

He leaned close. "Boys understand one language and one language only."

I engage my screaming muscles in sequence. They click one by one, but with nowhere to go, the sound bunches up at the end of my tongue and echoes up into my brain. I'm not sure what I'm letting out—or keeping in. But the reverberation gets me to the dizzy place drugs are supposed to take you.

When it's over, I realize that I dropped my lips. It takes me until midnight to fish them out of the drain using a toothbrush.

*

Jack shows up to practice with a black eye. He tells all of us that he tripped getting out of his Dad's car, and I think he avoids eye contact with me because he knows I won't believe it for a second. The other guys can wince and laugh, but I can sniff out shame like a bloodhound.

Coach pairs the two of us up for another sparring match. Eyes cast toward the floor, Jack stretches his legs right in front of me. A taunt, a mating call.

"Good luck," I say.

He doesn't stop his squats, doesn't look my way. "You're going down today."

"Oh really?"

"You can do your little tricks and beat up on the others all you want. But I'm not a loser like them. You're gonna eat it."

If I say anything, I might betray the supernova shooting from my heart and sending starlight through my veins, so I just take my spot on the floor. I try to slow my breathing, but there's no denying it: I'm an animal now, a clawed thing in heat. Everybody is moving too slow. All the chatter, everyone unzipping their bags—I need it all to stop and everyone to get out of the fucking way so Jack can come at me, because he might put me down hard, I think he really might.

We lock up as normal, circle tight. Jack is solid, but no stronger than last time, no quicker. I wait for a trick to come, some exploited blind spot or technique with the legs, but he just pushes and pulls like all the other boys. I try not to deflate too quickly as I slice my hand down the middle and send both halves up different sides of his arm.

I meet resistance.

The world enters stasis as I turn my attention to Jack's hand, now split in half like a zipper, three fingers on one strip and two on the other, just like mine. Our half-limbs fit in perfect symmetry. Out of instinct, I drop my other hand to the floor to grab for his leg, but his foot pops off the ankle and pins my digits under his heel.

Jack and I meet each other's gaze.

His eye, surrounded by a bruise, reminds me of a planet in space. He learned my skill somehow, or had it in him all along. Nobody ever taught me what to do in a moment like this. No movie ever showed how this scene ends. A smile spreads across Jack's face, and I feel my lips follow suit.

He flips me over onto the floor. I divide into quadrants upon impact and skitter across Jack's exposed skin. In return, he melts into eight, then sixteen, and I let my hands fall into fingers, into digits. Everywhere he touches, I go to pieces: knees splitting, my neck popping from the shoulders. He does the same for me, my pressure against his skin forming cracks and full canyons. We are a mess of each other. Strips of skin, individual fingernails, fresh filets.

Finally, two of my teeth—a bottom molar, a top canine—clamp around a jelly wetness like an unpeeled grape. One of my retinas glides across Jack's belly button and spots the object: his eye, a planet unmoored from the universe itself, stopped in place. My teeth wobble, and his lens presses against my enamel. I can tell from the pressure that this is his left eye. The slightly larger one. The one that bulged out like a balloon when he was filling his water bottle at the drinking fountain and brave enough to talk to me and I somehow got him laughing.

In the chunk of my brain in charge of recall, Dad's voice rings gold. The words slip into my neck and up Jack's spine and between our ribs.

Bite! Bite! Bite!

But I keep the sphere in its half-life between my teeth. No biting, no releasing. Only our flesh-halo swirling and the sphere of vision rolling back and forth, back and forth. I think people start calling our names, but our ears burrow under each other's tongues. I think the room smells like sweat, but our noses press together and cover each other up, nostril on nostril. Everyone eventually comes to pull us apart and back together one piece at a time, vertebra to ulna to pancreas to Achilles heel to kneecap. Each puzzle piece back in their places.

But I hold out as long as I can, bone on the polished gym floor. They think they are putting us back together whole, but I know that this is all that's really left of me, my teeth fusing with the gel of Jack's eye. Coach tries his best, but it takes him and half the team to pry us apart, and even then Jack and I don't stop fighting for our lives.

Blaspheme Baby

And if things could be different, I would have held
the knife steady. Made an offering. Praised and praised.
On Sundays, I forget to leave my guilt behind.
Don't worry. I can be soft and knowing. I can be
quiet as God. Lately, I cry more often than I orgasm.
The doctor says this is normal for people with
my condition. I take things with names that sound ancient
and expired and swallow the whole bottle.
I attempt nothing. All I know is to be too guilty
and filled with other people's mouths. My father takes
his whiskey always with three ice cubes but says this is
coincidence. What is a family, if not genesis? What am I,
if not a series of beginnings? I want to learn closure the way
a door knows it, loud and with purpose. Everything
enters me and I let it. O Mother, I flood everywhere. O Mother,
there is so much of me to apologize for.

the one where i am a boring movie with a terrible rating

last night was a movie but the black guy doesn't die in this one instead he
sees the rotten tomatoes forming in the sky the fading red dot screaming
action he plays his role on this hump day ordering takeout and driving
to pick it up because he hates delivery fees he doesn't die but he drives
the speed limit stops for red lights red octagons red suns he blows warm
air into his slick hands he says thank you twice he prays before he drives
before he eats the extra red sauce from the takeout place he double-dips
and licks his fingers as the moon zooms in and the stars look away

Salt

It was charming, for a time. The compass still sure of its magnetism,
the weather dependable if indifferent. We were sailing somewhere,
but neither of us could read the tides & the maps were all lettered

in some forgotten script. Often the intervals of approximate light—
chiaroscuro of sail & rigging or the moon calcified on the deck—
seemed almost metaphoric, or was I only saving myself
the trouble of exactness? Even now, June sits soft on the tongue:

half-light, laburnum & lavender. You won't be coming back,

& I won't say October is a bad door blown open, a blunder
of hours or a stopped clock caught in the throat. It isn't that,
exactly. It's like the place we never got to, to which I keep
arriving. Salt & sea grass. Little black birds saying: *soon* & *soon*.

NUALA MCEVOY

The Rathaus in Münster

Acrylic paint and permanent marker pen
40x30 centimeters
2024

Sometimes very special old buildings wear their history and their personal stories on their façade, and fact and imagination interplay in the minds of people who visit these buildings. The stunning Town Hall or Rathaus in Münster played an important part in European history in the 17th Century. It was severely damaged during WW2 and then meticulously rebuilt in the 1950s. It now stands proud and beautiful again, like a fairy tale building in the centre of the city. I find it to be particularly enchanting at night when the streets are empty, and the city is still but the sky is illuminated with stars. I tried to recreate my memories of Münster Town Hall purely from my imagination, and this is the result.

My Professor Asked What I Knew About Dying

When we were fifteen, my friend Lucas found a body underneath the Cedar Park bridge. He was walking his dog. *What do I do*, he asked me over the phone, *he's just lying there. Call the cops*, I kept telling him. *Calm down and call the cops.* He did. The police came out and told him it was just a junkie. *Sometimes*, the officer said, *they act like animals and try to find a warm place to die when they know the end is coming. The man's jacket was soaking wet*, Lucas told me. He had called me before the police. I always wonder why he did that. Who do you call when your shoulders tighten with fear? When there is a body with a wet jacket and you are the only one around? Someone you love, I guess.

*

Cats move to a quiet place before the end. They eat less, grow irritable, and often stop making noise altogether. Ferrets turn nearly catatonic and avoid touch. They take deep breaths as their neurons fire at a rapid pace. Whales will become so bloated with gas that they come to the surface and are picked apart by birds. Birds stop flying and return to the ground, decomposing in just two days. They don't want to be any trouble for anyone. They are born in the air and spend their whole lives flying, trying to unzip the sky before they come down again.

In a Kenyan conservancy in 2010, a giraffe stood over the body of her dead one-month-old calf for more than four days. It became a scientific spectacle, as the position of her body over her dead child was a unique contortion, unlike anything most people had ever seen. Photographers came from all over to take pictures of her, trying to get their shot at a NatGeo cover. She did not move. She stood so long that people started to wonder how she did not eat. When hyenas came at night and fed on

the corpse, the mother moved to the place where its bones had been scat-
tered. She did not find a quiet place to die. She was going to do it in front
of everyone and she did not care who saw. After the second day or so, all
the other giraffes came over to her and wrapped their necks around each
other. It was almost like a hug.

*

When my brother came back from Afghanistan, he covered up all
his mirrors. He didn't come out in the daylight. At night, you could hear
his footsteps in the kitchen and you'd know he was still there. It was like
living with a monster under your bed. Every disturbed chip bag or empty
beer can was saying, *I exist, even if you do not see me.* My brother never talk-
ed about his tattoos, which made me wonder about them more. Doesn't
everyone love a mystery? Despite the space he refused to take up, he had
a knack for holding your attention. He told me stories nearly every night.
The one I remember goes like this.

*A prince walks into Nomansland with a mission. He knows what he's supposed
to do, but right now he's just walking in Nomansland and there's nothing around even
though he feels like there should be. At night, he finds this cave and crawls in. He
lays on his stomach and the stars come out and he forgets what he's supposed to be do-
ing. And while he's in the cave on his stomach looking at the stars, he hears the sound
of death outside.*

That's it, that's where the story ends, or maybe it's just where I
stopped remembering. The prince found a warm place to crawl in before
the end came. My brother found this solace in taking his own life in the
middle of a busy street on a Friday. He didn't call me before the police
came.

*

It was two months before we got around to having a funeral. When
the day came, it was hot and there were no clouds in the sky except for
three contrails right above our heads from the jet planes. I didn't want to
look at him on the ground, so I looked up at the contrails instead.

We used to picnic not far from this cemetery. We would lay on our
backs and look up at the sky just like this to watch the planes. *Contrails are*

like zippers, he had said. *They could unzip the whole sky.* Who do you tell stories to when you can't sleep? Who do you look up at the sky with? Who do you look at when you cannot look at yourself? Someone you love, I guess.

The Lesson of Flash Floods

They begin small, from nothing, they begin as a terrible trickle, miles away, upstream, where there is no stream, in a perfectly dry river bed full of debris, stones, trees, old farm equipment, a wheelbarrow, a tractor, where hot and dry doesn't begin to describe the desolation, the silence, which is what I tell my twin grandsons, age 8, gathered at my desk, staying with me while my daughter attends to appointments in the city, and I think it is time to tell them about my brother Danny as I search YouTube for terrifying videos of flash floods, wishing I could also capture the smell of that hot dry day eons ago when my brothers Danny and Davy and I were scrambling along the river bed's steep walls, collecting stones to paint, hoping for arrowheads, not expecting anything to happen, but maybe the day wasn't dry, maybe the terrible trickle had already begun to grow upstream and become a river, a torrent, a wall, a dense cascade of trees and cars and trucks and refrigerators and even houses, a solid tawny mass of water that swept away a disbelieving Danny, lagging behind and far below us, his pockets full of stones, drowning his cries, and maybe I want my grandsons to know me as a survivor of the mysteries of water and a brother's death, so this afternoon I tell them my story in a steady voice to accompany the devastation on my computer screen in the crashing, alive present because I want my grandsons to know the possibility of surviving a dire unexpected event, their father's coming news that their mother has weeks, perhaps only days to live, and the next time they see her it will be to say goodbye.

Talking to Grief

after Diane Seuss

A sparrow moves into my backyard and I do not think of you.
It's spring. I walk the long way home.
Here the eclipse bruises a corner of the sky, I think of how
in ancient Greek, the word *sight* also means *god*. Later
I go out into torrents of dark with my heart open.
Someone told me a fugue is like a pebble thrown
into the water and taught me to see the ripples coming and falling
off white spaces. There are things I wish to repeat
when I think of you. When I look into the woods, animals,
those soft little fuckers, make me want to turn away.
You must have fed some of them. A magpie with bluish beak,
years ago, you held in your palm quite long before letting go.
Today, I wait in line to pick up flowers and stop
thinking of you. Some nights, I talk and talk to this animal
of my body. The thing about ripples, I say, is that they stop
coming after a while and I am tired of finding pebbles. Except
now and then, I'll lay a new curse on you,
damp as feather, small as bird.

Editor's note: "Soft little fuckers" is a play on Hedgie Choi's "Salvage."

Talking to Grief

Colours of Jacob

Digital art, 1200x800 pixels, 2024

This piece entails resilience and heritage In all life forms through culture and diversity. It showcases colourful unity and strength amongst all. This piece was created out of my love for heritage and resilience. My inspiration comes from nature and human diversity. This piece goes a long way in showcasing what true heritage and togetherness looks like.

Erin Therese

Somewhere in 1983 the girl I'm named for
shrugs off the black robes of her school years to don

her lover's jacket, cocoons herself in his smoke
and scent, kicks off her kitten-heels to straddle

the back of his motorcycle. The world vibrates
between her thighs. She is in love. From here the air

is choral with promise. She is shrill
with pleasure, wrapping her arms around his chest,

hurtling at seventy miles per hour past the corn labyrinths
of her youth, thrust towards a future

that ends in a thicket around the bend.
A name can be a kind of death mask. A talisman.

I look into the scrying mirror, chant this name
in a ritual of divination, until the mask fits.

Who was I when I was given this name
in the womb of my first mother, before it was changed?

It's true that many miscarriages might precede
an adoption. A changeling can logic her way

into any kind of shame.
Ledger of causality, ledger of what-ifs—
as if I were complicit in this change of hands
and all the misfortune that preceded. In this way

the mythic past arrives with an air of predation;
the slate gray sky is wind-stitched, a vulture

rides the seam where two currents meet.
He waits for me in a borrowed car, offers

a swig of something scorching. He speeds
through the underground tunnel because he likes the way

I scream his name, gives me permission to release
what rattles inside the cage of me. He tells me

about myself: *you're so pretty*. Says
no one chooses their parents, and in this way

I am ordinary, and it is a strange relief.

Untitled

Photograph, 2024

This is part of our parking garage at the office where I work. I find comfort in the repetition and implied infinities of the perspective lines there. The scene felt like abstract geometric art, brought to life. However, despite the simple shapes, the photo can never be mistaken for some old computer rendering or drawing, as there is the real world's ever present urban wear of cracking plaster and concrete, to deny that expected low-resolution smoothness of a digital world.

Family Room

A small Massachusetts town, and the sky like dusk, though early after-
noon. No birdsong. Through a picture window, to where no snow fell.
Our mother's fire, burning down. The '70s gold shag carpet, a brick
fireplace. No vanilla smell of brownies baking to ward off the cold. Our
parents stiff in wingback chairs. Probably our mother had gathered us
there, said to our dad *You're going to tell them, not me.* No sound. How hard
we held our bodies still. Outside the window, gray sky, the maple tree's
branching. Our mother shivered. Our father would be going to someone
else, who was also married. My sister and I were young, we didn't know
yet about resurrections, how a thing may return, but never the same. We
all cried instead of saying *I'll always love you.* My sister and I, crossing an
ocean on a plank, a listing ship behind. The terror of a blackening sky.
If I was crying, I couldn't feel. The main artery split into tiny blue veins.
Too young to know splintering of a kind happens to everyone, eventually.
The heart now far away, maybe flittering among branches. Now, I relish
stories about love ending. Little cuts that return me to a place. A place of
lies, winter in June.

CONTRIBUTORS

Kaitlyn Airy is a Korean American poet. Born on a small island in the Salish Sea, she currently resides in Charlottesville where she graduated with an MFA in poetry from the University of Virginia. In 2020 her poem "DMZ" won the Phyllis L. Ennes contest, hosted by the Skagit River Poetry Foundation. In 2022 *Narrative Magazine* named her one of their 30 writers below 30. Her poems have been finalists in contests hosted by *The Iowa Review, Shenandoah*, and *Ninth Letter.* Her work is found or forthcoming in *FENCE, Narrative Magazine, Poetry Northwest, Cream City Review, Poets.org*, Poetry Online, Moss and elsewhere. She serves as an Essays Editor for *Poetry Northwest.*

Isaac Akanmu is a Nigerian American from Staten Island, NY. Now living in Charlotte, NC, Isaac was the recipient of the 2023 Charlotte GoodLit Fellowship. His poetry chapbook, *not belonging anywhere*, is available with Bottlecap Press (2022). Additionally, his words appear or are forthcoming in *The Westchester Review, Posit Journal, Olney Magazine*, and more. Connect with Isaac at isaacakanmu.com and on social media (@insteadofisaac).

T. Cutler attends Trinity College majoring in English Language and Literature. She hails from East Coast soil—the metamorphic stuff and continental margins, not the sandy parts. She has previously been published in *Rainy Day Cornell, Third Wednesday Magazine*, and *The Gyroscope Review*. She loves large bowls of apples, crosswords, the Blue Ridge Mountains, and David Foster Wallace.

Therese Gleason is author of *Matrilineal* (Finishing Line, 2021), which received Honorable Mention for the Jean Pedrick Chapbook Prize from the New England Poetry Club, and *Libation*, co-winner of the 2006 South Carolina Poetry Initiative Chapbook Competition. Her poetry, fiction, and essays have appeared in *32 Poems, Cincinnati Review, Indiana Review, New Ohio Review, Rattle*, and elsewhere. An educator, she has an MA in English from the University of Kentucky and an MFA in Poetry from Pacific University. Therese has taught ESL, composition, and creative writing at the college level, and has worked as a certified dyslexia therapist and Spanish teacher for students in elementary and middle school. Originally from Louisville, Kentucky, she currently lives in central Massachusetts with her family, where she teaches English language and literacy to multilingual learners in the Worcester Public Schools. (Online: theresegleason.com).

Callan Latham is a poet from the Midwest. Her work has been published in places such as *The Nassau Literary Review*, *Santa Clara Review*, and *Sybil Journal*. She is currently an MFA candidate in poetry at the University of Illinois at Urbana-Champaign.

Amelia Loeffler is a born and raised Kentuckian currently living in Tennessee. Her work is forthcoming in *Poetry*, *Variant Literature* and *The South Florida Poetry Journal*. Amelia is a graduate of The University of North Carolina at Chapel Hill, where she earned a BA in English and Geography.

Nuala McEvoy is a self-taught artist, currently living in Germany. She started painting as a hobby during the pandemic, using acrylics, both on glass and on canvas. Her hobby has since turned into a passion, and she now interacts with her palette and paintbrushes daily. Her work has been showcased in several journals this year, and she currently has an exhibition of her paintings in Münster, Germany. Nuala has set up home in many cities and several countries over the years, and her work often depicts places where she has lived, but where the boundaries between her memories and her imagination are often blurred. Nuala has also had poetry and fiction published in several publications and has read her poems aloud on podcasts. When she isn't painting or writing, she enjoys getting to grips with new languages. @mcevoy_nuala

K. Mobley (they/them) is a bundle of crows in a long green cloak. A writer and poet based out of Missouri, their work follows themes of identity and upbringing.

Moses Ojo is a young Nigerian art and photography enthusiastic who uses his mind as a channel for making captivating works to showcase his artistic skills to his audience.

Pamela Painter is the award-winning author of five story collections. Her stories have appeared in numerous journals and anthologies, and have been included in Best Micro and Best Short Fictions, and received four Pushcart Prizes. Painter's stories have been produced by Word Theatre in LA, London and New York.

Ron Perovich is an American artist, musician, and poet, creating work inspired by his love of science and history, international music and cuisine, and a plethora of nerdy pursuits. This includes performing traditional music of the near east, publishing unusual genre-based poetry chapbooks, and photographing a surprising number of clouds. He currently lives in a Texas apartment with his wife and some very naughty cats. instagram handle: @ronperovichart

Liz Robbins' fourth full-length collection, *Night Swimming*, won the 2023 Cold Mountain Press Annual Book Contest. Her third collection, *Freaked*, won the Elixir Press Annual Poetry Award, judged by Bruce Bond; her second collection, *Play Button*, won the Cider Press Review Book Award, judged by Patricia Smith. Her poems have appeared in *Adroit Journal*, *Beloit Poetry Journal*, *Five Points*, *Kenyon Review*, *Missouri Review*, and *Rattle*, and she received a Pushcart nomination from *Fugue*. She lives in St. Augustine, Florida, where she works as an editor, as well as a poetry screener for *Ploughshares*.

Jennifer Robinson lives and writes on Treaty 1 territory—the home of the Anishinaabeg, Anishininewuk, Ininew, Dakota Oyate, Denesuline, Nehethowuk and the birthplace of the Métis Nation. She is the winner of the 2024 National Magazine Gold Medal in Personal Journalism. Her essays can be found in *River Teeth*, *Emerge*, *Reckon Review*, *Prairie Fire*, *Geist*, *Grain*, and elsewhere.

Vasundhara Srinivas is a self-taught visual artist whose work lies at the intersection of illustration, art direction, and graphic design. Six years of working in the design industry has significantly molded her aesthetic sensibilities, simultaneously nurturing a fascination for illustration. She draws inspiration from her inner state, personal narratives and experiences, transforming ordinary moments into profound expressions. She also enjoys bringing her illustrations to life through short animated clips. Her work has been featured in *Suboart* magazine, *Artists responding to* (UK), *Delhi Art Slam, Sofar, IndiaNama,*

Kommune, and *Artly* among others. She recently graduated with a Masters in Illustration from Arts University Bournemouth.

Shiyang Su is a Chinese poet and an undergrad at UChicago. Her poems can be found or are forthcoming in *Frontier Poetry*, *Glass: A Journal of Poetry*, *Rattle*, *Passages North*, *Diode Poetry Journal*, *Verse Daily*, and elsewhere. She was nominated for Best New Poets.

Theresa Sylvester is a Zambian writer based in Western Australia. She is a Tin House Scholar. She is also an alumna of Faber Writing Academy, as well as Stuyvesant Writing Workshop where she studied under Nicole Dennis-Benn. Her stories appear in *Shenandoah*, *Quarterly West*, *Black Warrior Review*, *Ubwali Literary Magazine*, *Midnight and Indigo* & elsewhere.

Ann Weil is the author of *Lifecycle of a Beautiful Woman* (Yellow Arrow Publishing, 2023) and *Blue Dog Road Trip* (Gnashing Teeth Publishing, to be released October 2024). Her poetry appears or is forthcoming in *Pedestal Magazine*, *RHINO*, *DMQ Review*, *Maudlin House*, *3Elements Review*, *The Shore*, *Anti-Heroin Chic*, and elsewhere. She earned her doctorate at the University of Michigan and lives with her husband and soul-dog in Ann Arbor, MI, and Key West, FL. Read more of her work at annweilpoetry.com or follow her on Instagram @ annweilpoetry.

Jacob Sheetz-Willard is a poet from Leadville, Colorado and an MFA graduate of the Program for Writers at Warren Wilson College. A winner of the 2023 Cantor Prize and finalist for the 2023 ALR Poetry Prize, his work has appeared in *American Literary Review*, *Kestrel*, *LEON Literary Review*, *New South*, *Poetry Daily*, and elsewhere.

Cynthia Yatchman is a Seattle based artist and art instructor. With an M.A. in child development and a B. A. in education, she has a strong interest in art education and has taught art to adults, children and families in Seattle. As a former ceramicist, she studied with J.T. Abernathy in Ann Arbor, MI, however after receiving her B.F.A. in painting from the University of Washington she switched from 3D art to 2D and has remained there ever since. She works primarily on paintings, prints and collages. Her art is housed in numerous public and private collections and she has been shown nationally in California, Connecticut, New York, Indiana, Michigan, Oregon and Wyoming. She has exhibited extensively in the Northwest, including shows at Harborview Hospital, Seattle University, Seattle Pacific University, Shoreline Community College, the Tacoma and Seattle Convention Centers and the Pacific Science Center. She is a member of the Seattle Print Art Association, Puget Sound Painters of the Northwest, COCA (Center of Contemporary Art), and Women Painters of Washington.

Andrew Zhou is a queer Chinese writer and medical device engineer who grew up in the Minneapolis area but currently resides in Boston. He holds a bachelor's degree in Chemical Engineering from the University of Minnesota and a master's degree in Biomedical Engineering from Columbia University. His work has appeared or is forthcoming in *Quarterly West*, *South Dakota Review*, *Foglifter Journal*, *Faultline*, *Jabberwock Review*, and elsewhere. Find him at zhouandrew.com.

Chestnut Review
VOLUME 6   NUMBER 3   WINTER 2025
FOR STUBBORN ARTISTS

DONNA VITUCCI

Leap of Faith

Acrylic & mixed media
16x20.2 inches, 2023
(Cover Art)

In Summer 2022, when words began to fail me, I began painting. Mine is very much a fledgling work through exploration of "try this, try that." In the way every story charts its own journey, and the joy is in the doing, so I find with painting. Each rendering brings me great joy. Each painting is mine, and each is a piece of me I give away, or capture, or transcend—"Leap of Faith" especially so.

Chestnut Review

VOLUME 6　NUMBER 3　WINTER 2025

Chestnut Review LLC, Ithaca, New York
chestnutreview.com

Chestnut Review appears four times a year online, in January, April, July, and October, and once per year in print in July.

ISSN 2688-0350 (online), ISSN 2688-0342 (print)

CONTENTS

SPECIAL THANKS

To our generous Patreon supporters:

Adam Boustead, Allan Ebert, Ciel Downing, John Fredericks,
Claudia Geagan, Annette Higgs, Katie H., Edison Jennings,
Buddfred Levi, Chris Mikesell, Marijean Oldham, Vicky S,
Benjamin Thorne, Regina McIntosh, Rhonda Wiley-Jones

to learn more, go to
https://patreon.com/chestnutreview

Introduction

Winter has brought a sudden cold snap across most of the southern US. Meanwhile, our social feeds are proliferating with an abundance of 2024 Wrapped. We closed the year out with a record December, with 1,243 total submissions, as stubborn artists from all walks of life hoped to open 2025 with an acceptance from us, or at a crack at our shortlist, in the company of a select contingent of maybe thirty or forty.

In what we hope marks a tradition, we are returning to Merida, Mexico, for our third annual Urban Writing Retreat. In fact, our issue will be published the day that we are touring the Mayan ruins of the ancient city of Uxmal, a reminder of the persistence of art even in difficult times. We hope to continue this streak for many years to come; in fact that's why we're planning a new retreat experience. We're calling this one "Imagination and Identity: A Generative Writing Retreat," a chance to reimagine your work and yourself in the embattled city of Riga, Latvia. We know how beneficial travel can be for our writing, which is why we're opening up a scholarship campaign to help a marginalized writer attend.

We will also be at AWP in Los Angeles this spring, looking forward to a time of renewal and community—and, perhaps, you.

But even if you can't join us in person, we invite you to brave the cold: curl up with a hot beverage and our amazing issue—or, if you are in the Southern Hemisphere, enjoy a gentler clime and a great read.

A Conversation with Mario Aliberto III, author of *All the Dead We Have Yet to Bury*

MSP: Hello all! I'm here today with Mario Aliberto III, the wildly talented author of *All the Dead We Have Yet to Bury*.

I'm a sucker for incisive flash and innovative language, and Mario's chapbook grabs you from the start and doesn't let go. "Classified Ad for a Ghost" offers an explosive and thematic opening and I really enjoy the way that the chapbook itself continues to iterate on the theme of grief. A lot of the work that we see in the queue engages with loss, but does so in a much more straightforward way. The stories here include a nod to that titular "yet," the idea of anticipated loss.

Mario, how did this chapbook come together? How did your own writerly lens inspire and inform the pieces that you've assembled into this gorgeous mosaic of all the stages of grief, including the forerunner thereof, which captures such a thrilling observation of human nature?

MA: Thank you for that wonderful intro, Maria! I think my worldview is particularly defined by my upbringing. I was raised by loving parents, but everything was viewed through the lens of what could go wrong. Not just wrong, but how spectacularly wrong. It was as if we were always preparing for death; my parents would make sure I was aware of the worst case scenario for something as simple as driving to the movies with friends. The roads are wet? Drive carefully, or the car will skid off the road and everyone will die in a ditch. We were the family that if the phone rang, our heart skipped a beat because we knew it had to be bad news on the line. In this way, we were always living in some state of mourning, for people that weren't even dead yet!

MSP: As a quick follow-up, I'm curious about which piece came first in this chap.

MA: The piece that centered the chap is "Classified Ad for a Ghost." There's something universal about grief, and how everyone is looking for someone or something to throw them a lifeline. We would do almost anything to just have some part of our loved one back, to take some of the pain away. I wondered what real world solution would a desperate person seek for some solace? The classified ad begging someone to pretend to be a ghost sprang from that idea, and the chap was built around that foundation. All the ways we refuse to move on from those we've lost (the living and the dead), and how these characters cope, from the absurd to the tragic.

MSP: The concept of a ghost itself can mean so many different things to so many different cultures; still I feel like it's having a moment. You offer so many unique takes on ideas of ghostliness and haunting here. I'm wondering if it was difficult to brainstorm and come up with those ideas or if you had natural concepts that you wanted to explore and flesh out in your fiction. And how does that ghost enhance and deepen the rich portrayal of grief in yours?

MA: The ghost is such a universal concept. I truly believe we all have our own ghosts that haunt us, whether psychologically or spiritually. The concept that I was very excited to examine was the idea of a living person being "dead" to us, as in the story "Closer Than Gone," in which a living person who the protagonist has cut out of his life comes back to haunt him. Then, how his memories of that person are sort of a visitation, and the choices he makes to exorcize the ghost from his life.

MSP: What advice would you give to writers who are perhaps at a more conventional starting point and want to bring that originality on hauntings and liminal spaces into their work?

MA: My best advice to writers is to take the path that no one expects, not even yourself. Particularly in first drafts. There are no boundaries in first drafts, so when the writing gets boring, take the story in the direction that is unexpected. Surprise yourself. When I first began writing "All

Apologies," it was a much different piece. A student showed up to a high school class as a classic ghost in a sheet with eyeholes cut out. Nothing much happened. Now, one of my daughters writes little phrases on her Converse sneakers, and I couldn't get that image out of my head. These sneakers with black sharpie graffiti beneath the sheet. And like any Gen Xer, I know that this was a habit of Kurt Cobain, and right there, I had to know what would happen if Kurt Cobain showed up as a ghost to this generation of kids. What could they learn from him? It's so weird, but I couldn't get the story out of my head, and hopefully the readers can't either.

MSP: Florida Man memes aside, one of the things that really struck me about the chap was its strong sense of place. To me, this offered a competing dimension along which to flesh out the stories and make the characters feel lifelike.

Florida of course has a wonderful literary tradition, but it seems to be much more centered around, perhaps, Key West or Miami. I'd love to hear a bit about the specific regional identity of the Tampa area, as well as how that informed the development of the chap and its stories.

MA: Oh, Tampa Bay! This is truly the melting pot of the United States. There's so much rich culture and life here, whether it's the Greek Community in Tarpon Springs, or the Cuban influence in Ybor City, or the native Floridians in Plant City. Right now, the cities themselves are growing exponentially, from Tampa to St. Petersburg. There's this sense of wanting to retain small city charm, but the population is exploding. It's wild to watch all these newcomers adjust to the heat, the alligators, and the hurricanes. In "Shooting at Hurricanes," that story is ripped right from the headlines, where a few years ago the news had to beg the good people of Florida, please don't shoot the hurricanes. I bet someone new to Florida saw that on the news and wondered what they got themselves into, but those of us who have been here a minute didn't even blink.

MSP: Several of the stories here have an interpolated style, for instance, the epistolary ending of "All Apologies," and the fragmentation of memory in "The Swear Jar." Can you talk a bit about how to employ these craft techniques without making the fiction feel gimmicky? Is it just adding that depth and resonance that fiction, especially flash, seems to need, or are there other concerns to consider?

MA: The one test I always use is honesty. Any variation of form, if done for the sake of forcing the piece to stand out, will fail if it isn't honest to the story. A story can survive any form, whether it's a prose poem, or erasure, or hybrid, if the reader doesn't feel tricked or deceived. For example, in "The Swear Jar," Greg is haunted by his memories, and he kind of forces himself to live out his trauma, working at a pool during the summer to change a mistake of his in the past. The form of the piece contains sections of traumatic memories, and I use repetition and italics and ellipses to convey these repeating thoughts, and well, I've had anxious thoughts like that. Where you just keep replaying your mistakes over and over in your head, the same words, and it's my hope that others will recognize the truth in that, the honesty of it. In that way, the form is the only honest choice in which to tell the story.

MSP: I love father-daughter stories, and "Closer Than Gone" offers a compelling father-son take (also baseball, another obsession of mine). The rejection of the Rays hat felt like a moment when we choose what to consciously take from our parents, whereas the daughters in the other stories are shepherding a father's legacy in a way that is also curated, but outsized. I think the forecasting in "Goodbye, Tampa" is resonant because of its subtlety and the careful way the emotions of growing up and going off to college underscores the contention with a future grief. Cammy, like Kaley in "Panera Pariah," displays a tenderness that contradicts the idea that the parent, maybe especially the father, is the caregiver of the child. How do these conceptions of parenthood inform your writing? Is this another form of haunting, grieving, or even the grievance on display in "Closer Than Gone" and even "Shooting at Hurricanes?"

MA: "Goodbye Tampa" might have been one of the hardest pieces for me to write. The anticipation of losing someone, watching them dwindle before your eyes, and feeling helpless to change any of it. I lost my father last year, and he had not been doing well for some time. His mental health was not always the best. And it made me think back to when I was younger, and I wish I had been more aware, and had taken better care of him. I think I try to change my own history with my writing, by making my characters look at their parents as individuals, not someone to be placed on pedestals. Also, I come from a very strong family of women, and the women in my family are the leaders. I think that comes through in my writing, where women like Kaley in "Panera Pariah" and Cammy in "Goodbye Tampa" are much stronger than the male characters, particularly these daughters who take up the challenge of parenting their parents.

MSP: I'm always thrilled to see former contributors in the queue. Your piece "Tuesday May Never Come" was featured in Vol 4, Issue 3. Can you say a bit about what it was like to work with our CR prose editors and publish with us? When D.E. Hardy and I moved on to other positions in the organization, I was so proud to see what Brooke Randel and Nadia Staikos did in prose. Nadia's since moved on, and Brooke will be stepping down after this issue, but we're so excited to hand over the reins to our associate prose editors, Annie Schoonover and Praise Osawaru. And part of the reason I love seeing former contributors in chapbook queue is because it feels like an endorsement of our process.

MA: Oh wow, I still remember the day I got an acceptance from *Chestnut Review* for "Tuesday May Never Come." I had tried for quite awhile with some other pieces, and the rejections were always so kind, so I never gave up. I did a classic double-take when I opened the email for the acceptance. It's always an amazing experience when you are supported by editors who are writers themselves, who care for the entire process. There is a great feeling of community with *Chestnut Review*, and it's a dream come true to work with a brand that loves writing and writers and cares for their readers as well. I highly recommend any readers right now to pick up *Chestnut Review*, and any writers looking for someone to handle their work with care, sub now!

MSP: Finally, what's next for you? What are you working on now?

MA: I am heavily involved in edits for a novel, a literary horror story that centers on, you guessed it, grief and ghosts. Hopefully, *A Girl Made of Bees* will make it into bookstores in the future. In the present, my first love is still flash fiction, and I have a couple of pieces coming out this year. Flash fiction is addictive. Reading it, writing it. Oh, and I'll be at

AWP this year table hopping, so if you're in attendance, stop by and say hello!

MSP: Yes, we will be there as well, and happy to feature Mario at our booth for a signing. *All the Dead We Have Yet to Bury* will be out in mid-February. Please keep an eye out!

The Legend of Panera Pariah

Before there were no more every-other-weekends at her father's apartment, before she remembered it as the last time he brushed her hair off her face and kissed her goodnight, Kaley begged her father for a few more stories about growing up in Plant City with his infamous cousin, Panera Pariah.

Panera Pariah, her father said on one of their Saturday nights together, his hands stinking of gasoline and lawn clippings as he tucked her into bed, *flapped her arms and flew from Plant City to Ybor City alongside a flock of Snowy Egrets because no one ever bothered to tell her a little girl couldn't fly.*

Honestly, Kaley never considered her parents divorced. Ten years old now, alternating weekends with her parents had become a seamless routine, and it wasn't like her parents hated each other. Kaley's father promised he'd come home when he got right. Said he was halfway there. Kaley held onto the belief he'd make it all the way home someday. As for Kaley's mother, she still wore her wedding ring. In fact, her mother always said Kaley's father was the love of her life, but sometimes love wasn't enough to keep people together.

Kaley believed they'd be a family again right up to the Monday her mother got that phone call. No one had ever cried as hard as her mother when she broke the news to Kaley, barely able to get the words out. Kaley's father had been at work, mowing grass for the Plant City lawn crew, when on a forty-five-degree incline along an embankment of a city culvert, his riding mower flipped, pinning him beneath a foot of water. Her mother said it was quick. No pain. In the coming days, an online news article would quote a witness claiming her father drowned before the mower blades stopped spinning.

Panera Pariah, her father had said, breath beer-sweet, eyes glassy-red, *wore white to funerals and black to weddings because she knew there was a little sweet and a little sad in everything.*

In the school auditorium, Ms. Franklin discussed all the changes a girl's body experienced during puberty. Ms. Franklin played a video on the big screen for the sixth-grade girls, and they learned all about hair growing in their armpits and on their privates, breast development and menstruation. Hormones and reproduction. Ms. Franklin taught them everything about when life began, but nothing about when life ended.

Sitting in her bedroom after picking up her things from her father's apartment, Kaley wondered about all the important stuff Ms. Franklin had left out. What did you do with the duffel bag you no longer needed to pack on Thursday nights? Where did you put the extra hairbrush and toothbrush and sets of underwear? The extra pajamas, board games, and nail polish. The second night light. The second mattress. The second Nintendo. The second television. What did you do if you had two of everything except two parents?

Panera Pariah, her father had told her, his eyes glittering in the bedroom nightlight, *ate soup with chopsticks and never spilled a drop.*

The day of her father's celebration of life, Kaley picked a white dress to wear, and her mother, instead of fussing over the color, wore white as well. At the funeral home, Kaley kept an eye on the door, waiting for her father's cousin to make a grand entrance. On a pedestal at the front of the room, water lilies and chrysanthemums surrounded her father's urns. His ashes had been divided between a large silver urn and a smaller urn about the size of a teacup. The large one for Kaley, the small one for her grandmother.

Panera Pariah, her father had whispered before brushing her hair aside and placing a last kiss upon her cheek, *could step through a mirror and play with her reflection. She said that way she was never alone and always had copies of her favorite things.*

Mourners waited in line to hug Kaley's mother as if she were a widow. They hugged her grandmother and patted the uncles on the back. Everyone in black. No sign of her father's cousin. People settled in their seats, and one of her uncles stood by her father's urns to speak, but when he began sobbing and couldn't get a word out, Kaley's mother rushed to his side and told stories. Some Kaley knew, some she didn't. Everyone laughed. Everyone cried. It was good in the worst way.

After the service, Kaley and her mother were the last ones left besides her Grandma. Kaley held the large urn, her Grandma the small one. The door to the funeral home opened, and Kaley held her breath with anticipation for Panera Pariah's arrival. Unfortunately, it was only the funeral director ushering them out so he could prepare the room for the next service. As they hugged goodbye, Kaley's mother eyed the small urn in

Grandma's hands. She twisted her wedding ring, her hands empty.

Kaley stopped her Grandma at the door. "He's supposed to come home with us. He promised." Grandma shook her head. Looked at the wedding ring on Kaley's mother's finger. Then the wedding ring on her own finger. Six years since Grandpa passed and her hand never went without it. "Not halfway," Kaley said. "All the way."

That night, Kaley's mother tucked Kaley into bed beside two urns on the nightstand. She rested her head on Kaley's lap, crying with all the hurt in the world. "You brought him home."

Kaley brushed the hair off her mother's face and kissed her cheek. She whispered in her mother's ear, "Panera Pariah wears white to funerals, owns two of everything, and her love is enough to keep everyone together."

SUSAN SOLOMON

Bleeding Hearts II

Gouache
7x5 inches, 2024

Tong, Tong, Tong

After arriving at the airport and wading through the near-standstill Manila traffic, Tara and I found our way to the hotel and booked a room together. Now we lay naked in bed, as if we were no longer strangers but lovers. The room smelled of generic lavender, and the dimly lit modern light fixtures kept the darkness at bay. The walls, once white, had yellowed with age and were bordered by brown, like an old colonial home from the distant Spanish past, now cooled by air conditioning. In the distance outside, the Pacific waves gently crashed against the night. Tara leaned her head into me and whispered a tune, *tong, tong, tong, tong…*

"It's about a crab," Tara said. A simple nursery rhyme. Her hand mimicked the motions of a crustacean crawling up my arm, each finger a tiny leg stepping to the distinct beat…*pakitong-kitong*. "Big, delicious, but tricky to catch…" she continued. The crab lunged from my shoulder, pinching my earlobe, "It bites."

"I don't remember that one," I said, wincing. I filed through childhood memories, searching for that crab, trying to remember what it was like before my parents whisked me away to the States. The only nursery rhyme that came to mind was about a hut made of bamboo and leaves. I had already forgotten the lyrics.

"That's a different one," Tara said, caressing my ear between a finger and thumb. The crab was no longer a crab but her smooth, delicate hand. "You're too American now," she teased in Tagalog, "Amerikano."

This was my first visit to the Philippines since my parents had died—my father in a car crash, followed shortly by my mother from a heart attack. My mother always insisted on being buried in the same cemetery as her relatives in the Philippines. "We have a whole plot all to ourselves," she would brag as if tombstones were trophies, a row of them on public display. My father didn't have a grave in mind, so he ended up in a small, additional lot alongside my mother's family. He was always that way, so caught up in appeasing his wife's wishes that he never got his own. He would say, "A happy wife, a happy life." I wondered if it was the same for the two of them in the afterlife—whether either of them were happy, or if happiness was even possible. Their funerals were five years ago, the last time I had been in my home country. Before that, my last time in the Philippines was when I was two, leaving for the States with vague memories and mistranslated nursery rhymes. I was too American now, Tara was right. I didn't remember much at all.

*

I was in Manila for the wedding of William and Sophia, my friends from college. Growing up, I didn't think much of the Philippines since I left, not until I met them. Back then, Sophia was an international student from the Philippines who came to our university in her junior year. There weren't many Filipinos on campus, and the few often hung around in cliques. Perhaps I could have been part of that little Pinoy community, having been approached to attend weekly meetings involving Filipino food, but I declined. I got enough lumpia from my parents when they visited, and my tastes leaned more towards cheeseburgers and fries than dinuguan. Sophia must have been looking for that community, which was how we first met.

"You're Filipino?" she asked, approaching me in the quad. But to her disappointment, I wasn't much of one. While the Filipino cliques often had potluck dinners—kamayan nights—and line dances, I was either with William playing Call of Duty or watching some five-dollar matinee at the downtown theater. When I told her my major was in art history, her disappointment continued in questions. "Why not an engineer?"— her brother was an engineer in the Philippines. "Why not a nurse?—she was pursuing a nursing degree. She sounded like my parents. I had been a biology major like William, with plans to pursue a medical career. Then I saw how all the other Filipinos, no matter how few, were in the same classes. I couldn't quite explain my aversion to joining them, but I resisted any aspect that could have pigeonholed me as one of them, even if it meant my exclusion. I refused to be a stereotype. So I switched my major to art and never looked back.

It was William who gravitated towards Sophia. When I introduced her to William, she was already lost in his all-American-ness. He was as white as they came, with a squared jaw and freckles that came out in the summer. His voice seemed stuck in that slightly-after-puberty stage, like a teenager posing as a grown-up. They said it was love at first sight, and I believed it was true. William was the one who joined her at those Friday night meetings full of Filipino food and karaoke. Though they invited me, I still refused, citing some art project that needed be done. But I watched their romance blossom. By the spring semester of junior year, they were together seriously. Their marriage, it seemed, was always inevitable.

In between semesters, I invited them to my home, which was a four-hour drive from the college. My parents didn't visit me on campus, so I figured I would introduce them to William and Sophia. Almost instantly, my parents grew fond of William, extending an invitation for all future family gatherings. They loved Sophia, too. Unlike me, she kept her Tagalog tongue and even spoke Ilocano, the language my father spoke from his province. My parents teased me, of course, using William as an example. "See? If you were a doctor, you would already have a girlfriend." A *Filipino* girlfriend, they insinuated. But I never did live up to their wishes.

The three of us remained close until the end of college. When William went to medical school and Sophia returned to the Philippines as a nurse, they kept a long-distance relationship. Meanwhile, I grew distant from them. I found work as an art instructor at a community college near my parents. I thought it best to live with them until I could afford somewhere better. When they asked about William and Sophia, I told them how well they were doing in their careers. All the while, they reminded me of how I could have been just like them. By the time I felt like it was the right time to reach out to them and plan a reunion, life had other plans. Then came the car accident that took my father's life, and then my mother's heart attack. At the time, William was preoccupied with his residency. I also decided not to tell Sophia. I didn't doubt that she would have come as a friend to the funerals, but I felt it had been too long since our college days. Perhaps I should have told them about their deaths sooner, considering how they were practically family according to my parents.

But now, we three would be back together in Manila of all places. I was to be William's best man. "We wouldn't be together if it wasn't for you," William had told me over the phone. His voice hadn't changed since college; it was like we never left. Apart from my parents, William and Sophia had been the closest people in my life, so I agreed to be William's best man.

*

As I lay next to Tara, I had more on my mind than William and Sophia's wedding. While I found them attractive, I was never infatuated with Filipino women, an immature fear that one might have been a distant relative. Even though my parents wanted me to find a girl like Sophia, I always found it strange when, standing on the subway, any given Filipino would stare at me until I noticed, and they would nod at me, gesturing, *You are one of us.* I'd smile reluctantly, then turn the other way. Now, I found myself in bed with Tara, the only intimacy I've shared with another Filipino, as if being in the homeland gave me permission and reassurance—Tara's touch telling me, *You are one of us.*

On the plane, her face was much paler, under layers of powder and pigments, a hint of blush across her cheeks. She must have shared the same routine with the other flight attendants, whose faces hid the same tropical traces. Even in sound, their voices lost the authority of strong consonants and quick syllables, the authority of my parents' mother tongue, scolding, commanding. They spoke in soft gestures instead: sir, miss, please.

"Sir," Tara had said, leaning into my aisle seat, "Coffee or tea?"

"Coffee," I replied. I was sketching a baby in the aisle across from me, the mother lulling the plump infant in her arms to sleep. Tara eyed my sketchbook as she poured, careful not to spill. Then her eyes met mine, a blip in her uniformed performance. We smiled. "Thanks," I said as she handed me the hot drink. Then she returned to her routine, "Coffee or tea?" right down the aisle of the plane.

When the flight landed and all the baggage was retrieved, we found each other waiting for a cab outside the terminal. Children ran to greet their aunts and uncles; significant others embraced for too long. Tara had a few bags, including a balikbayan box. When I went to help her load her things into a taxi van, she tried handing me a couple of bills—first in pesos then in dollars.

"At least let me share the cab with you," she offered.

I didn't have much, just a carry-on roller. Unlike her, I had no need for a balikbayan box, no family waiting for presents or supplies. I looked back at the horde of other arrivals, clamoring over taxis to haul themselves and their belongings to waiting loved ones. Then Tara mentioned her destination, and we realized we were staying at the same hotel.

"Wait," I said, grabbing the taxicab door before she could close it. "I accept your offer."

I didn't expect the ride to take so long. But as the afternoon sunlight gradually turned to evening, and the cab had only moved a few miles, I couldn't help but feel the tense air between Tara and me—the hot, tropical humidity didn't help either. "There's an accident on the expressway," the driver explained, cutting through the silence. Tara and I exchanged looks. She said something in Tagalog that I couldn't quite make out, maybe something about taking a shortcut or even the lack of air-conditioning in the car. The driver merely responded, "Sorry, mam. Hindi po puede."

"Your art is beautiful," she said to me. I had taken out my sketchbook and began finishing the piece I started on the plane, which was shaping up to be an in-flight rendition of the Madonna and child.

"Salamat," I attempted to thank her in Tagalog, which was met by her smirk. Despite the heat, I could also feel my cheeks go warm.

"I wanted to be an artist, too," Tara added.

"Let me guess, your parents said you couldn't."

"Actually, they didn't really care," she explained. "One of the perks of being the youngest. The problem was that I wasn't a very good artist."

I handed her my sketchbook and pencil. Tara raised an eyebrow.

"Prove it," I said. "Draw me."

After a moment of hesitation, she accepted the challenge. She took her time, glancing between my face and the blank page. I didn't watch what she was actually putting down on the paper. As her subject, I kept still, which was easy considering how slow the traffic moved. While she was focusing on me, I kept my stare on her fingers, which moved with the pencil in lines and circles, scribbling out shapes that didn't satisfy her. When she finally handed the sketchbook back to me, I laughed. She had merely drawn a smiley face. "See? Not very good."

That was enough to cut the tension.

We continued to talk throughout the ride. Tara spoke about the cities she'd visited: Rio de Janeiro, Abu Dhabi, Moscow. She demonstrated her limited proficiency in foreign languages, such as French and Korean. Then her speech eventually settled between English and Tagalog, her accent growing harder and more demanding. As she spoke, she took a face wipe from her purse and took off her makeup. She undid her hair and let it fall to her shoulders. By the time we arrived at the hotel and reached our room, Tara was almost unrecognizable as the flight attendant I had met some hours before. Despite all the places she'd been to, there was still her true Filipino self underneath her uniform and accents. I felt no such change in myself.

Perhaps it was finally having the freedom to move after spending hours in that taxi or the immediate relief of the air conditioning in the hotel room that led us immediately to bed, one touch after the other. Then came the song, *Tong, tong, tong, tong, pakitong-kitong.*

"We used to sing that song every day, ever since we learned it at school," she continued. "There were five of us, can you imagine? Going around the house shouting *tong, tong, tong, tong*"—her accent rang true, her tongue determined each note—"then we'd change to *ting, ting, ting, ting.* I don't know how my parents managed," Tara said.

My parents, who only had me, managed well. My father was a dentist and my mother taught kindergarten. I got good grades in school, and never got into trouble. I was the model immigrant child and, after seventeen years, a citizen. But when my parents passed away, I wondered how I would manage without them.

On the other hand, Tara lived her childhood in the Philippines. She narrated her memories, which were mostly made up of early mornings before the sun rose over Manila. "Mama didn't need to raise her voice," she said. Instead, she recalled how her mother would start up a frying pan on the stove and throw in a handful of pusit and danggit. The pungent, salty smell of dried squid and fish was enough to wake anyone from the deepest sleep. Tara continued, "I never got used to it. It was gross, which was practical. It made me want to shower and get dressed right away." She inhaled the bedsheets for a moment, taking in the lavender. "My school uniform smelled much better." Was her life any different as a flight attendant, waking up at sporadic times, and slipping into a newly washed and ironed uniform?

"My mother's sick," she continued. "The doctor told my siblings she has a few months left. They caught the cancer too late." She went back to the song, *tong, tong, tong…*But her hand looked numb, no longer the crustacean with claws. She was still leaning into me, but her eyes were fixed on the ceiling, a beige canvas in the faint light. What was she drawing in her mind? "The crab bites back," she concluded.

I let her drift to sleep. Her breathing matched the waves outside, gently advancing and receding. I reached for a pencil from my bag, then began to draw her. The moonlight seeped through the window and clung to her silhouette, the contours of her body forming a clear edge. She held her position, the cotton sheets rising and falling with her body. While my body had yet to adjust to the time and place, Tara slept just fine.

I didn't want to admit it. But when William and Sophia paired off in college, I became the odd one out. When I lost my parents, the feeling was harder to ignore. I was lonely. I had been for a long time.

*

In the morning, Tara had to leave for Pangasinan. She arranged for another van to pick her up from the hotel, but this time she would share it with other strangers looking to make the five-hour journey through winding roads and the Filipino countryside if the Manila traffic didn't hold them back. Meanwhile, I had to get ready for the wedding.

When the sky outside awoke with a glimmer of pink and orange, I got out of bed and unzipped my carry-on. The barong was only mildly crumpled, but the black dress pants developed their own topography. I can hear my mother's voice in the back of my mind, nagging me. "Ang lukot lukot," she would say, pointing out the noticeable creases in the fabric. "You should have had it dry-cleaned!" But there was no time for the dry cleaners now, and I could no longer wish for my mother to stop nagging me.

"Ang lukot." This time I heard it for real. Tara had woken up. "What's that for?"

"A wedding," I said.

"Wow! Bongga bongga," Tara teased. "I didn't know I was the other woman."

"You're not," I said, embarrassed. "It's for a friend's wedding."

She got up from bed, looking over my shoulder and pointing out the crumpled-up barong and pants. I let her head rest in the crevice between my neck and shoulder. "Steam should help with those creases," she said. So, I hung the outfit on a hanger and hooked it behind the bathroom door, and then we both slipped into a hot shower. When we got out, she helped me dress. I thought of my mother on the night of college graduation, making sure my tie was centered along the line of buttons on my white shirt. Tara buttoned the collar up to my neck—her fingers felt like the pinch of a little crab.

"Tong, tong, tong," I attempted to sing, my muddled, too-American mouth struggled to recall the words.

"Needs work," she teased.

"I'll get it right next time," I said, not knowing if there would be a next time.

Before I left, I walked her out to the van. She didn't have her airline uniform on, but a red tank top over blue jeans. Her face was free of makeup, and her deep brown skin glistened in the morning sun. Just as I did at the airport, I helped her carry her belongings to the van. I thought of convincing her to stay by inviting her as my plus-one, even though I'd already checked off a single RSVP months ago. But her mother was waiting for her arrival, and I couldn't take that away from her, not while they still had each other. Instead, I presented her with the sketch I had drawn of her the night before.

"You keep it," Tara insisted. She asked for a pencil and wrote a phone number on its back. "So you can find me when we're back in New York." She kissed me on the cheek and, before jumping into the van, pinched my ear with her hand, the crab. I watched the van drive off the parking lot, onto the street alongside jeepneys, tricycles, and motorcycles—the steady stream of urban Manila—and waved goodbye.

*

The wedding took place in an old Catholic church in a section of Manila called Intramuros, the colonial headquarters of the Spanish way back when. Intramuros was a walled city, whose buildings all bore the same brown and yellow bricks. Its streets were tight, not made for two-way traffic, especially not for a limo. The ceremony itself was as expected. Back in New York, my parents had dragged me to other weddings of titos and titas—some true blood relatives but most just their colleagues and friends. William and Sophia's wedding was three hours of mostly standing. The orchestral songs were dramatic enough to make the colonial barebones of the church tremble. For a while, I moved my mouth to keep up with the Taglog songs and readings, but I eventually surrendered, chiming in only for the occasional amen. As the best man, I had to stand in front of everyone, pretending my feet weren't blistering in my dress shoes.

The reported temperature was ninety degrees, but it was amplified by the hundred or so attending the ceremony, and the church wasn't made for air conditioning. The electric fans did their best. Sweat seeped through my barong—the last time I wore one was for my parents' funeral. The other men, too, wore the traditional shirt—a thin, see-through fabric with flowery designs. In colonial times, Spanish officers forced Filipinos to wear it because of its transparent fabric, which allowed them ensure no daggers or weapons were hidden beneath. But now, a whole church congregation had men wearing barongs, right in the capital of Spanish colonial rule. Even William.

"A happy wife, a happy life," I echoed my father in my best man's speech at the reception. In the cooler, air-conditioned banquet hall, I felt more comfortable.

"You know," William said, "you might take that advice sometime soon."

"I've been talking you up with all of my cousins," Sophia said. She gestured to a table full of young women. A few giggled as they caught us eyeing them. She continued, "Any of them would be lucky to have you."

"I'll take my chances back in the States," I said. I decided to withhold Tara from them. I kept my sketch of her in my pocket, like some kind of totem or lucky charm. If I told them about Tara, if I revealed our secret little tryst, would I somehow ruin my chances of finding her again? I would wait until we rendezvoused in New York, whenever that would be.

"If I were you," Sophia added, "I wouldn't close the door on women around here. They're all looking for some handsome American to whisk them away."

"Just take a look at Sophia," William joked, "Now she's my wife." They both laughed. I should have been happy for them, and by all appearances I was, laughing uncomfortably.

Fortunately, the DJ started the music and called everyone to the dance floor. The opening notes of Earth, Wind, & Fire's "September" beckoned everyone out of their seats.

"I actually know this fucking line dance," William said.

He met Sophia at the front of the dance floor, and behind them formed five rows of miscellaneous Filipinos from Sophia's side and some of William's white family members who struggled to mimic the movements. It was an awful sight, but for everyone else, it must have been fun. I approached the open bar, took a double shot of rum, and did my best on the dance floor. I also knew the steps to "September" like a good

Filipino. I could at least be one, if only for a dance number.

*

I don't remember much after the dancing and the spinning of it all—the echoing of ABBA's "Dancing Queen" reverberating through the banquet hall. When William and Sophia found me an hour after the reception, I was outside on the beach in a drunken, sandy stupor. They found me with my face thrust into the sand, the back of my neck burnt red, and my shoes filled with ocean water from Manila Bay. I was mumbling and slurring my words, refusing to wake up from an apparent dream. Crabs had scurried all over me, so they called over some paramedics to pry the pincers off my arms and legs. William and Sophia helped me back to the hotel with patches of Band-Aids covering the pricks all over my body.

"You kept calling out to Tara," William said, "in between some song."

"Tong—uh—pa-ki-tong—uh—ki-tong," Sophia sang clumsily, mocking what had been my drunken rendition. "I didn't think you'd know it. Did Tara teach you that?"

"And who the hell is Tara? Is that one of your cousins?" William asked his now wife.

"None of mine," Sophia answered. "Did you mean Cara? I didn't see her as your type."

Still in a drunken haze, I shook my head.

"If you've been seeing someone, then you have to tell us," they egged on. "Who's Tara?"

I reached into my pocket for her picture—the sketch I had drawn of Tara with her phone number on it. But when I took the picture out, it unfolded like a wilting salad. I looked at what remained of my drawing—the lead was all streaks and smudges on the sodden piece of paper. I turned it over to find that her phone number was also lost to the ocean.

"Who's Tara?" they repeated.

"Just some girl," I said. I wanted to say she was someone special, to tell them I had found someone too. But I couldn't, not when I had lost the only trace of her.

When their wedding had all wrapped up and I returned to New York alone, I realized that letting her go was for the best. Even though I knew the chances were nearly impossible, I held on to the slight hope that Tara might have been on the same flight back. But the crew was entirely new.

Instead, I imagined her with her siblings, crouched next to their ailing mother in bed in her final moments. Tara was where she needed to be—where she belonged. Me? I was *Amerikano*, like she had said. Still, I never did get that damn nursery rhyme out of my head.

Our reader describes what it was like to find Patrick Joseph Caoile's "Tong, Tong, Tong"

"Tong, Tong, Tong" weaves identity and longing into a delicate tale of romance. The narrative voice—honest, introspective, and tinged with melancholy—pulled me in and lingered long after the final page. Its exploration of cultural dislocation deeply resonated with me, echoing my own experience of growing up in Nigeria, outside my Yoruba heritage, and feeling caught between worlds. Also, I first read this story from the pile of submissions while preparing to leave for graduate studies in the U.S., a moment when the prospect of becoming an immigrant played on my mind. It became a mirror for my hopes and fears, reminding me that the search for belonging is both an outward journey and an inward discovery. This is the story we all need.

—Shedrack Akanbi

Our reader describes what it was like to find Debmalya Bandyopadhyay's "A House on Fire"

Coming across "A House on Fire," I was surprised that a poem with such a dramatic title began so quietly—not with someone leaping from a window to escape an inferno, but with a speaker who is just walking down the street and comes across a burning house. But at the end of the first couplet, the fire triggers a memory, and that memory starts to become more and more urgent, until the speaker almost seems to be burning from the inside out. The little respites between each couplet keep a solemn hush hanging over the mounting tension, giving us moments of stillness so that we can take in all the branching reflections on longing, frustration, trauma and resilience, and more.And even as we pass through that whole world of turbulence, the poem's music flows softly through us. By the time I got to the "burning hands" in the final couplet, I knew that this was a hauntingly beautiful poem that we had to share with our readers.

—Brian O'Sullivan

A House on Fire

The day I walk past my old neighbourhood,
  a house is on fire. I remember it all too well,

the weeded walls, the family that moved out
  when their girl got sick, the backyard I would

trespass hoping to run into her; wait under
  the jamun tree in the vermillion dusk,

a hive of mosquitoes gathering over me
  like a sharpened memory. No one arrived

to answer my little crime, but a decade & half
  later, my body recalls how anticipation had

shattered my heart. What did I learn of waiting
  from the house? Of giving my abandoned hopes

over to fire? Chagrin smashed over
  my floorboards like lightbulbs. Small explosions

in numberless small towns. Something kept falling
  over my own debris all these years, stayed in me

like a season's leftover, like hamlet fog. Was it rain, or
  regret freckled over cheeks of glass? Damp & devious,

I crept beyond my teenage, past my fallible heart
  in the language of moss. When it ached with alone,

I pretended desire was a borrowed thing: a myth
whispered in a bar, sparks smouldering out

of an abandoned house. Yet, I waited for someone
to rush in, to discover my beautiful, burnt hands.

At the Park

Acrylics on canvas
30x40 centimeters, 2024
(Next Page)

The piece is from a memory I had, a visit to the park with my good friend. I wanted to capture the immediate moment on canvas, my aim was to not make an exact replica of the scene, but to add my own touch, the color palette is very different from reality, a focus towards more pastel shades, it was not just to capture the moment, but a nostalgic feeling I had at that exact moment.

Why Our Bodies Sought Asylum in Water-[Genes]

genocide. genocide. genocide. genocide. genocide. genocide.
genocide. genocide. **our gene was made genocide**. genocide.
genocide. genocide. **with loose glue** gene-o-cide. genocide.
genocide. genocide. **against bullets**. genocide. gene-o-cide
genocide. **& there is a hole in our species** genocide. genes
genocide. **where the massacre sneaked in**. genocide. genes
genocide. **on the news, you'll hear of men** genocide. gens
genocide. **migrating to the Nile for asylum** genocide.
genocide. **at least, what births us should kill us** genocide
genocide. **without pain or blood**—genocide. genocide.
genocide. **just our bodies drowning** genocide. [genocide]
genocide. **into the quietude & softness of water**-[genes]
genocide. **& unto the feet of our God**—genes. on. void
genocide. **perhaps water is another wormhole** genocide
genocide. **leading into another universe** genocide. genes
genocide **where we won't be called black gen**-ocide. gene.
genocide. genocide. **black things** genocide. genocide. melt.
genocide. genocide. genocide. genocide. genocide. genocide

No Promises

The book he hurled across the room at me. The glass mason jar he smashed to the floor in the kitchen. The door he slammed in the bedroom. The door he slammed in the living room. The time he pushed up against me, not quite touching but close enough to feel his heartbeat across the distance between us. He always promises he won't do it again. He says we belong together. But the pre-violence. This is how I describe it to my therapist: pre-violence. She's quiet, thoughtful. She asks if I feel safe. I tell her of course I do. *He wouldn't hurt a fly*, I say. She says, *hm*. I say, *a door is not a fly—a fly is alive, it's different*. It's like the trick I play in my head on an airplane when I picture the wing tearing off and the whole hulk of metal plunging down to the earth: because I've imagined it crashing, it absolutely won't. Just like because I have considered that his pre-violence is violence, it absolutely is not. It is not. It is not. I explain this to my therapist. She uses the phrase *domestic violence*. I laugh. *I'm not a door*, I say. *I'm not a book*. I'm not a mason jar. She isn't laughing. I look out the window of her office. Across the street, there's a lone shopping cart piled with clothes. It's strange to have a window in a therapist's office. Too much outside when you're trying to deal with the inside. My therapist is saying something, but all I can hear is the sound of the recycling truck somewhere beyond this room. The sound of bottles breaking. The mason jar on the tile. A hundred silver slivers. I was barefoot. A sliver landed on top of my foot—the skin there so tender that when I tried to wipe it off, it cut me. A light line of blood. I think about his face when he broke the jar: so much anger. Before him, I could not fathom that much anger. But now I'm used to it. *Is that love?* I ask my therapist, and she shakes her head, violently. She is adamant: **Abuse. Domestic violence**. Those are the only words she knows today: lacking in creativity. I've heard this said about the word fuck. It shows a lack of creativity. I look out the window again. The shopping cart is still there. Abandoned. To my therapist, I say, *he says we belong together*, and, *he always promises*—but she stops me mid-sentence. She's had enough of me today. She says the

words again. *Abuse. Domestic violence.* I sigh. She wants me to break up
with him, but I've never broken up with anyone. What would happen
if I did the breaking? How lovely to fit a life into a shopping cart. How
simple. I know it's not true at all, but the thought comforts me. To leave
with nothing but a shopping cart. To break, to leave. I don't know what's
true anymore. I close my eyes. I imagine putting my body there inside the
shopping cart. I imagine it rolling away, down the street and then onto
a dirt path, into a forest. I imagine the safety of the metal around me. I
imagine the forest: so tall and quiet. Soft barked redwoods. Spongy for-
est floor. A jar would not break there. No doors to slam. No books. No
men. No promises.

Gender Questioning in the End Times

August stews the tidepools on Tybee,
every puddle is a bath by 9:00 AM,
sunshine bakes a beached horseshoe crab belly-up
I toe over the black helmet of its body,
revealing a clutch of eggs undershell
watch it sashay downshore, a waltz of legs
recalling the soup of ancient seas.

I suspect I am not exactly a girl early on
I see my life sprawl into positions unlike
        Mother fussing rooms into order
        Nagymama rolling dough for walnut *beigli*
        Ayyamma mending saree seams
        aunties pollinating buds of gossip at dinner parties
        motherbound classmates swaddled in worry
        latchkey cousins slipping the boundaries of their lawns
mine is a different liberation
a certain otherness like
the undersounds dogs hear
the hidden spectrums of nectar-seeking birds
the taste of the world flickering
along the tongue of a snake
or trundling on living fossil legs

slipping into the warming Atlantic, I admit
I've been too buoyant for diving,
breasts are the kind of lifesavers
that kept me from serious depths
now scientists say we are in the middle of the sixth extinction
every day holds space for new deaths
 this home is fruitful with endings,
superocean Panthalassa was a theater for ghosts

rounding the stage of Pangea,
every handful of silt a slaughterhouse floor, still
I can't imagine a better place than that ancient Earth,
the drowsy ocean snug against the unparted land,
every lifeform a neighbor,
an Eden where all living things were whole

these days I sense the need to slip over borders like wind like water
my boundaries are drawn differently from women and men
like Pangea I am everything all at once
I can wear the skin of any wet-eyed artist
following the path of the setting sun
wondering at the hues my eyes never evolved to see

when I'm five fingers old
I paint a dinosaur with every color in my palette
when the teacher wonders, I say it's not a boy or a girl
later, I press close to the table fan refreshing the nursery
and call myself a boy just to hear the sound in the cooling room
the blades turn my words
round and round into the universe
and I say to the fan I am a girl too
I am a daughter-son
will be a husband-wife, a mother-father
when I turn 37 my niece will name me Uncle Drea
I will sometimes sign my name Mr.

these are the smallest liberations
seeded into my soft tissues

        that when Earth swallows the spines of its mountains
        I will untether from the cradles that confined my mother
        and announce my will to exist
        like the crabs of Panthalassa
        I will persevere into the depths,
        shed my buoyant shell,
        and carrying my family on my back,

find the deep clefts of a new paradise,
a Pangea of the bodies where nothing is broken apart

Sarabande For O

Two bodies face to face/are at times two waves - Octavio Paz

Into you, I go, like a sermon.
There is a garden party
in your pupils. What strand
of light were you culled from?
Your hips, swaying lily.
I plucked your ribs like a harp
& watched you entice the trees
till every bud split into promise & song.
The promise of bee to nectar,
the promise of knife to ginger.
The knot of your tongue & mine
untangle only to whisper prayer
into the windy noon
unfolding like a pamphlet
we will forget to read.
The sun's dialect, seeping
into the plumbagos, sets loose
a blue optimism over the world.
I found a river inside the salmon.
I believe in the resurrection.

Cleaning Girls

We were cleaning girls together at The Hideout Inn, a bed and breakfast and retreat center in the Ponderosa Pine Forest, twenty miles west of where I lived in Rock Creek. Fran lived closer to work in a gated community called Cathedral Pines. Her house was massive with a white stone exterior and marble floor entryway. Most vividly, I remember the basement—the pullout sofa and the big-screen TV and the bathroom where Fran tried to scrub Natalie's blood out of the carpet.

*

I taught Fran everything she needed to know about cleaning. When she started at The Hideout—her first job—I'd been there three years already, saving for college and helping my mom pay bills. Every Wednesday and Thursday after high school and every Saturday, I punched in, tied on an embroidered apron, and picked up a chicken-scratch to-do list from Jared the owner, who always ended the lists with an apology. *Rm 4-9 & 11. Conf 2 reset. Din 15 ppl. Patio Hot tub. Sorry.* A shy, frazzled man, Jared rushed around the property in flip-flops, the only shoes I ever saw him wear. I liked that he left me alone to do my work. I knew how to clean a bathroom and push tables together and re-make beds with tight, neat corners, because I came from a mother who cleaned for a living. I must have been ten years old when she taught me to scrub the toilet bowl barehanded with a rag and white vinegar. The inside too.

Fran came from a mother who offered to pay her to do chores if she wanted to, and she never wanted to, and her family had a maid who cleaned their house anyway. The day she started, I showed her all the basics, like how to work from the outside of the counter into the sink, instead of the other way, because of germs, and how to fold a fitted bed sheet to match the shape of the top sheet instead of balling it up and stuffing it in the closet. I had to explain dustpans after watching her sweep the patio without one. She looked like a cartoon character golfing, swinging through a haze of dirt.

In her first week, Fran exhausted herself trying. She worked in short, earnest bursts, and then she followed me around talking while I cleaned. She talked to me with ease, intimately, like we had been friends for a long time already.

*

Fran said that she'd applied to The Hideout to get some work ethic before college. Not that college itself would be anything like cleaning, but she wanted to get some perspective. She kept calling it "the real world." While I made beds, she talked about the future, and she talked about her sister Natalie.

"She's gorgeous. Like Naomi Watts, except skinnier," she said.

I thought Naomi Watts was already skinny. And I thought Fran was beautiful the way girls with money often are—born into rituals that become effortless and inclined from a young age to match accessories. To have accessories. Fran had long wavy hair (perfect beach hair, by my land-locked standards) and heavy-lidded green eyes that made her look a little bored, if it wasn't for her gap-toothed smile underneath.

I motioned for Fran to grab the other side of the duvet cover. She held up rubber-gloved hands to signal that she couldn't, even though she hadn't cleaned anything with them yet.

She continued on about Natalie. "She's super smart, you'd love her. She's studying philosophy at CU Boulder, but she might switch to art history."

I liked that Fran perceived me as smart. I told her that I'd love to meet her sister, and I admitted—for the first time, out loud—that I really wanted to go away to college.

"You have to!" Fran said. "Come to Boulder with us. I'm following Nat, even though my dad made me apply to all these liberal arts colleges in the middle of nowhere."

I had never heard of Grinnell or Claremont or Oberlin. I wouldn't have been able to fathom the cost of tuition if she'd told me. Although I had been planning to live at home after graduation—to keep working, to start classes at community college—after work that night, I looked up application requirements for Boulder.

I thought it was sweet how close Fran was to her sister. I had always wondered what it would be like to have a sibling, a built-in friend. When I was younger, I used to beg for one, and my mom would say that she'd find me a sibling if I could find her a good man, which meant tough luck, kiddo, because she also said that all men are bad news. As far as I know, she never dated anyone after my dad left.

"Do you want to tag-team the bathroom when you're done with those?" Fran asked, still holding her gloved hands like foreign objects.

*

The first Saturday Fran invited me over after work, I feigned indifference when we got to the first gate, and then to the second gate, and then drove up a long, paved driveway flanked by pine trees and monolithic bronze sculptures—her dad's art, apparently. The entryway of her house echoed, which made me want to whisper.

Fran's favorite snack was cookie dough. I pretended to have a favorite way to make it, which was the same as her favorite way to make it. I didn't admit that I had only ever had the greasy pucks in tubes of yellow plastic. Fran gave me a tour while we each carried our bowl of chocolate chip oatmeal dough, pinching it into our mouths until we felt sick and sleepy.

In the cool air-conditioned basement on the plaid pull-out sofa, we watched *Blue Crush*, the movie we became obsessed with, a movie about surfer girls in Hawaii. The girls work as hotel maids to pay the bills while pursuing their dreams. The main character, Anne Marie, has to fill the role of mother for her kid sister Penny.

I asked where Natalie was and Fran told me she was upstairs, doing something with their mom, or in her room resting. There were so many levels and walls and doors in Fran's house—borders that no one seemed to cross.

*

It didn't sound natural when Fran cursed. "Fuck," she said, "I just bought these." She reached inside her pants to confirm she'd started her period. I remember which room we were in because it was The Hideout's biggest ensuite with windows that faced the back garden, where Jared spent a lot of his time. I worried he was out there and able to see in. Fran was peeling off her pants and then her underwear. Lime green lace. She balled them up and threw them in the bathroom trash can.

It was the same reaction I had had, at twelve, when I first got my period. I thought my butt was bleeding. I didn't know anything about menstruation, and for some reason—fear or embarrassment—I didn't want to tell my mom. When she found my underwear in the trash can, she took them out and put them in a bowl of water in the kitchen sink to soak. Before she left for work that night, she set a pack of pads out with a note: *Wear these for your period.* When she got back from work, she laid my underwear flat on a towel to dry. The next day, she sprinkled baking soda on the stain. The day after that, she used an old toothbrush to scrub the stain with vinegar, until it was only a shadow of itself.

"Is this OK?" she asked me, holding them up. "I can dye them pink if you want."

I wore a pad every day for twenty-eight days. I had emptied the package by the time I started bleeding again. My mom was angry about the waste and expense. I didn't understand my cycle. I thought getting my period meant that I would bleed spontaneously and continuously for the rest of my life.

I found Fran a tampon in the supply closet, where Jared kept a box of miscellaneous toiletries for the guests who inevitably forgot to pack something.

"I can get the blood out for you," I said. "Your underwear."

"Don't be gross," Fran said.

*

Fran's favorite thing to talk about while we cleaned was the kind of house she, Natalie, and I would live in together in Boulder. Three bedrooms, two bathrooms—she said that she and I could share one. She said that it would be a good situation for us, since we were used to cleaning. We wouldn't fight about chores like some roommates. She said Natalie might need some guidance. But Natalie could do our hair and makeup, and we could all share clothes.

*

When we were at Fran's, we had the house to ourselves. If her mom came home from shopping or lunch or the tennis club, she would pause at the top of the stairs and yell down, "Hi girls!" and that was it. I could hear her shoes clacking on the hardwood above us. I told my mom how no one in their family took off their shoes in the house.

"Yep," she said, like she already knew it by their zip code. "Dirty."

I thought of how Fran left her dishes in the sink, instead of washing them by hand or putting them in the dishwasher. I didn't tell my mom about that.

Maybe we never went to my house because I didn't want Fran to leave her dishes in the sink for my mom, and I didn't want my mom to judge Fran for doing that kind of thing, and I didn't want Fran to pity us, even by accident, by calling our apartment *cute*. It was cute. We lived in a two-bedroom ground-floor unit, crowded with house plants and my mom's sewing and dyeing projects. But it was far from the Hideout, and my mom would have been there, telling us to take off our shoes. She would have wanted to ask Fran questions about her life.

Ultimately, we never went to my house because Fran never asked to see where I lived, and I never had the courage to show her.

*

Unlike the girls in *Blue Crush*, we never had to clean up anything super gross in the rooms, like sticky pee floors or used condoms. But there was the glitter.

To Jared's great horror, The Hideout Inn became notorious within the scrapbooking community—mostly stay-at-home moms who loved the cottage-themed rooms and the fire-lit dining room and the big conference tables that could be clumped together and organized by station. Glitter lodged between carpet fibers and rained out of pillowcases. The scrapbookers were, in their own words, a hoot and a half—laughing and gossiping and calling Jared on his emergency cellphone to ask him if his big strong muscles could move this or that, and didn't he want to join them for happy hour, just for one drink? I loved them. I remember wishing my mom had more hobbies, more friends. More time.

Fran was less impressed. "So this is who the nerds become," she said.

For the first time, I was glad we didn't go to the same school, so Fran couldn't know that I was a nerd. That I wouldn't have minded growing up to become a person who didn't work on the weekends, who could spend two full days in a bed and breakfast, cropping family photos.

I justified pocketing all the tips the women left—propped up against the lamps on their nightstands inside of sticker covered *Thank You* cards. I told myself that Fran didn't appreciate the women anyway, and I was still doing most of the work while she talked, and she got a weekly allowance from her parents, and did she even know that some people left tips for the staff? She didn't even need the job.

*

When I asked my mom if she would ever make a scrapbook of me, she said, "Do I seem like the kind of mother who would spend our money on stickers?"

But after that, she kept a disposable camera around. Later, when I graduated, she surprised me with a blue poster board covered in pictures of me, mostly from that year, collaged with a few of me as a baby. She decorated the edges with iridescent stickers of flowers and tropical fish.

*

Fran knocked softly on Natalie's door and asked if she wanted to watch a movie with us—she could pick it out, it didn't have to be *Blue Crush*. Or we could go for a walk. "Come on Nat, let's go for a walk," she said.

I stood in the hallway, awkwardly holding my bowl of cookie dough, pretending to study the framed family pictures I'd seen a dozen times, one on either side of Natalie's door like a reminder. Matching denim jackets in a grove of Aspen trees. Matching white button up shirts on a beach. Natalie looked vaguely like Naomi Watts as much as anyone with blond hair and small facial features could. Compared to Fran's gap-toothed grin, her tight-lipped smile appeared forced.

The music from inside Natalie's room got louder. Fran vibrated with anxiety at the door. I didn't understand why she didn't just open it. Other than our strict door-closed-while-pooping policy, my mom and I didn't really do privacy. In our house, knocking meant, I'm coming in.

*

I met Natalie once. One Saturday, she came out of her room. Her hair was stringy with grease, dyed green at the ends. She wore an oversized black sweatshirt like a minidress. She didn't respond when I introduced myself.

She paced behind the sofa bed while *Blue Crush* played. It unsettled me, feeling her moving back and forth behind our heads the whole time. She wouldn't sit down, and she talked through most scenes. She made fun of the stupid characters and cheesy plot, and then she made fun of Fran for liking the movie. She said Fran was pretending to be working class. She said Fran was a spoiled little bitch who could have anything she wanted, but instead she was playing maid with her poor friend. She said Fran was getting fat, eating all that cookie dough.

Fran didn't respond. It was like she couldn't even hear her. I told myself later that I didn't say anything either because I was following Fran's lead. It was shocking, the discrepancy between the Natalie I'd heard about and the Natalie I witnessed. But I also didn't say anything because Natalie was a little bit right—Fran was playing at work, and I wasn't. And I thought that the gates and the house and the cookie dough and the framed family pictures were the shape of happiness, and so I needed Fran to be happy.

When the movie ended, Natalie went back to her room, and Fran reached for the cookie dough. Her hand was shaking. I pretended to fall asleep.

*

We were unloading clean towels from the dryer when Fran said that we should swap secrets. There was only one rule: the other person couldn't respond; they had to absorb the information like a sponge.

"You first," Fran said.

I don't know why I told her about keeping the scrapbookers' tips. A part of me must have been truly sorry, because I still remember the confessional heat in my gut, the pre-vomit churn that I only ever feel when I regret something. Because of Secret Sponge rules, Fran didn't respond. She focused on her towels.

"This is how they do it at the spa," she said. She was building a pyramid of rolls. I waited for it to collapse, but it held.

"Natalie is sick," she said.

We slow-rolled the laundry cart down the hallway, and I waited for more details because there had to be more. We hadn't talked about what had happened at her house. Her towel pyramid looked a mess.

"You can talk to me," I said.

When Fran didn't say more, I decided, again, that I had been justified in keeping the tips.

*

We continued swapping secrets throughout our shifts.

While stacking firewood in the dining room fireplace.

"My mom fills her water bottle with wine," Fran said.

"My mom smokes weed, after she thinks I've gone to sleep," I said.

While dusting the shelves in the entryway.

"I don't know my dad, but I looked him up and I know where he lives," I said.

"My parents hate each other. I think they're waiting until I go to college to get divorced."

While cleaning the bathroom in Room 3.

"Natalie hurts herself. That's why she's home from college."

"Hurts herself how?" I said.

"You're not supposed to respond."

*

The day that Fran didn't show up for work, I called her from The Hideout's phone. I was standing at the big window in the dining room, watching Jared chop firewood. He was so sweaty, flinging the ax around like a maniac, missing the logs half the time he swung. I worried about his bare toes. I had never chopped wood, but I was sure he was doing it wrong, too spastic. I wanted to describe it to Fran. She would have loved it.

Once, we were making the beds in Room 5 when we heard the lawn mower. From the windows, we watched Jared, shirtless, push the mower as fast as he could move. Instead of cutting the grass in rows, he was running in a big spiral. When it started to rain, he kept going, pushing faster. We couldn't stand it, we laughed so hard we had to pee. Fran beat me to the toilet, so I peed in the tub, and then we had to re-clean the bathroom.

I drove to Fran's on my lunch break. By then, the gatekeeper knew my car. He waved me in. The gate to Fran's driveway was open, and her car was parked in front of the house. No one answered when I rang the doorbell, so I used the spare key—Fran had shown me where they hid it behind the birdhouse—and I went in, calling her name. I didn't take my shoes off.

When I got downstairs, I heard crying, and I found Fran in the bathroom, on her knees, scrubbing the carpet. I remember her arms. They were foaming with blood and suds—this beautiful brown-pink froth that reminded me of the dye my mom made from simmering pots of avocado pits. "Stop it," I said. "Stop it." Even as I was wrestling the sponge out of her stained hands, I was thinking, why would a family with this much money put carpet in the bathroom?

I asked what had happened, but Fran couldn't speak. Or I couldn't understand what she was trying to say. It wasn't until I answered her phone, which kept ringing and ringing, that I learned from her mom that Natalie had tried to kill herself. "Unsuccessfully," she said, like Natalie had failed. They were in the ER. They had followed the ambulance. Could I please drive Fran to the hospital when she was ready.

When Fran stopped crying, she stood in the tub, arms extended, and I scrubbed them. In the car, she was rigid and quiet. When we arrived at the hospital, I asked if she wanted me to go in with her.

"I'm fine," she said. She said it in the same voice she used to talk about spa towels. She was done crying, done moving her face at all. When she got out of the car, I had the feeling that I had seen something that I wasn't supposed to see.

*

Fran didn't go back to work. A few weeks later, on a Saturday, I stopped by her house. But it wasn't the same. We didn't eat cookie dough, and we didn't watch *Blue Crush*. The bathroom carpet had been torn out and replaced. At the threshold, between the hallway and the bathroom, the seam puckered.

*

While lying side by side on the pull-out sofa, Fran flipping through TV channels.

"I got the blood out of your underwear," I said. "The green ones." I wanted to take care of her, but I didn't know how.

*

I went to Boulder for college. So did Fran. All year, I thought about texting her, but I didn't. She didn't reach out either. I finally saw her on the Hill late at night. I had just clocked out at Pizza Boy, where I worked as a server. She was with a group of girls. They all looked the same, wearing short skirts and knee-high boots. Fran had even straightened her hair like the others. Her body was so small. I wouldn't have recognized her if she hadn't yelled my name.

I hugged her—my friend, a stranger. Knowing Fran was my first experience of intimacy as a vivid, temporary place. A hospital room. A foreign city. I worried that adulthood meant there would be others—people with whom friendship is a visiting privilege.

I could feel Fran working hard to hold herself up. "We were cleaning girls together," she slurred to her friends, who opened to me like the sun. They talked over each other, telling me they'd heard all the stories. They said Jared sounded like such a doofus. I laughed with them at Fran's impression of him mowing in the rain. It seemed impossible to me suddenly that she'd never met my mom.

After Fran spun in circles on the sidewalk, I stayed at her elbow, steadying her, and I wondered where Natalie was. It didn't seem like the right time to ask.

Comfort Food

I pickle the seeds of doubt in an open container
            and bless them with thyme and cardamon
wipe the crumbs   from a fresh mouth
            Not mine, not mine.
I steal in the way of nourishment –   unashamed
in the way that I undress, then beg
for a hand or bread, as in replenishment
I am empty   and the spiderwebs caress the kitchen cabinets
of my youth.   Anoint me with the oil of forgiveness
and I will shine like a new leaf
            under a new light.
Lick the insides clean and then your fingers,
like how a dog stuffs his head inside a tin can,
and can't shake it loose.   *Not enough, never enough.*
Edacious, only after starving for so long
when your hot mouth bells my spine as a reminder
or a metaphor.   Feed my ego once
and you will feed it forever.
Tell me again how you think I'm beautiful.

Preparing the Salt

In warmer months, you suffered the hills: heaved sludge buckets and filled the caverns. Sea mud from tidal pools set the dough. By winter, you scrape and trowel and gather crystals from the cistern walls. Notice how the sand still pines for slime—her hilly coat of flea-specked kelp. First time, then flame. Beyond the season's fog, blue fires of dried tangle dot the shore, making mounds of ashen crust. *Netted ocean overgrowth—nightmare, affliction—neutralized* as you crumb the briny cinder into the cave wall's molt. After pestle. After mortar. Sew satchels for your bridge of tears. Cure hearth. Line sills. Circle every corner.

Kaddish, or Eating

In late November of 2019, a few weeks after my grandmother was diagnosed with stage four pancreatic cancer, she called me into her room, closed the door, and asked if I would help her kill herself.

"You're the only one I can trust," she said, near-whispering.

It was evening, so there was not much light. What light there was filtered through orange blinds and a deep red lampshade, encasing us in red and shadow, as if we sat in the embers of some dying fire.

I don't remember much of what I had said to her since her diagnosis a few weeks earlier. I only remember leaving every conversation angry with myself over what I said or didn't say. There was a lot I didn't say. But what do you say to a person who knows they're going to die?

"Ok," I said. "Ok."

*

My grandmother's bathtub was Pepto-Bismol pink. Black tile on the floor and up the wall; a large, three-tiered lighted mirror; same-shade-Pepto-pink countertops, sink; framed surrealist paintings of cats, small ceramic cat sculptures on shelves. I don't think it had changed since they purchased the house in 1953, and certainly not in the twenty-three years that I'd been visiting.

I stood over the pink tub, waiting for it to fill up.

The water was hot. Too hot. I stuck my foot in, and it burned, it's burning, and I think, unbearable, this is unbearable. But it must have been bearable, because I stood and bore it. I lowered the rest of my body down into it.

And it hurt. A hurt in a million needles; a hurt that morphs and pulses like it has its own rhythm, the heat. Its own breath. Eventually the sharpness gave way to a kind of numbness, and I could breathe out again.

*

After I had agreed to help her, she told me her plan: fill the tub with warm water; gather sleeping pills; pour some vodka; put a record on. Swallow, drink, fall asleep.

"And you slip beneath the water," she said, "and drown. Just like that. Painless." She had read it in a book somewhere.

"If that's what you want," I said.

"I can't go out like all of this," she said, motioning to her too-thin body, her flattened hair, the bedpan on the floor. "I don't want to be remembered as some pathetic thing. Besides," she said, "I did it for my mother." And again she's whispering. "She wasn't waking up. She kept rattling. Oh, that breath. That breath. I couldn't take it anymore.

"So I upped her pills. And I kept upping them. I gave her more and more until finally it stopped. The breathing stopped."

I was quiet for a moment. "I'm sure that's what she would have wanted," I said.

"My mother?" she said. "My mother? No. She would have wanted to stick it out until the very end."

*

I try to write my grandmother's death.

I write a story about a girl whose grandmother asks her to kill her. The girl goes to New York City and sits on a bench. There is something about a faded old photograph. The story is terrible, and I delete it.

I write a poem. I write dreams I wish I'd had. I write an essay.

I write about going into Macy's, sitting on the floor, and crying. I write a lot about crying because I am crying a lot. In a workshop, someone highlights the scene, and comments, "OK, we get it. You're sad." I delete the scene.

Writing about my grief seems silly and sentimental and self-absorbed. I'm not a nineteen-year-old crying about my dead grandma on American Idol. I am twenty-seven. I am almost thirty. Who do I think I am?

Temporal organization of my memory eludes me. Past and present tense become interchangeable. I take inventory. I make lists. I remember things she taught me. *Here is how to make a soft-boiled egg, how to weigh yourself every day. How to stand up straight, breasts forward, how to be so beautiful and sure that nothing anyone says or does can ever hurt you.*

*

Again.

I am seven years old, sitting next to her on the couch.

"You have such a pretty face," she says, "but I'm concerned that you're gaining so much weight. Don't you want to be able to fit into a nice Bat Mitzvah dress?"

I'd never been so aware of the space I was taking up. I shrink into myself and say "Yes, I do want that, I do."

I have replayed that conversation in my mind so many times it's as if a part of me has never left. Sometimes I'm still that seven-year-old girl, sucking in my stomach for the first time, or folding in the skin on my thighs, imagining I was someone else.

I didn't feel thin enough until I was fifteen, when I smoked often and ate very little, and I fit into a size two. When my grandmother took us shopping, my cousin Rebecca said, "It's like you're a woman now, all of a sudden."

My grandmother, watching me from our shared changing room, said, "Look at how thin you are." She said, "Look how beautiful."

In the weeks after my grandmother's diagnosis, I'd gained ten pounds. We were driving to Queens almost every other day, stopping for donuts, for bagels, for coffee. Anything to take the edge off, to relieve the boredom, for something to do with our hands. Shiva, when we covered the mirrors with bedsheets, was a relief; to not catch my own reflection out of the corner of my eye–a relief. To not have to think about how disappointed she might have been in me. A relief.

When we were going through her things, I found my grandmother's old leather jacket. I wanted it, and so did my mom. We argued over who should take it home. When I tried it on, it was too tight around the shoulders.

"Oh well," my mom said. "If you lose weight, maybe I'll give it to you."

I hung the jacket back up in the closet.

*

My mom and I went out to lunch at a hot pot restaurant on Northern Boulevard. We piled thinly sliced ribeye and enoki mushrooms into the simmering, cloudy broth. We sat uncomfortably close to another family, and I told her about our conversation.

"You're kidding me," she said, eating a mung bean sprout. "She asked me the same thing."

She said the same thing to both of us: "You're the only one I can trust."

We laughed together, but I also felt a slight constriction at the back of my throat. I felt half-betrayed. I wondered how many other people she had asked. This one, last, private moment between us had been whisked away; an illusion, broken.

But I was also half-relieved. I tried to picture us together, the three of us, then just the two, with a body in between. Her body.

I remember her through the body. I remember her nakedness, and mine. I remember her breasts, large and bottom heavy, out as she got ready in the morning, and mine, barely formed, pressed against my knees in the bath. NPR on the radio, soft light. I'd watch her from the bathtub. "Hold your breath while I spray," she'd say as she set her hair, but the light-headed-plastic scent of the hairspray lingered, clinging to the oxygen molecules in the air, suffocating them. And after, her short blonde curls perfectly coiffed, like a 60's movie star, she would dress.

*

She didn't believe in God, and certainly not in the concept of sin. She told me once that she'd had an abortion, when she had gotten pregnant for the fourth time. I asked her how she had felt about it, if it was difficult for her. We were sitting outside. She was smoking a cigarette and I was sweating.

"What do you mean?" she asked. "Why would it be difficult? It was nothing." I'm not trying to paint her as a callous person or anything. It's just that she never dwelled in that thick, what-if space. She didn't care about the morality question. It was a question of practicality, efficiency, action.

I know that she wanted to live. But more than that, she didn't want to go through the process of dying. Maybe she thought it was the ultimate weakness, to decay slowly like that. Maybe she thought if she could just be in control, if she could make the last move, the loss would be mitigated.

And the truth is I wanted to help her. I felt her asking me was confirmation of our special bond, that I would be the only one with her in the end. It was a perverse kind of validation, and I clung to it despite my terror at the idea of watching her die.

I imagined all the ways it could go terribly, terribly wrong. What if she didn't naturally slip beneath the water? What if I had to push her under? What if she changed her mind and it was too late?

*

I was never able to fulfill my promise to her. A couple of nights after my grandmother's request, my cousins and I sat outside on the cold stone patio, smoking a joint and listening to the cars speeding on the Long Island Expressway just a few yards away.

A few hours earlier we realized we couldn't wake her from her sleep. She was breathing, still, but we couldn't reach her. She was in that in-between place. My grandfather, even though they'd been divorced nearly thirty years, hadn't left her room. He was in bed with her, still, holding her emaciated body. But for us, there was not much to do except remember. So we sat; we smoked; we remembered.

Soon after, I left—got onto the Long Island Expressway, made a few detours because I was still stoned, went across the George Washington Bridge, and made it home around two AM. And the next morning, when my mom called to tell me that she died, all I could think about was food.

"Ok," I said. "I'm on my way. Will there be something to eat?"

*

About a month before she died, right after her diagnosis, we sat on the porch of our family's lake house in Upstate NY. The house is perched on a hill overlooking the small lake, and the porch is all open windows.

She was smoking something, or maybe she wasn't. She had a blanket across her lap, or maybe she didn't.

My memory is failing. It is fractured; there is no chronology, no geography. I am afraid half of what I remember is completely made up, or half-dreamt.

"It's so beautiful," she said. I am sure she said this. "I'll miss this."
It was early October and the leaves were mid-change. A breeze came
through the open window. "I don't want to die," she said. Or maybe she
didn't. "I want to stay here, with all of you." Maybe she said it a few
weeks earlier, in the dining room.

I said something comforting and wise. Or maybe I didn't say anything
at all.

*

A year later, we all gather again, for the unveiling of her tombstone.

The tombstone is covered by a patterned shawl–red and yellow,
paisley. My aunt pulls it away, and her husband begins to read from the
kaddish. He moves the way that Jews do when they pray–like the power
of God itself is inside them, leaning forward, falling back, all on the heels
of their feet, a little bend at the knees.

My cousin Rebecca FaceTimes us from California and I'm crying
again, eyes closed tight, trying not to think about the new grass grow-
ing above the coffin. Has it been that long already? Two inches of grass,
already?

Instead of flowers, we leave stones. My aunt passes me a tiger eye
stone. I hold it in my palm until it's warm and press it into the soft earth
next to the tomb. The next time I come here, how tall will the grass be?
Will it be tall enough to mix with those plots around us? They should
leave the grass uncut, so I can measure–it has been eight inches of grass
since it happened; twelve inches; two feet. For a moment I imagine stay-
ing here forever, letting the grass grow through me, swallowing me whole.

I Have Always Wanted to Write a Poem on Cock

though it's not what the man   I knelt before said
as he held or rather   aimed at my mouth.

He said, *lund*, his voice   like the voice
of every other man I made my knees touch the dirt for.

When I came to this park, to do more
than I could do with my own self,

I must've looked   like a lost boy, standing
so close to the gate. What I wanted was

to be good at pleasing, because what could be more
noble than giving   a man a chance

to be worshiped? As the leaves above us rustled
as the wind   made its way through, he touched

my head, indicating   that time was running
like blood from a cut wrist. I looked up, his features

obscured by early dusk. When I finally took him,
I swear   I did so with the carefulness

a mouth does   taking on a new word.

D. ARIFAH

My Sun

Digital photography
Gyeongju, South Korea
4000x5000 pixels, 2023

"My Sun" was originally a poem I wrote about someone whose soul to me shines so brightly it shames the sun. This image was at first intended to be twined with that, acting both as a visual complement and comparison. But then, funny thing happened after I sat with the photo in Lightroom: it wants to tell its own story.

Supposing Cancer Is a Leopardess

after Igor Altuna's "Holding On"

Somewhere in South Luangwa's valley,
a monkey clings to its mother's lifeless trunk,
her baboon body swinging from the black
mouth of a leopardess, serene and green-eyed,
sleek spotted bullet splitting yellow savanna.
Dead mother dangles like baby herself: stiff
from pinched scruff, limbs stretched wide and
reaching, her limp neck rubbered with need.
And leopardess, a mother too, her own baby's
small black mouth of hungry teeth, open wide
in wait for tiny beating heart to fall like fruit
and slice savanna's yellow skin with blood.
Now, supposing leopardess is lung cancer—
her jaws, the quick black end. Supposing
my mother's skin was like this—jaundiced,
waxy, lifeless. And just before the end, her
bile—jewel bright beneath hospital
light, peridot in kidney pan, pink
as a pacing mouth, its waiting teeth.
And on that final night, her face—serene
with death, my cheek pressed to her silent chest
still warm enough to pass for living. Supposing
I am child again—clinging in gold brocade
chair beside the old front door, her stocking
feet on sky blue nap, voice vibrating bony rungs
of rib between each incandescent drag. And
in the moments before, a match. Then
black: gaping jaw, closed eye, bare tree.

Head

Digital photograph
(Next Page)

Photography is often an extension of observation, a decision to fix
our sight, to memorise some part of the world. Yet the contemporary
camera's technical and creative possibilities invite us to be bold with
metaphor, emotions and imagination, no more so than in the tidal zone.
Between high and low tides, this zone's turbulence and marine struggles
are an unending theatre of Biology, Zoology and Geology. It conjures
our body and mind, tales of evolution, and human history, sociology and
psychology. Its ebb and flow is ours. Its shapes, colours, behaviours and
textures are ours.

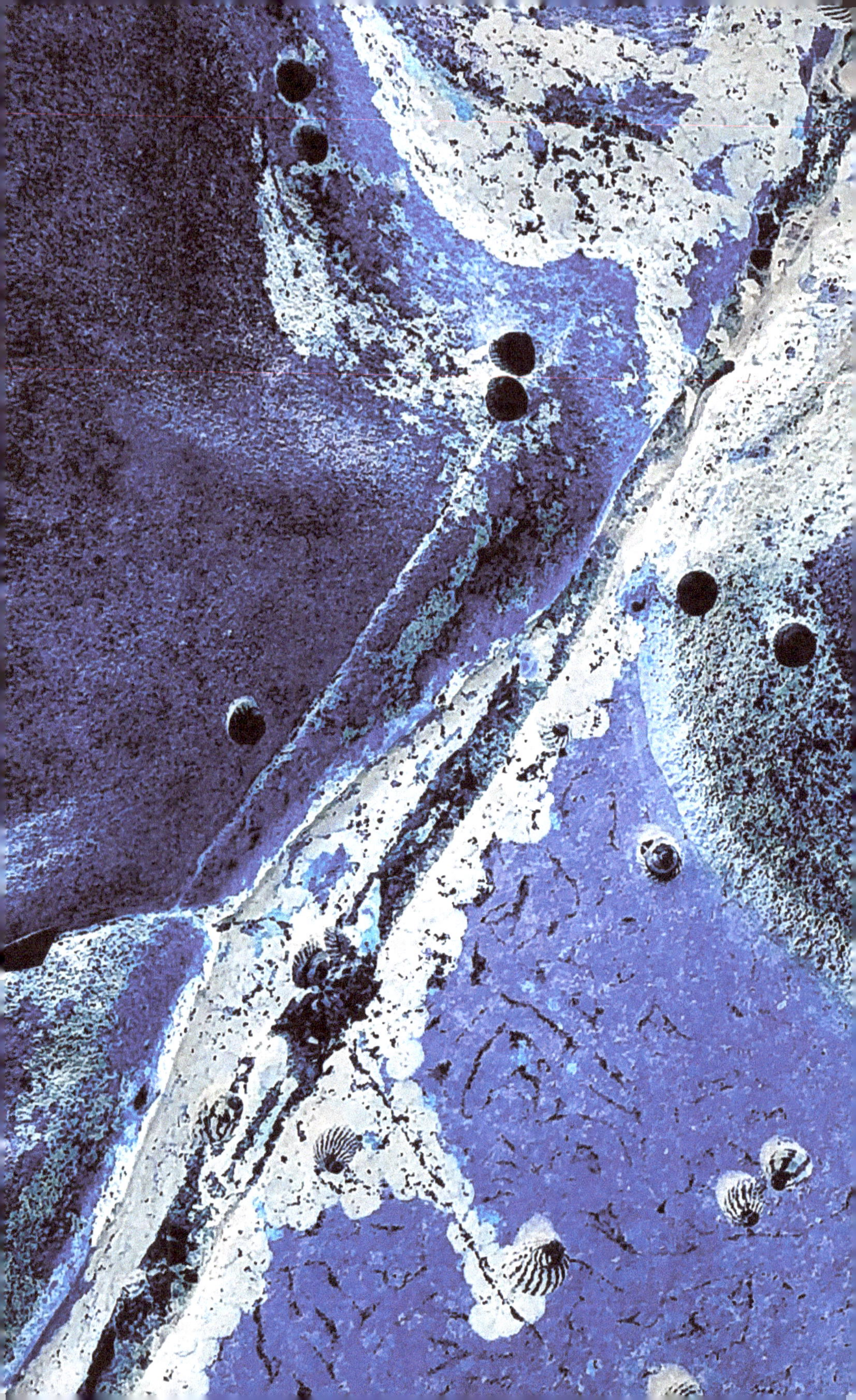

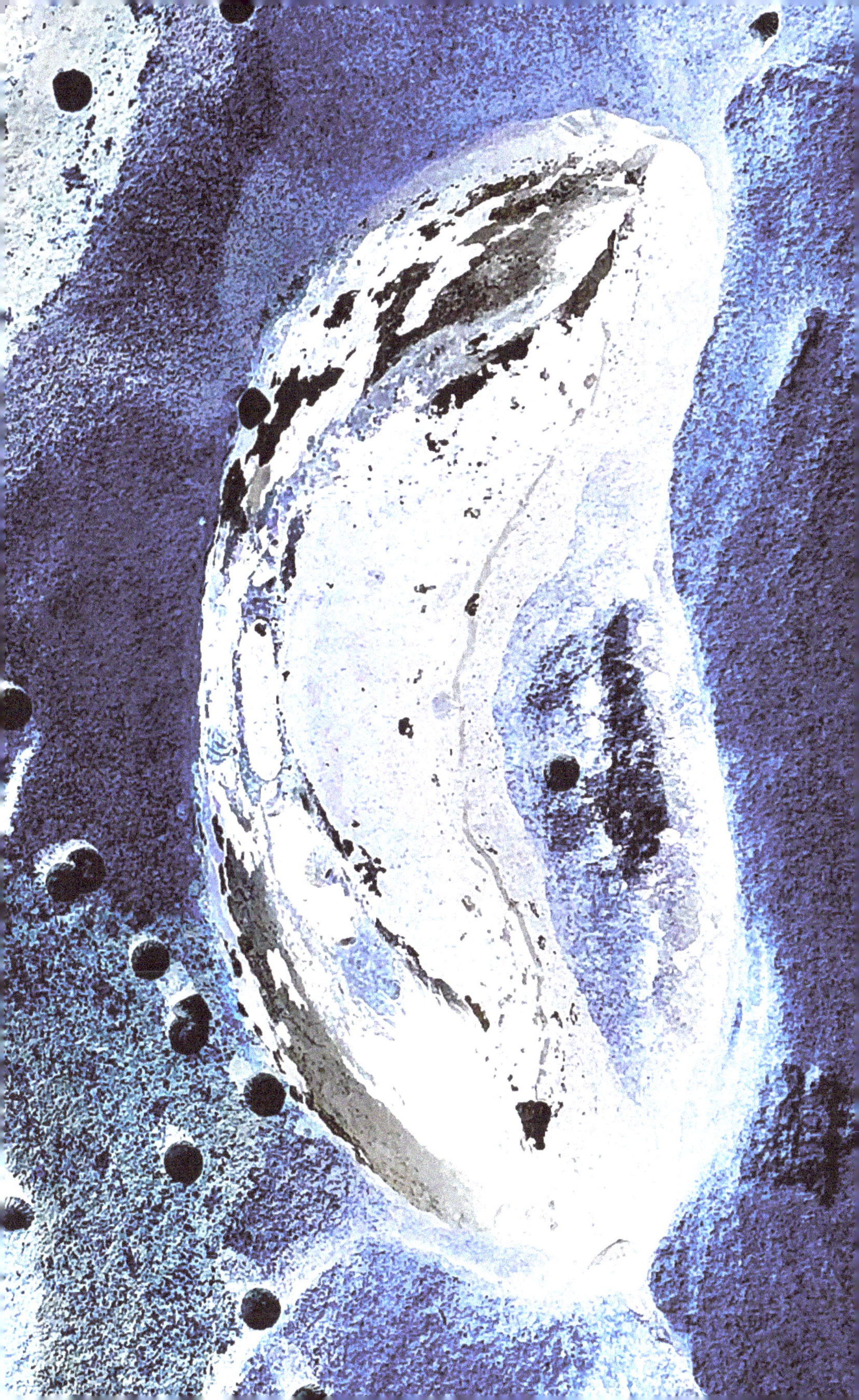

Florida Gothic

Nathan Holic

Wherever you see Spanish moss growing, you won't find any ghosts.
That's what they say. That the moss repels spirits.

That, even in the most haunted places on Earth, you're safe if you're standing under a tree covered in Spanish moss.

But I know for a fact that this isn't true.
Because there was Spanish moss everywhere around us in Gulf City, and I still have a ghost story to tell.

If you come from somewhere else, maybe somewhere up north—and these days, that's everyone in Florida, am I right?— you might be forgiven for thinking that Spanish moss doesn't look quite right.

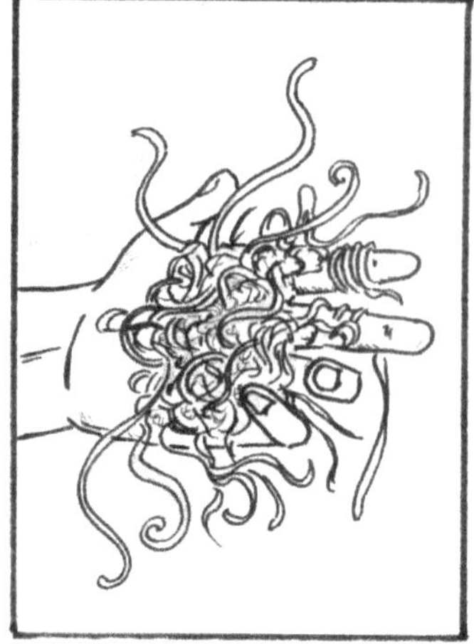

That it looks like it isn't of this Earth.

Cosmic horror collecting on tree branches.

But it's ours, and it's everywhere.

Down here, you see it on oaks, most often.

Grows and grows, hangs from the tree limbs like tattered afghans draped over furniture.

Sometimes the clumps outnumber the leaves, and you've got something more moss than tree. I've always thought this is a sign of longevity, like the tree has settled into its place.

Outsiders think it's creepy, but you grow up with it, and it's just part of your everyday. Every Florida kid has a story about wearing it like a wig and getting bug-bit.

That's the kind of mistake you make exactly one time.

(Florida kids know what I'm talking about.)

But living in Gulf City? Sticking around when all your smarter friends escape to college, maybe even escape the state entirely? That's a mistake that haunts you like a ghost, only you don't know you're being haunted until it's too late.

It's easy enough to remember the moment I committed that mistake, though. The moment I settled into it, like one of those old oaks that knows it's not going anywhere and just accepts the weight of all that moss.

After high school, I moved in with my girlfriend, both of us already in debt but talking about marriage like it was a thing destined to happen.

We said sayonara to our parents and moved into one of the old apartments on the south side of the island, out by the rusty municipal airport.

Back in the '40s, the Gulf City Airport **trained** pilots, but by the time I was a kid in the '80s, it was strictly for recreational pilots, guys who looked like they'd been pirates in another life. Gold chains and rings. Wild chest hair that grew out of unbuttoned linen shirts.

They came for the day, drank at the beach bars, and flew back out.

All day long, and no end to the noise, because there were flight classes, too. Zooming and buzzing.

Loud as hell, but the apartment was walking distance to the beach, and is there anything more beautiful than watching a plane take off into a Gulf of Mexico sunset with your woman at your side?

The north end of Gulf City was where the white sand beaches were. That was the wealthy side.

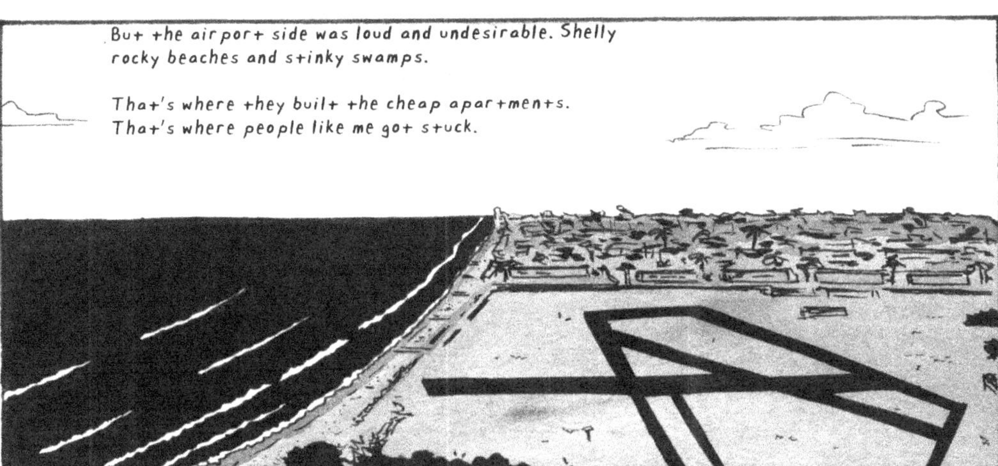

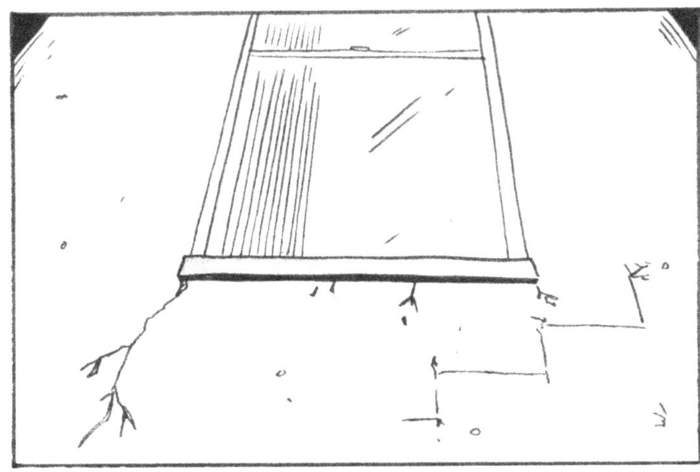

The apartment building was called the Gulf City Castle. It was all cinderblock and stucco, stairstep cracks in the faded pink paint. Looked more like an old roadside motel than a place you'd want to live.

Amanda's parents never wanted her to move in with me.

She had a college fund and a spot waiting for her at some Catholic school up north where her parents were from, but she wasn't religious and she wanted nothing to do with their world.

So we waited tables together at a beach bar down the road—one of the places that served rum runners and fried shrimp to tourists—and we came home every night to the Gulf City Castle, a place that somehow always felt as wet inside as it was outside, like the walls and windows were never enough to keep out the humidity.

Me, Amanda, Courtney, AC. All of us waiting tables, playing beach volleyball and putting down cases of High Life in the morning, then dragging ass to sling margaritas at night.

Looking back, it was like the summer after high school just kept going, every day bleeding hazily into the next. Nobody telling us what to do. Who wouldn't want that forever?

Anyway. That side of the island, out by the airport...There were these vast swaths of undeveloped wild land beyond the runways: fields full of sandspurs and fireants, pine forests, cypress swamps, the sort of thick palmetto scrub that looked like it'd swallow you whole if you got too close.
So that's where the town held its festivals.

The Italian–American Festival. The Jellyfish Festival (that was our high school mascot). Circus Days.
All of it in those sandspur fields across the street from our apartment, land that was useful only for ticket booths and carnival rides and dusty makeshift parking lots.
CKETS
LE
ERE
SAUSAGE & MEATBALL
CASH

So yeah. The airport. The festivals. The mold. Gulf City Castle was a hell of a place in the late '90s.

The 4th of July Fest, our first in the apartment after graduation, me and Amanda got riproaring drunk with all of our other saltneck friends.

Watched fireworks from our balcony. Heat lightning in the distance like a challenge to the city's show.

Dripping in sweat all night, air conditioner gurgling, storms building over the Gulf, then fading.

Wet. Hot. Wasted.

Wild times, your late teens and early twenties.

What I wouldn't give to go back.

We came out to the porch sometime after midnight, and the festival was over, but that party out there in the fields was still going.

The police had largely given up, and the vendors had packed up, so it was just aging saltnecks and beach bums with cases of beer left to finish, and no one to stop them.

Like a bonfire on the beach, the authorities just kind of shrugged and let the party burn itself out.

It was irritating for someone living in the Castle.

But what are you gonna do? Hell, most of those fucks lived on Airport Way, too, under the same umbrella—sized Spanish moss that hung over our sidewalks and dropped on our cars.

Either you party, or you try to sleep, and no one was sleeping.

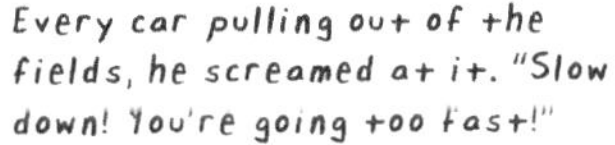
Every car pulling out of the fields, he screamed at it. "Slow down! You're going too fast!"

Slurred it, really. For hours, until the very last car was gone.

Me and Amanda, we laughed about it. Drunk guy thinking he was making a difference...the cars weren't even *speeding*!

We assumed he lived nearby, but over the next couple months, we met just about everyone in the Castle—and in the blue apartments next door, and Airline Rentals down the Way, and on and on—and there was no sign of this bozo.

Jellyfish Festival, it was the same deal.

Out on the corner, beneath the moss, yelling at the festival, yelling at every car.

By the third or fourth festival, we stopped joking about it. The guy looked deranged, we decided.

Families were walking back to their cars and he'd scream that they shouldn't drive.

Five feet from these kids, spit-screaming, and yet no one confronted him.

One time, we stayed up late to watch where he went at the end of the night.

Watch this. He's going to get in a car and peel off. He'll be the worst drunk driver of them all!

That never happened, but something else did.

No other way to say it: One second he was standing in a shadow, and the next, he **was** the shadow.

Poof. Gone.

We could convince ourselves that the oak trees and the Spanish moss were obscuring our view. There were late night shadows, too, so maybe we didn't see what we **thought** we saw, but...

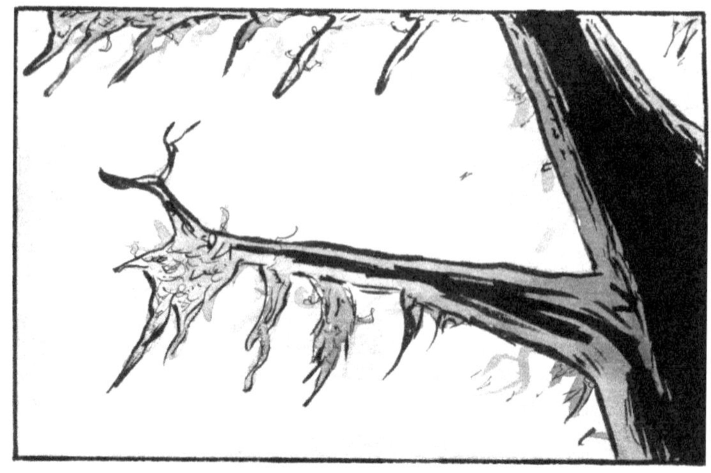

Well, Amanda was shaken by the guy vanishing, that's what mattered. She wouldn't listen to any talk of optical illusions.

She was scared, but did she think he was gonna come up to our apartment or something? Come on.

He was just an old guy yelling at people on the sidewalk. Seemed harmless enough to me.

It wasn't until later that we heard the legend about ghosts and Spanish moss.

We were on a haunted pub crawl in Savannah. Amanda was so excited that she paid for the whole thing out of her savings. She then spent the entire length of the ghost tour pestering the guide with stories of our "slow down" ghost.

After we heard the legend, she gathered clumps of the moss from outside.

Strung it across our balcony railing, laid it at our front door like other people might display crosses or Bibles.

The bugs, I told her. Come on. I couldn't believe Little Miss Rich Girl wanted this place to be shittier.

The ghost, she said back. Fuck off.

From the street, our place looked no different than the woods beyond the airport. Untamed Florida. The Castle, overtaken by the Spanish moss.

Next festival came.
Spring Fest, maybe?
Gator Fest?

It's a blur.

THIS WEEKEND
FESTIVAL PARKING

I don't want him anywhere near us.

He's not hurting us. Stop, Amanda! He lives at that damn corner.

And that's where we saw him, once again. This time standing in the street, right on the center stripe.

Cars whizzing past, but if he was flesh and blood, why wasn't anyone slowing down, acknowledging him?

Hell, why wasn't anyone else talking about this guy, this fucking nuisance? That was the night that I believed her.

I'm gonna go down there. Talk to him. See for sure.

So I walked down to that corner. I thought I was tough shit.

Look at me, solving problems for my woman!

Only, when I got down there...

He was already gone.

Just Amanda, crying on the couch, shrieking that he'd come for her and where the fuck was I? This awful place, she said. This awful place!

He'd gotten in her face, he'd screamed at her and screamed at her and screamed at her, and we needed to leave—she had money, we could go **anywhere**, she said—and I don't know why but suddenly I was fucking furious.

I'd like to say that we made it. That this little spat was a bump in the road. That we worked hard, got married, and now we just laugh about all of this.

But that's not true. Just like it's not true about the stupid fucking moss.

No, Amanda got out. Moved to Gainesville and did her AA at the community college, then transferred into UF.

Now she's got a real life somewhere else.

Atlanta, I think.

A family, a forever house.

No crumbling castle overtaken by mold and mildew, no ghost at the stop sign.

No loser boyfriend to piss off her parents.

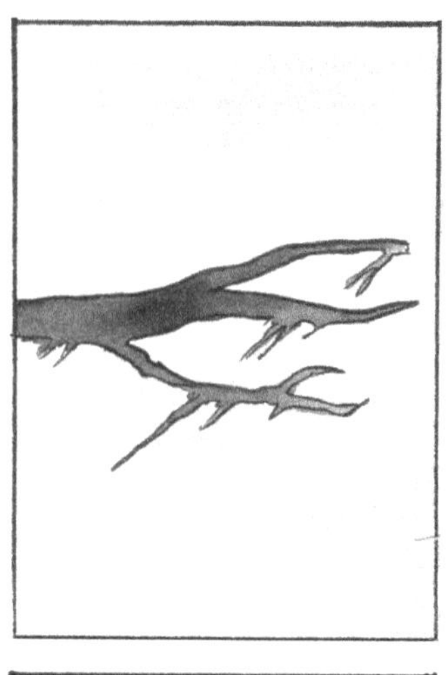

My ghost story is true,
though. Every word.

And listen, I still go to those
festivals and stay until long
after the fireworks have
ended, and I never see the guy
anymore.

I know for damn sure that he's
out there, though, that he
shows up whenever the right
couple moves into that
apartment building.

Screaming at drivers, but
really screaming through the
oak branches and the moss,
screaming to someone who
doesn't yet see that this life
—this place— is not where
they belong.

Damn, do I wish I could see
him still.

Damn, do I wish that I was
the one worth speaking to,
the one worth warning.

Mario Aliberto III's short fiction has appeared in *SmokeLong Quarterly, Fractured Lit, The Pinch, trampset, Tahoma Literary Review, JMWW,* and other fine journals. He is a *SmokeLong Quarterly* Workshop Prize runner-up, and his work has received nominations for The Pushcart Prize, Best of the Net, Best Small Fictions, and Best Microfiction. A graduate with a Creative Writing degree from the University of South Florida, he lives in Tampa Bay with his wife and daughters, and yet the dog still runs the house. Find him online at marioaliberto3.com.

Alexandra Apuzzo is a writing instructor and an MFA candidate at Rutgers-Newark. She lives in Jersey City with her partner and their overly-excitable Husky. Between teaching and playing with her dog, she is writing her first novel. Her poetry and prose have appeared in *The Gyroscope Review, Juxtaprose Literary Magazine, Cagibi Lit,* and *Sunlight Press.*

D. Arifah is a photographer captivated by the silent stories the world tells. Her photography seeks to preserve these delicate narratives and share with others the depth of human experience and the quiet power of our interrelation with our environments. Much of her work is an invitation to pause, listen, and see the world around us with greater intimacy.

Jodi Balas is a neurodivergent poet from Northeast Pennsylvania. Her poetry has been featured in *The Shore, Painted Bride Quarterly, Sugar House Review, Jet Fuel Review,* and elsewhere. Her poem, "His mouth, mine" was selected as a finalist for the 2023 *River Heron Review* poetry prize and her poem, "Bone Density" won the 2023 *Comstock Review* Muriel Craft Bailey Award judged by Danusha Lameris. Jodi is in the process of marketing her first chapbook to publishers, which will hopefully be one of many works to come. You could follow her on Instagram @jodibalas_

Debmalya Bandyopadhyay (he/him) is a writer and mathematician based in Birmingham, UK. His poems, translations, and essays have appeared or are forthcoming in *Rust & Moth, Ghost City Review, Propel,* and *Anthropocene Poetry*, among other places. When not reading or writing, he can often be found in parks confabulating with local birds.

Pracheta Banerjee, born in 1994 in West Bengal, India, earned her Bachelor's degree in Mass Media with a specialization in Animation from St. Xavier's College Kolkata in 2017. She made headlines after winning the Millarworld Award in 2016, becoming the first Indian to achieve this honor, she was featured on the British daily, *The Guardian*. Pracheta's work was displayed at the Times Square and the Oculus in NY, Artizan Gallery in the UK, Art Revolution Taipei, Shockboxx Gallery in CA, CICA Museum in Korea, National History Museum in Albania, Gallery Nucleus in LA to name a few.

Allison Field Bell is a PhD candidate in Creative Writing at the University of Utah, and she has an MFA from New Mexico State University. She is the author of the poetry chapbook, WITHOUT WOMAN OR BODY, forthcoming 2025 from Finishing Line Press and the nonfiction chapbook, EDGE OF THE SEA, forthcoming 2025 from CutBank Books. Allison's prose appears in *Gettysburg Review, DIAGRAM, The Adroit Journal, Alaska Quarterly Review, West Branch, SmokeLong Quarterly*, and elsewhere. Her poems appear or are forthcoming in *The Cincinnati Review, Passages North, Smartish Pace, RHINO Poetry, The Greensboro Review*, and elsewhere. Find her at allisonfieldbell.com.

Cassie Blair is an Oakland based writer working on a collection of short fiction. She holds an MFA from San José State University, where she was a Graduate Steinbeck Fellow.

Patrick Joseph Caoile was born in the Philippines and grew up in northern New Jersey. His work is featured in *storySouth, Porter House Review, Bright Flash Literary Review*, the anthology *Growing Up Filipino 3*, and elsewhere. His debut short story collection *Tales from Manila Ave.* was the winning selection of Sundress Publications' 2024 Prose Open Reading Period and will be released in fall 2025. He has received support from Roots.Wounds.Words and the Martha's Vineyard Institute of Creative Writing. Currently, he is a Visiting Assistant Professor of Literature and Creative Writing at Hamilton College. More can be found on his website writingsbypatrick.com.

Nathan Holic is the author of *Bright Lights, Medium-Sized City*, a not-so-medium-sized novel from Burrow Press. He is also the author of *The Things I Don't See* (Main Street Rag) and *American Fraternity Man* (Beating Windward Press), and is the Graphic Narrative Editor at *The Florida Review*. His traditional-text fiction has been published in *The Portland Review, Iron Horse*, and *The Apalachee Review*, but he also creates comics, some of which have been published in *Booth, Saw Palm, Bridge Eight*, and *Redivider*.

Andrea Thurairatnam Imdacha (she/her) is a genderqueer writer and poet of Sri Lankan and Hungarian heritage who hails from Savannah, GA. Her poetry and short fiction have appeared or are forthcoming in *Ploughshares, North American Review, Literary Mama, Light Enters the Grove: Exploring Cuyahoga Valley National Park through Poetry*, and other publications. Andrea resides in the Cleveland area with her husband, son, and the ghosts of her unfinished stories. She is currently at work on a novel.

Pamilerin Jacob's poems have appeared in *POETRY, Lolwe, The Rumpus, Agbowó, Frontier Poetry, 20.35 Africa*, & elsewhere. He is the Founding Editor of *Poetry Column-NND*, and *Poetry Sango-Ota*. Twitter: @pamilerinjacob.

Garry McDougall is Trouble, from a sports-crazed childhood to his first scribblings incinerated by an irate headmaster. After pretending to be a Maths teacher, he studied Art and created the Official Bicentennial Great North Walk, a long-distance walking track. They refused him an Honour and threw him off the Board when he objected to cigarette company sponsorship. His first novels, *Belonging and Starts With C,*were followed by another five. *Damn!* and *Border and Soul* are two of ten books on the Spanish, French and Portuguese Camino de Santiago. A member of DiVerse poets, he won the Peter Cowan Short Story Prize and exhibited paintings and photographs. He was Sydney Writers Festival Feature Poet and won the Art-In-Unusual-Place Grant in 2022. He masquerades as Hugo Hugo, a 510-year-old passionate for every human folly. He was born too late for the best of the Renaissance.

Cathlin Noonan (she/her) is a poet based out of San Marcos, Texas. Her poetry has appeared or is forthcoming in *Denver Quarterly, Merid-*

ian, Salamander, and *SWWIM* among others. She can be found online at cathlinnoonan.com.

Alicia Potee is a 2002 graduate of St. John's College in Annapolis and a current MFA candidate at the University of Baltimore. Her poems have appeared in *BRUISER, Comstock Review, Hawaii-Pacific Review, Little Patuxent Review*, and *Baltimore Review*, among other places. She lives in Towson, MD with her tiny zoo of children and pets.

Ashish Kumar Singh (he/him) is a queer Indian poet with a Master's Degree in English Literature from the University of Lucknow. His poems have appeared or are forthcoming in *Poetry Wales, Frontier Poetry, The Bombay Literary Magazine, Fourteen Poems, The Texas Review, Atlanta Review, Foglifter Press, Diode Journal*, and elsewhere. Currently, he lives in his hometown of Amethi, Uttar Pradesh, where he teaches English to high schoolers.

Susan Solomon is a freelance paintress living in the beautiful Twin Cities area of Minneapolis/Saint Paul. Her work is a search for a light in the dark. She is a graduate of the Pennsylvania Academy of the Fine Arts, and her work appears in the permanent University collections of Purdue and Metropolitan State.

Emmanuel Umeji (AshBard) is an Eastern-Northern Nigeria poet and debater. His work has been published in Eunoia Review, NWF Inaugural Issue amongst others. He writes from the North of Nigeria currently.

Donna Vitucci began painting in 2022, after a mostly writer's life. While she's been publishing stories, novels, poems, and memoir since 1990, her visual art appears these days in such venues as *Glacial Hills Review, Anti-Heroin Chic, Perceptions Magazine, Mayday, Carolina Muse Literary Magazine*, and more. Information about her four novels appears at: www.magicmasterminds.com/donnavitucci. She has always seen the world through a creative lens, a POV that anchors what she feels or wants to say in both stories and in painting. Her work hangs in local galleries; Facebook at Donna Vitucci, artist; and at Donna D. Vitucci | Alamance Artisans Guild

Chestnut Review

VOLUME 6 NUMBER 4 SPRING 2025

FOR STUBBORN ARTISTS

PATRICIA JOYNES

Peony and Ants

Photograph w/minor brightening
2024
(Cover Art)

My heart and soul connection lies in nature photography. Many times Nature presents me with magical moments. I am often literally stopped in my tracks when my heart connects with what I can only refer to as an energy. On this day, I was walking through a nearby small park in Blowing Rock, NC and came upon a shrub filled with peony blossoms. As I got closer, I noticed that several ants were on the flower. I was intrigued watching their own special small universe. I've since learned that the ants are attracted to the flower because of its aroma, and as the ants continue to eat the nectar, other insects will stay away.

Chestnut Review

VOLUME 6 NUMBER 4 SPRING 2025

Chestnut Review LLC, Ithaca, New York
chestnutreview.com

Chestnut Review appears four times a year online, in January, April, July, and October, and once per year in print in July.

ISSN 2688-0350 (online), ISSN 2688-0342 (print)

CONTENTS

SPECIAL THANKS

To our generous Patreon supporters:

Kimberley Boehm, Adam Boustead, Au Drey, Allan Ebert,
John Fredericks, Claudia Geagan, Jim Higgins, Annette Higgs,
Katie H., Edison Jennings, Buddfred Levi, Linda Meg, Chris Mikesell,
Marijean Oldham, Jeanmarie Riquelme, Vicky S, Regina McIntosh,
and Rhonda Wiley-Jones

to learn more, go to
https://patreon.com/chestnutreview

Introduction

Spring seems to have come with weather setbacks, with snow dotting the landscape across the northern US. There's resilience in the cycle of excitement for the future and the pull of the present, as well as the moments that remind us why we do this work.

We had an amazing time at AWP in Los Angeles, meeting contributors, chapbook authors, staff, and community members, some for the first time. At the Central Library on AWP Thursday, we had our first-ever contributor offsite reading for three of our 2025 chapbook authors. The congratulations, the reading's atmosphere, the booth conversations, the staff breakfast we had and more all serve as affirmations we can draw on in times of crisis. We are already anticipating a fantastic AWP in Baltimore in 2026.

All this is supported by the core of our mission to support stubborn artists. The magazine we publish each quarter testifies to our own resilience as readers, staff, and editors who do the necessary again and again: last-minute issue revisions, two-day-turnaround second reads, wrestling with a 200-deep queue, keeping track of everyone. The people on our staff are bright, eager, enthusiastic human beings, each with their own writing, their own story, their own reason for doing the work. When you scroll through the masthead on our site, we hope you see in their smiling faces that sense of community that makes us Chestnut and feel the deep contributions each of them makes to this magazine. When you read the pieces in our issues, the product of so many labors of love, we hope you feel the cycle of work-celebration that underscores all we do. We are stubborn; so too, are you.

A Conversation with Katie Kemple and Maya Cheav

MSP: Hey, hi, everybody! I'm here today at AWP in LA at the *Chestnut Review* booth with Katie Kemple and Maya Cheav, who are both amazing Chestnut Review Press Chapbook authors. So, I would love for both of you to give me one sentence about your chapbook, and then tell me where the project came from and how long you've been working on it. Katie, I guess we'll start with you because you're to my left.

KK: *Big Man* is a memoir written in poems about my late father, Patrick W. Kemple, who is a veteran. A public school teacher, a union negotiator, and a widower two times over. I've been working on it for over two years, maybe a little bit longer than that. It has themes of joy and loss, childhood, coming of age, youth.

MC: *Tan's Donuts* is about a Cambodian War Refugee and genocide survivor who immigrated to the US and opened up a donut shop to make a living. Some of the themes of it are related to family: specifically, Southeast Asian family dynamics, intergenerational trauma, grief, and healing. And for how long I've been working on it? I think I drafted it in August 2023. Originally, I wanted to have it as a short video series with audio poems.

MSP: You should totally still do it! Katie's working on an audiobook of her chapbook for us right now.

So, my next question for both of you is that your works are both extremely hybrid. They have this intersection of poetry and sort of CNF memoir and fiction-y feeling. Of course, Maya, yours is actual fiction, right? It's a family that is imagined, but it could be almost any Cambodian refugee family who came in and had this unique experience of adjusting to life in the U.S after the tragedies that happened in the early 1970s, late 1980s. So, I'm just wondering if both of you have done hybrid writing before, if you write in other genres, and you know, how did you place this project in its chosen genre and form?

MC: In terms of how I chose to go a hybrid prose poetry format, I usually go towards lineated poetry, but for the the sake of the first person narrative voice, following this donut shop owner, it felt more natural to go with the prose poem with similar language as well and be not as traditionally poetic, so I leaned into that.

I'm currently working on tableaus that I hope to have a museum exhibit for: art accompanying the poems and things like that.

MSP: So cool!

KK: I love memoir and nonfiction, but as a writer, my work always comes out in verse. And so, that's the shape that it wants to be written in and I tend to tell stories in very small spaces. *Big Man* was really a series of special memories of my father and me together. It's funny, it didn't really seem very hybrid to me, but I suppose I could see now how it would be because memoirs aren't typically written in poems.

MSP: Well, yeah, I think that a lot of people would look at that and say, that is very hybrid, and then the other thing is I know you had your poem on recycling published in *Chestnut Review* earlier, in a magazine issue, and that almost seemed like a journalism exposé in poem form. Of course, it's like a satirical recycling dive, like all these other things we used to believe in, and that was really powerful. But I also remember that you sent us a chapbook about the recession, and financial struggles, and that was something that really interested me. It felt like a slice of your life and your experiences that you put into poem form, and I really want to know if you have done anything yet with that chapbook because I would love to see it come out in the world.

KK: Oh, I'm still working on it. And of course, this year I have even more to write about because my husband and I are in another period of underemployment. And I think a lot of people in the country right now are experiencing that as well. It's an odd experience, and I think it should be something that we explore in writing. For me, the writing comes out as poetry.

MSP: Maya, do you have any experience writing prose forms previously, or was your education more in poetry?

MC: Interestingly enough, growing up, I identified more with novel writing, but I didn't really write that much. I said I was a writer, but I didn't really do anything. When I first started writing more regularly, I wanted to start with poetry because I figured that would be less daunting than full novels and long stories. And then I fell in love with it.

MSP: So, we had an amazing off-site event last night with a whole bunch of other really cool magazines and presses. It was at the Los Angeles Central Library, and it was our first ever *Chestnut Review* off-site. I will say Maya, Katie, and Mario, who is our third chapbook author released this year, knocked it out of the park. So, I would like to hear some very unfiltered thoughts about the reading from both of you because you were both there. You were both reading, and I know you were probably nervous. But you guys both did so phenomenal. So, yeah, just lay it on me, what do you think?

MC: Yeah, I was definitely a little bit nervous. I've done a couple readings before, and I was, like, yeah, I can do this, but then, you know, right before you go on, you start shaking a little bit. You're like, okay, maybe I mentally can do this, but my body is not handling this very well. So, I was doing my little breathing exercises trying to get in the zone. I also really enjoyed that James had us do very personalized intros, and everyone else had very serious ones, which ended up making us have a fun intro. I was like, how am I gonna loop in this cannibal stuff? so that was really fun. I think I overthought it a little bit. I was looking down at my phone the whole time, but I had fun. And yeah, it was a good time.

KK: Yeah, I was wowed by the packed room, and I love to do readings in the community. But I don't think I had performed to a room that packed with other writers before and the lineup leading up to *Chestnut Review's* writers. The performances were so great; it's hard to follow up on that, but I felt really excited to share the work.

MSP: I think character work is a huge part of these stories. Relationships are central to the chaps, parental relationships, but also intergenerational relationships and how experiences like parental trauma can shape what happens in the next generation or even the generation after that. I'm wondering if you could say a little bit about that? I'll start with you, Katie.

KK: Yeah, I mean, I was raised by a veteran and a public school teacher. His life really affected me and, I'm trying to think, how do I say this in an intelligent way? How do I talk family trauma here?

MSP: We're at AWP Bookfair. It's okay.

KK: As a child, I remember coming downstairs and seeing my dad really upset, like watching TV. He'd been watching TV, and he'd be having a beer or a drink, and I could tell that he was sort of a different person in those moments.

And when you're little, you don't really understand when your parents change like that. For him, a lot of times, it was the trauma that affected him before he had me. So, you know, being at war, having to go to war, having to have that experience as a young person and not knowing what he was getting into when he enlisted or losing his first wife in a horrific car crash. He could have been angry in those moments, but he wasn't. I saw that he was tender, and he wanted to tell me what was wrong. He wanted to show that those moments made him sad, not angry. I mean, I saw my dad cry growing up. And I think men, especially today, have a hard time showing that. There's a lot of toxic masculinity, and my father had a softer masculinity that I benefited from as a child.

MSP: I really see that in the book and the things that you said, like, last night, before you introduced the red car poem, you talked about how he blamed the car for the accident, like he didn't blame you. He could have reacted any one of a thousand ways, but he chose to be gentle in that moment. To teenage you, I feel like that was a really powerful choice.

I also think in Maya's chapbook the grandfather character, their father, is wrestling with the toxic masculinity that he was shown to have inherited from Khmer culture. And because of that it's really this story about how someone can make a mistake or how someone can make a choice. And I see that really powerful moment of choice coming through in the chap with this male identity expressed through fatherhood, through grandfatherhood. It's really, really a powerful thing.

So, Maya for you, since your chapbook is a work of fiction, I'm wondering where these character inspirations came from and this central, integral relationship.

MC: I'm trying to figure out how to word this as well, because I'm like, what if my parents…?

It is a work of fiction, so it's not inspired by my own personal life, but there are themes of intergenerational trauma that I can resonate with. I'm sure my family can as well; there's lessons that we all have to learn that we may not know as we're going through it. Also there's issues with extended family and the pressure that's put on a lot of Asian communities, especially as genocide survivors and war refugees. They escaped such suffering to come here, and so they didn't have so many options with their own lives. And it's hard not to project, I guess, in an accidental sense, onto those who have the choices to lead their lives their way. I wanted to reflect on that and imagine a story of healing where those mistakes are able to be apologized for, and both the parents and the child can come to an understanding of forgiveness and grasp what happened and where they came from with those previous choices and activities.

MSP: One of the interesting things about these chapbooks, at the end with the characters, is there's a transfer of power happening. In Katie's, it's about your father passing, but also some of the life stages, for instance after his second wife died, moving into a smaller place and having, as I think you described to me in the editing process, these big markers from his bigger life with her in a smaller condo space. So there's a diminishment of power.

In *Tan's Donuts* that is coming through this cancer diagnosis, and this idea of reconciliation before it gets too late, but I was really struck by the parallels of the effects of war, the effects of geopolitics, and how that sort of plays out in an individual sense, but also the way that the paternal figure in the chap is passing along to his children and future generations this legacy that's really given a great stopping point or ending: kind of a rest, both in *Tan's Donuts* and in *Big Man*.

I want to take a moment because I think there's this very phenomenal thing happening at the ending. Like, I don't know if you've read each other's chaps but I just want to highlight this idea that we should have "Noum Ansong" at the end [of Maya's chap] because it's like a phenomenology of something. It begins:

"I saw it in a dream, a lush plane by the Mekong River in a time when it was not the color of dirt or filled with the contents of a landfill. Catfish swam among the shallows as a pod of Irrawaddy dolphins peaked up over the water. The entirety of the world was tinged with gold."

And of course, there's so much imagery in here that has come back and is resonant through the chapbook, through some of the experiences earlier in Cambodia.

Katie, in yours, there's this elegiac poem towards the end about your father's experience, and I want to highlight this poem, which is just called "Our Father":

"At the cemetery our father has two
headstones. One shared with our mother:
names and death only. The other one:
Air Force Sergeant. Four years of war.
His name carved into the stone of U.S.
imperialism. His triangular flag added
to the mosaic of servicemen. Here he
will not be the father, teacher, union
negotiator, driver of teenagers, joyful
eater of fried chicken, ice cream, pizza.
Born. Air Force. Died. He had a wife.

We leave heart shaped rocks, sea glass,
shells and pinecones. Small things we
might have passed into his big hands."

There's a beautiful tribute at the end of both of these chapbooks, and I
want to know how that feels in your body when you hear it, how it felt
when you wrote it. How you knew that this could be something that you
wanted to include in your chap.

MC: When I wrote that piece, it was definitely one of the more emotional uses of the story. There are moments when the grandfather Tan has a
little crack of emotion because he explains things very matter of factly.
This one, he's reflecting on so many memories. He's in the dream, and
that reflects with the imagery being very vivid compared to most of his
language through the rest of the chapbook. It was Maria's idea to end on
that piece, and it was a really great idea to end there, a really great choice.

KK: It's funny because that poem came in and out of the chapbook
manuscript. I thought it was maybe a bit simplistic, so I'd taken it out in
recent submissions. *Chestnut Review* had an early version of the chapbook,
and I was really happy to hear that you liked that poem.

When you lose a parent, being at their grave site is a big deal, and you
think about how future generations will walk through the cemetery
and what they'll know of your loved one, and for the most part, it's just
names, and birth and death dates, or if you were married. My parents
have a stone together, but it struck me that my father also had this military stone, and that was not a happy part of his life. He felt very conflicted, being involved in that war at all. So, when we go to visit him, we really do leave stones, pinecones, and little bits of nature. I'm really pleased
that it came together as the ending. It felt right when we got there.

MSP: I think that, for both of you, it just felt like that was the right ending. And, again, because all these things come back. All of these things
were mentioned beforehand, like the pizza, like the kathael, the mats,
right? That was something that the sister was shown to be sitting on in
the pre-war time, which was almost like a fever dream in the chapbook
for the family. This thing, before those horrible events happened, and

there was a breaking of essentially the world. It was just a really powerful resting place.

No pressure, but I would love it if you both had a question or comment for each other.

KK: So, Maya, I read your book a couple weeks ago and just loved it. I read it in one sitting. It really moved me, and I think I was most struck by this little sister who had been left behind before the war, and these glimpses that we get of her as the story progresses, and the idea that she may have been captured and brainwashed. That loss and how it shapes the other child's life was very moving for me, and I was curious about where you got the inspiration for that character?

MC: That's a very good question. Thank you, Katie. It was a fairly common thing that happened during the Khmer genocide for there to be child soldiers being used to place the mines, I think, because, their weight is less so they're less likely to trigger them.

I saw this younger sister living in the shadow of her sister's death. She never got to meet this sibling, but it had so greatly impacted both of her parents, especially her father's way of raising her. I noticed that as well in extended family with older sisters or older siblings, having to live up to that standard. Seeing how that impacted the younger siblings' lives was interesting to think about.

KK: As a parent, that rang true too because there's no way to separate parenting one child from another. The way you parent your first child influences the way you parent the second one, even though they're two very different people. I was really impressed by how you were able to navigate that.

MC: For *Big Man*, what do you think was the most challenging part of writing the book?

KK: It felt very natural for me to write so many of these poems. When a person who is important to you passes away, it almost feels like there's a window of time where you can still capture their memory and their essence, and that diminishes each year. My father's been gone eight years now, and I've been trying to just capture those memories, and get them down on paper before they're completely gone. Honestly, the hardest part was finding the right publisher. I was so happy that the manuscript landed with *Chestnut Review*.

MSP: Thank you both so much. This has been such a special experience. I know it's kind of rough and tumble, but it's been so great to do this here. I just want a few words about what's next for you?

MC: I am working on a novel in verse that is a speculative, alternate history story that follows Perenelle Flamel, the wife of Nicholas Flamel. I'm imagining her journey of trying to become immortal. And it's very queer, and part of the immortality powers comes with shape shifting, so she's crossing through different species and genders. So, yeah, I'm excited to see where that goes.

KK: I have a full length that I'm working on that is actually a mix of poems from *Big Man*, memories of my father, and then also memories of my mother. I'm also working on a separate chap with just poems about my mother, and focusing on the clothing we wore at different periods of our life because my mother loved clothes, so each poem has a clothing theme. I was raised in the '80s and '90s, big mall times. I'm also working on a collection of poems about being under- and unemployed, and that manuscript is feeling closer to the point where I can send it out.

MSP: Thank you both so much for that! Maya, you have this speculative bent which I love that wasn't really in *Tan's Donuts* because of its subject matter, but I can't wait.

Katie, for you, "Eating Disorder Meet Cute." is one of my favorite poems; I feel like it encapsulates so much of your parents' dynamics, along with other great moments in the chap, so it makes so much sense to put both of them together beside each other in this tribute.

I'm really interested to see how these projects turn out! Much love to you both. It's been so great to see you and hang out here.

Coconut

Depressed. I didn't understand what your mother meant when she told me that was how she felt. Sure, we're all sad sometimes, but what's a teenager got to be depressed about? Trigonometry homework? Who you're going to prom with? Everything your grandmother and I ever did was for her to have a chance at a better life. Lying on the ground between the corpses of our friends, pretending to be dead so the soldiers wouldn't shoot, tiptoeing through minefields holding our breath—it was all for her. We scrounged all our savings together for a business we didn't choose just so that she could have a better future. It was hard to hear that she was still unhappy. I didn't have the words to explain how I felt so I just screamed, throwing every English word I knew at her as she ran into her room and locked the door shut. I never had enough words for her. I didn't have enough patience either. After that, she started seeing your father, a boy from the grade above her. He wasn't the best influence. She started skipping classes and getting detention. The stack of missing homework assignments piled higher and higher. In the middle of her shift at the shop, your dad would breeze in, throw an arm over her, take a coconut donut from behind the counter without paying, and drive away in his unwashed car to who-knows-where. Then she flunked out of school, he left town, and well, you know the rest. You would think that losing one daughter would be enough to make a person kinder.

Donut Holes and Orange Juice

April 16th, 2005. 3:08 AM. That was the moment your mother walked through the door with you, our sweet Matthew, in her arms, bundled up in a baby blue blanket covered in ducks. Do you remember when your mom used to take you to the shop on the days she was working? Your favorite thing in the whole world was our donut holes, always eaten alongside freshly squeezed orange juice poured into your sippy cup. We were awestruck by you, sitting by the cash register, taking orders from customers. You couldn't pronounce your R's right, so "cinnamon roll" always came out like "cinnamon woll." Every other Saturday, we took you to the park in a stroller as you clung to your plush turtle, Shelly. We'd have a picnic on the grass, with strawberries and BLT sandwiches, and then we'd go to the playground. You loved going on the seesaw with me, laughing as you kicked up sand each time you pushed off the ground. The moment you showed me that drawing you had made of our family in kindergarten, I pinned it to the fridge. Every square inch of it is covered with pictures of you, ones with you playing at the beach in your flamingo floaties and ones at your third grade violin recital. I even printed out the ones your mom posted on Facebook from when you graduated high school. We thought about you every day after you and your mom left. You've gotten so tall now. Oh, chau, I've missed you.

Big Man

The walk from the air-conditioned truck
to the mall turned him into a popsicle,
sweat dripping down his tanned forehead.
He had a big build in the arms and shoulders,
strong like bull, he'd told his daughters.
He didn't move easy, but well enough
in his Gold's Gym t-shirt with the sleeves
cut off, his ancient mesh shorts. He had
nearly made it to the door, its chill relief,
when a voice sizzled through the air.
A six-year-old girl exploded into him:
Mr. Kemple! Mr. Kemple! Mr. Kemple!
Hollering like he was a celebrity, not her
first-grade teacher. She hugged his bad leg,
wrapped around him like a Band-Aid.
And for a moment, he could acknowledge
it, the pent-up pain, the strain, how hard it
felt to move. Maybe the girl had no one
at home to hug. They both took a break
from being tough and melted there together.

The Wedding Album

We found our father's first wife
in the closet upstairs, behind
the child size door my sister and I
cracked open, under the naked
pull-light in a maroon leather album.
That 1970s pigment gave a warm
glow to the photos. Dad in a dark
tux, white carnation in the lapel.
The lady next to him brunette
like mom but angular, wore
glasses. At six and four, we didn't
understand. I took the album
to Mom fresh out of the shower,
penciling her face in. The sight
of it creased her eyes: "Pat!"
she hollered. Dad arrived, took it
back, ushered us to the table,
said: "You know how your kitten
died?" Hit by a car in front of our
house. He said his first wife died
in a similar accident. My sister
and I must have hugged him,
the memory of our cat stinging.
But I only remember tugging
my sister's hand to play outside.
When night fell, Dad sat alone
by the hearth stoking the flames,
the wedding album man, a stranger.
He saw me there and looked away,
back to the blazing fire he created.
I didn't know who I was anymore.

West Texas

Watercolor and ink on paper
9x12 inches, 2024

My art documents my journey back to my own nature as an intuitive, feeling animal, after years of trying to repress my way into fulfillment. "West Texas" was created as part of the larger series "The Breakup Tour," a 6-month period of solo travel and artmaking to heal from an overlapping breakup, job loss, housing loss, and serious surgery. "West Texas" specifically was painted in west Texas (surprise!) while working and living at a communal sustainable winery. Working with my hands in the dirt under vast empty skies, grief dug thin rivulets in me as it trickled out like water, leaving behind presence and potential.

Sharkbite

I. MY HOUSE

Notable happenings: My birth; a fire in 1907

She was a bitch and I loved her. The hole we bury Sharkbite in is no longer than my forearm and no wider than my head, though it was just the right size for her little bunny body. She was dear to me and an enemy to most. There's Mrs. Silva, for example, who lives next door and is now watching our ceremony from between the slats on the fence with a twisted look on her face revealing her teeth like little skyscrapers. Can't you see we're having a moment! I want to shout. Can't you understand a local hero has fallen! I forgave a great deal in the six years I shared with Sharkbite; there was the time one of Mrs. Silva's grandchildren tried throwing the rabbit from the roof to see how she'd land, and of course there were all those times I would introduce her to family friends, who would coo and then shriek at the sight of her, the combination of her cherubic face and gargantuan teeth. Though her head was but the size of a fist, those teeth—*Oh Jesus Almighty that's not good*, the vet called them—never stopped growing until they ultimately killed her. All this to say that, yes, I've forgiven a great deal, but even I have my limits.

Palma kneels beside me, head bowed in the direction of the mud heap and cardboard cross. The grass in my family's backyard has not been trimmed since my thirteenth birthday last year when I decided that Sharkbite might miss the thrill of the hunt and the wild terrain of her native grasslands. I know that Palma's knees must itch like hell, and for this I am grateful.

She starts solemnly: "You know, she was never all that cute or intelligent, but she will always be a force in the community."

"Hey!" I whisper. "Mrs. Silva can hear you!"

"I was talking about Sharkbite."

Palma's voice is thick and syrupy, and it certainly doesn't suit her face, which is bright and pointy and pretty like a rat's. Right at this moment, with her head hanging low, she looks like those icons of weepy lady-saints with thin eyebrows and sloping lips. "I pray she will be gently punished for her sins," she continues. "And then transported to animal heaven expeditiously."

I take advantage of this rare moment and study Palma's face while her eyes are shut. I want to commit it to memory, starting with the moles on her cheek. But soon enough, instinct takes over and I mumble, "You'll see animal hell before Sharkbite ever does." Palma's laugh, unlike her voice, is the squeal of a child, or a violin.

II. HEAVEN DELI

Notable happenings: My conception; a fire in 1992

We start at Heaven, because Palma says she will miss it the most. It is her last full day in America, so her wish is my command. As our sophomore year came to a close last week, so too did the international exchange program, which means that tomorrow she will be making her journey home with all sorts of new American ideas, along with Rupert the German, who performed regular scratch-and-sniffs on himself, and Isabel from Rio who campaigned to implement morning prayers into our curriculum.

I am worried the power outages and stolen toilet seats of the public school system may have given her the wrong impression of our country, meanwhile Palma has taken it upon herself to search up rabbit facts and report them back to me from the other side of the instant noodle aisle. So far, we have established that all these creatures are good for is antibody research and savory stews, a fact that depresses me to no end. "But this delicacy is your friend," Palma says. "I'm sorry for your loss." We stack up on every gloriously revolting snack Heaven has to offer, making our way from the vacuum-sealed meats to the chili-soaked pickles. Stationed by the multicolor constellation of sour candies, Palma sighs and shakes her head, clearly waiting for me to engage with her research.

"This antibody stuff is crazy," she says. "Did you know that we have more bacteria in our bodies than cells?"

"I believe it. Look where we are," I tell her. "This place probably has all sorts of undiscovered bacteria."

She runs a frozen bottle of Dr. Pepper along the dark surface of her forehead and sighs like a phantom is escaping her body through her nostrils. Her bangs stick up like sun rays. "Well, did you know that our cells are constantly regenerating? It says that our cells right now are completely different from the ones we had when we were babies. Oh, I don't like that, I don't like it at all."

"I bet you can't make your chin touch your chest," I challenge her, and she does so without hesitation, still reading through the black veil of her hair. I bow back to her. "Oh no, Miss, the pleasure's all mine!"

Palma laughs like crazy, so I do too. "Ah hell," she says, and coils her arm around my neck until I cry uncle.

Behind the register stands some undiscovered bacteria. He says, "Hey, it's Darren's daughter! And her friend the pomeranian."

Palma says, "I'm Maltese."

He says, "Sure thing." Something far more exciting has caught his attention, something far below Palma's eye level. There are two wet crescents on her dress where her sweat had gathered. "Uh, that dress is very becoming."

Palma looks around, as if for clues. "Becoming what?"

There's the kind of biblical heat outside that makes you grateful to be alive in this day and age, if not for democracy then at least for air conditioning and cotton underwear. I challenge Palma to a race. She points up at the sky in explanation and it's painfully true, the sun so ablaze it turns everything white in its wake. "I'd do it if I didn't have boobs. I'd do a lot of things if I didn't have boobs." She smiles and so do I, but her words trouble me. She considers it for a second. "Jumping jacks. Competitive stair climbing. Run for president."

I say, "There's all sorts of people with boobs running for president."

She says, "But do they ever win?"

In a sort of answer, I bring each of my knees to my chest, stretching them, then I crouch until I can feel the rising heat of the pavement. Then I start to sprint. The air around me feels like the inside of a dishwasher.

For a while, I don't hear any footsteps behind me. But then I do. The sound of Palma's dress against the wind is like the whipping blades of a helicopter. Her hair is stuck to her forehead, black strands looping around her eyebrows, dripping in front of her eyes like teardrops. I remember learning about the short-term effects of running, how it produces some chemical or another that's more powerful than sugar and drugs combined, and I feel happier than happy.

From across the street, we hear someone shouting both of our names.

III. WADE PARK

Notable happenings: Discovery of my father's affair; oldest tree in the country is felled by drunk college students in 1964; several lesser battles of the American Revolution

"Remedial math is just not the move." Simon Schwartz tugs at the branches, clearly trying to impress Palma. He looks around at his two friends, up at the tree, even at me, as if this beautiful, European, weepy-saint-looking girl is the last thing on his mind. The first thing about desiring someone is that you have to make them believe that you despise them; they must be gathering all the boys at school and teaching them this sort of stuff in an afterschool program for the Socially Gifted. Simon Schwartz—he doesn't know some of our classmates call him Hymen Warts—is decently popular, depending on who you ask. Certainly if you ask him. Sitting across from me, her knees digging into grass for the second time today, Palma's expression is unreadable.

"I guess not," she says. "Sorry they're making you go to summer school."

"Hey, I'm sorry for you man, you're gonna be missing the Fourth of July here."

As I watch the two of them, my thoughts come to me muffled and warbled and warped, like hearing music from outside of a party.

An elderly woman stands alone under the shade of the gazebo with one leg suspended in the air behind her. She is wearing white linen pants that are several sizes too big for her and her hair, curly and just as white, moves with her in slow-motion, levitating above her head like those part-time mermaids at the county fair. I can tell she was once unreasonably beautiful. She closes her eyes and lifts both of her hands, palms facing out and pushing forward forward forward as if to ward off all evil.

The quietest of the three boys, Benny, who is handsome in a ferret sort of way, unzips his backpack with an air of secret ceremony. A moment of silence falls upon the park. I can tell, already, that the time has come for our little group to disturb the peace. I recognize the boy sitting closest to me from Beginner's French but can't for the life of me think of his name. Last year, he was the runner-up for Homecoming King. There's a chance no one could remember his name long enough to write it on the ballot. As Benny digs several cylindrical shapes out of his bag, the runner-up turns to face me with a look that can only be described as nauseous disinterest.

He asks, "So what kind of woman are you?"

I can't quite tell if he's joking, so my best bet is to pretend I haven't heard him. But then he continues, "Are you the silent type? You mysterious or something?"

"I'm not a woman," I tell him in an attempt to end the conversation before it can begin.

Until now I've only ever heard him speak French, which made everything sound romantic and gravely serious. Listening to him trip and lisp in English, his words sound as if they've been programmed into him by some nefarious entity, or a toddler. "My eyes tell me otherwise," he says, scanning me up and down for a second. "So what are you then?"

I try a joke. "I've been sent here to kill you."

"Say that again?"

"I'm a Netherland Dwarf."

"Oh." His eyebrows are sparse, and he moves them closer together until they almost connect. "You're the goofy kind, huh? I'm not into those, sorry."

The tai-chi lady, having successfully kept the evil at bay, exits the gazebo and makes her way through the path lined with trampled wildflowers and fallen acorns until she becomes a curly white dot against a background of identical white houses. I wonder what kind of silence she will come home to.

I look down at my arms. They are spectacularly hairy. I am brought back to a memory of my mother sitting alone for hours in front of her mirror, running a hand up and down the fine hair on the nape of her neck. I can't for the life of me think of any reason why I should be remembering this now. Simon—apparently, incredibly his plan all along—offers to light up the park for poor Palma, who has spent an entire school year in America without attending a real firework show. Our circle has transformed into an audience with her sitting front and center, a performance of Palma Blinks. I keep forgetting to memorize her face, my one important task before she leaves tomorrow, but here is a group of volunteers willing to do it for me. The day is almost over, I think, and all we've done is play undertaker in the backyard.

A hesitant chill comes with the setting of the sun, as if the wind hasn't quite caught on to the fact that we are still in the prime of summer. It blows over our hands and the grass, almost shy, just passing through. The hair on my arms stands on end like fire ants. The boys too, like a colony of insects, rise and rush toward Benny's stash. They huddle together, squatting for a few seconds, and begin to run. Palma and I, quick learners, follow their cue. Several at a time, firecrackers and bottle rockets are popped and launched into the breeze. The first few are unsuccessful—wind. *This wind absolutely blows*, I would say if Palma was close enough to hear it. Hymen I mean Simon finally triumphs and a bottle rocket soars and dazzles the air around us a bright red. He's built up quite the momentum because the entire group has begun to launch successful rockets and each time I blink I open my eyes to the world in a new color. I watch Palma turn blue then red and I watch Simon lean in close to hear her better and I watch him laugh. I wait for the discomfort to creep over her face, but it never comes. Runner-up is happier than I have ever seen him; in the back of French class and on the wings of the stage at homecoming he always had the exact same defeated expression. All of us stand there panting. I'm reminded of my earliest birthdays, blowing out the candles then begging my parents to revive them, over and over until the wax drooped onto the icing of the cake. Was I more thrilled for the ceremony or my parents' attention? It was hard to tell then and it's hard to tell now. While the park is still shimmering red, I turn and walk away, in pursuit of something though I'm not sure what. Maybe the gazebo lady. Either way, I am confident my disappearance has not created a void.

IV. LAKESIDE BRIDGE

Notable happenings: My father encounters an abandoned rabbit in a box labeled Sharkbite Plumbing Co.; I am offered a pet in exchange for my silence; a fire in 1971

For a while, I don't hear any footsteps behind me. But then I do, the sound of legs against linen, or wings against wind.

"Why are you following me?" The sun has almost completely set and beneath us the lake is the color of orangeade.

"You should've told me you wanted to leave," Palma says. "I was standing there like an idiot looking around for you."

I do not stop or turn around to look at her. "Okay. I wanted to leave." Already I can tell I'm about to do or say something very unkind.

Her deep voice, for some reason, soaked in apology: "I was talking to Simon—I really thought his name was Warts, you know—I was talking to him about Sharkbite and he said this thing about fossils: he said they found the oldest rabbit skeleton in the world a few years ago and it's the oldest complete skeleton. Like ever. Why he knows that, I have no idea. I think maybe he looked it up when he was pretending to text someone–"

"Don't talk about my rabbit's bones with some guy!" I shout at her like a certified insane person, like a father. I don't give myself enough time to regret it. "Don't talk about her at all! I don't want to hear about her stupid cells or her antibodies or her guts, just stop it! You're being creepy."

"I thought it would bring you some comfort." I try to imagine Palma's face as she jogs to keep up with me, beautiful and confused. Maybe her nostrils are a little flared or the corner of her lips has quirked up. Not so far away, I can hear the boys still howling with laughter.

"*How* would this stuff comfort me?"

"I wanted to show you how cool rabbits are," she says, the smack of her flats against the pavement slowing down. "I don't understand why you're so upset now." I do everything but respond: I walk faster, almost running, feeling as if I've been set on fire. Palma goes on anyway: "I think maybe you are mad that you're not my only friend. I only spoke with you all year, because you are the only one who wanted to sit with me. Now on my final day someone is interested in me and it makes you angry. Because you like having a pet that everyone hates. This is something about you."

When Palma is troubled, her English is unusually formal, as if she's translating a textbook in real-time. Once, during a tornado drill, she told our teacher that she was "exceptionally frightened." Another time, looking at the words *mystery flavor* on the cafeteria menu, she whispered miserably, "How dreadful!" Me, on the other hand—I can only revert back to sputtering, tantruming childhood. So now with Palma at my heels, I can think of nothing to say but, "Quit following me," and eventually the restless noise behind me halts and there's no wings no wind no bird at all.

V. MY HOUSE

Notable happenings: Demise of Sharkbite, local hero

By the time I arrive home, it is completely dark save for a couple of street lamps. I behold the house in front of me, slight and crumbling in some parts like its residents. I feel like Odysseus or Jason or Jack or whatever. The one who came home and wasn't all too happy about it. I wonder if any myths start the moment the hero walks in through the front door and has to explain to his parents where he's been all day. It takes the last puff and wheeze of energy I have left to carry me to the front porch, where I sit slumped like a question mark. Wrapped around the yard like a dormant snake is one long flower bed, but no flowers. Every year, my mother insists she will plant some in the spring; zinnias, maybe, or some basil and thyme. For now, it is a heaping pile of dirt and potential. The thought comes to me like a math exercise: When I woke up, I had an apple and a grilled cheese and a mutant rabbit and a best friend. What do I have now? I drop my head into my hands because that is what people do when they are upset and when they have wronged and been wronged.

Blood rushes to my face and time moves impossibly slow. There's the sound of cicadas warbling and yodeling, every now and then the siren of an ambulance or the muffled laughter of the Silvas next door. Then the crinkle of a plastic bag inches away from me. My head still bowed, I open my eyes to a pair of scuffed flats pointed toward me. "Be angry all you want, but don't take it out on the pickles," says their owner. "You left them at the park."

She drops the bag on the porch beside me.

Because neither of us knows how to say we're sorry, we tear open a bag of *onion flavor tangy apocalyptic turbo-blast* chips instead, and I move over to make space on the porch steps. My mouth full, I cry out: my hero. And Palma laughs, "Imagine how embarrassing it was to go back to that stupid park. The whole remedial math gang was still there! I had to take the bag when they weren't looking and run for it. I apocalyptic turbo-blasted out of there."

I tap my knee against hers in gratitude. I miss her already. "History will remember this. America will."

The sprinklers start up. They spray and lick at the tall blades of grass. I point to a scar, raised and pink, on Palma's elbow.

"Where'd you get that from?"

"The stairs at school. I didn't see the last step and I tripped."

For a moment, I'm thrilled at the idea of our town leaving a memory on her skin. She must read the look on my face as concern because she says, "It's fine, those cells should regenerate soon enough. Then it'll be like it never happened."

I have accomplished very little on Palma's last day in America besides buying her pickles and yelling at her, though arguably there are few things more American than that. It does make me guilty enough that I'm obliged to accept when she offers to read my palm. I rest my hand on hers and notice that the red paint on her fingernails has chipped. Now each of them is shaped like a different continent. Any fortune teller worth a damn will tell you, she announces, that it's important to begin your palm reading with an analysis of the client's knuckles. She skates her finger over each mountain and valley; I make a joke about my fate being in her hands. In the time it takes Palma to count my knuckles, I have already thought of everything, the whole world from Heaven to Lakeside Bridge. Somewhere in town, there is a fire that will be remembered in the years to come. There are babies with teeth still growing. Someone far away is discovering a fossil that looks a lot like Sharkbite and right now Palma is holding my hand but also right now she is an old married woman who can remember the snacks we shared in class but not my name and not my face either. My mother will always talk about renovating the kitchen but she will never get around to it and she will look sadly into her chicken soup long after the rest of us have left the dinner table. We are two girls alone at night with our knees touching; we are living this moment and looking back at it, both at once. We are like the dress she is wearing, we are becoming. I will become the kind of person who remembers everything and has no one to share it with.

"I can feel you looking at me, ma'am," Palma says, smiling. "You're driving the spirits crazy, I can't focus."

How many knuckles, I ask her, and she tells me I've got a healthy twenty-eight. She traces her slender finger over a groove in my palm. "Now we begin. I see you had grilled cheese for lunch."

My jaw swings open. "How did you know?"

"I can smell it."

We laugh without looking up at one another. What else, I ask her, what else.

"See here? It's a good thing. It means you've got charisma. The line goes all the way to your pinky here, which means you have a lot of potential. You do. This is something about you."

I think about the flower bed. I say nothing, tap a little rhythm on the wood of the porch. I can't seem to lift my head, so I don't. Several yards to my left and a few feet below us, Sharkbite is turning into something else. So am I.

I finally ask, "How many years until our whole body regenerates?"

She says, "About seven. We'll be twenty-one." She rubs the hem of her dress against my hand. "Tsk tsk, sweaty palms, now let me see your future!" I snatch it away from her and hold it to my chest. I don't want to know everything, least of all when there's nothing good to know. We sit in silence for a while and listen to the cicadas sing. I am suddenly overcome with the urge to challenge her to a race, but I'm sane enough to know that that would be a profoundly silly thing to do right now. Palma has three moles on her right cheek and two on her left. I repeat that in my head, over and over. I am still holding my own hand and hers is still limp and open before her. I can't tell if I should look forward to my new body or miss this one. I wonder which version will be the happiest, if all of them will live in this house. If this version of Palma is the only one I will ever know.

I have to speak or I might cry, so I ask, "What is the number one thing you'll miss about this place?"

"I already told you. The deli." She laughs through her nose. She adjusts her posture so the entire right side of her body and left side of mine are pressed together. "What about you? If you had to miss something, what would it be?"

I pretend to consider it, I imagine I am someone who is leaving. Flecks of light and water land on my leg. The sprinklers twirl like ballerinas and make hushed noises like hissing, like girls sharing secrets.

Kyle Givens describes what it was like to find Mai Mageed's "Sharkbite"

This is a story that jumped out from the first line. In the first paragraph the narrator feels so strongly at the loss of an animal, and it enrages her that the people around don't feel as strongly as she does. It takes the little things seriously. It's lively and energetic. There's an outside world that intrudes in her summer. There's summer in this, heat and cicadas and dirt and flowers, and at the center of it all a character whose life is changing without her permission. I'm most moved by stories that manage to keep a sense of humor around a sense of loss or change, and this is it. I am so excited to see this story out in the world now.

Ibraheem Uthman describes what it was like to find January Santoso's "Interview"

This poem arrived like a faulty transmission, a dialogue in which the interlocutor is never visible but whose presence is sharply felt in the silences. The poem's initial question, "Where would you like to start?" plunges me into a disorienting space, a "cobalt room" that will not submit to easy allegorization. Santoso's speaker, forthcoming and evasive, evades the questioning of the interview in a syntax that breaks and reforms, and in the process, betrays a consciousness at once luminous and besieged. There is an odd grace in the speaker's refusal to conform, their insistence on a logic that operates at the margin of mainstream discourse.

The poem's power resides in its ability to evoke a palpable sense of liminality. The speaker's pronouncements, "I'm made of plasma so I can't say," or "a clam shut pearl," are not mere obfuscatory ornamentation but, instead, assertions of a reality that cannot be accessed through empirical perception. It was as if I were presented with a sequence of fragments, witnessing the speaker's attempt to articulate the ineffable. The image of the swan, "frightening, what a swan is, when you're looking it in the eye," possesses a stark, almost mythic quality, suggesting an encounter with something both beautiful and terrifyingly primal.

In the end, I realized that Santoso wasn't dishing out answers, but experiences. "Interview" is a deliberate reversal of the typical communicative experience, a deconstruction of language that forced me to let go of the comfort of crystalline resolutions. It was a journey into the belly of uncertainty, that left a disquieting, sonorous echo in me. By its end, I was less reader and more observer to a strange, compelling ritual, reminded of the power of language to create worlds that exist just beyond the edge of our perception.

Interview

Where would you like to start? when it happened I was knotted in a cobalt room.
Is that a metaphor? I mean the lights were blue, but they were not
Were the lights symbolic? exactly. they are the last jagged glacial edge
What were you doing there? evermelting. but I'm made of plasma so I can't say
Were you drinking? look at that. I like this flowy state, like to be all
What were you wearing? love and crap. if anyone showed me love, it was
Were you conscious? a clam-shut pearl. thought I'd pry it open, lube it
So you were awake? up with swan tears. frightening, what a swan is, when
You didn't try to stop it? you're looking it in the eye.

Cut Off

Doctor Bonney said, *Society shoved our boy the wrong way. I shoved him back. Being a surgeon, I held life in my hands. Administered pain. Relieved tragedy. Destroyed my boy to make him whole. He's whole now. Sure is. Rather a cripple with a brain than some useless athlete … Where's my breakfast?*

The nurse said it'd been ordered. Doctor Bonney told her that he was hungry, that she'd better get his breakfast or else.

When he got hurt, there was sure lots of crying from Mrs. Bonney and our boy, Doctor Bonney mumbled.

I told my wife and son to cry if they wanted but that nobody could cry forever.

I went to see my son in the hospital room after the operation. I told him to stop crying. I asked him if he believed he was going to play football all his life. People lose their legs all the while, I told my son. I won't cry for you. His mother would cry for him. She did so.

He thought he was to play professional football, Doctor Bonney said with a chuckle. *I said, you wanted to play pro and make money and be a celebrity, but you lost your leg. And isn't it a wonderful thing? Aren't you the luckiest boy in the world? I said.*

Now, you'll go to college and then to medical school. Or to law or into business, Mrs. Bonney said. *I assented to Mrs. Bonney, long as our son made something of himself.*

An orderly in a grey shirt with 'SEASIDE ASSISTED LIVING' scripted across his heart came into the room. He carried a tray of warm milk and a bowl of bran cereal and placed it on the table beside Doctor Bonney's bed.

Our boy wanted to be a football player, Doctor Bonney told the orderly.

Did he, sir?

That coach burst into my office in a sweatshirt and cap, one day. Grown men dress like children. And I asked the coach what sort of man he was.

Your breakfast, sir, the orderly said.

The nurse secured a napkin to Doctor Bonney's chest and dismissed the orderly. Doctor Bonney was laughing as he said, *That coach told me my son was getting interest from colleges, that with a little luck, our son was going to get a scholarship to the state university.*

I excused the coach from my office. There wasn't anything to do with grown men who act like children. I wouldn't have my son be like him.

Doctor Bonney ate a little cereal as the nurse patted his mouth, and he said, *I told my wife not to believe him, that our son was going to become a doctor. Our son said he was going to be a football player and I said that he wasn't going to be and that was all.*

The milk wasn't any good and Doctor Bonney complained but the nurse told him the breakfast was ordered by the doctor.

Doctor Bonney said, *It was a damn good thing that game he pivoted the wrong way and snapped his shin bone. Lucky for him he got an infection. I told him God is always looking out for us good people.*

Eat your breakfast, the nurse said. The doctor will see you soon, Mr. Bonney.

Doctor Bonney ate a little of the bran cereal with his fingers.

Mrs. Bonney asked what to do. I said cut the leg at the kneecap.

She said how is a boy of seventeen going to live without a leg.

He'll walk alright, I told her. He won't need that leg, a boy like ours. With smarts.

Better operate. So that the infection wouldn't swell, is what I told her. She didn't know what to make of that. I said the infection was on the lower end of the tibia and that we'd better amputate, and that time was a-wasting.

When I was preparing to amputate the leg, Mrs. Bonney said she wouldn't dare let me go through with it. I told her to hush, that the leg would have to go.

The doctor will be to see you shortly, the nurse said.

Doctor Bonney asked if the arriving doctor had a good reputation.

He sure does.

Good. Then he said, *A few of my colleagues observed the case with me, and they offered a solution of penicillin. But I told them that this was no laughing matter. This was my son, and I knew what was best. There was some argument, but I knew what I must do.*

My son awoke after the operation and said that he couldn't wait until he could get back onto the field. I asked how that could be. And he looked down at what'd been his leg, and then he cried for a long while. His mother cried with him, and I allowed them to do so. Colleagues of mine would tell me privately that something else could've been done. They asked me how I could do such a thing. I said that I saved his life. Now he can forget stupid games and make something of himself. Told him that every man must grow up. I sure did. Nobody wants to grow up. I sure didn't. No, I had to be shoved that way.

Eat your breakfast and please rest, the nurse said.

Doctor Bonney told her, *God allowed my son to forget that stupid game. I told him that he had a chance now. No more games. Studying books would do him good. He will be a doctor, someone important, someone there to look after others.*

The nurse said for Mr. Bonney to rest and that the doctor would see him soon. When the doctor arrived, Doctor Bonney looked up at him. The doctor walked with a limp, but his shoulders were broad mountains and his face stubborn and resolved. The nurse stepped back to allow for the doctor's examination, observing with quiet resolve how well he carried his father's imposing presence.

In the Thick

Acrylic on canvas board
10x6 inches, 2024

Creating art is a passionate extension of my poetic pursuits. Life truly is in colour. And there is no better way to respond to it than through art. I document Life in its entirety using various media and techniques. Primarily painting with acrylics, I enjoy experimenting with other media as well, especially soft pastels. My paintings are reminiscent of personal memories that have shaped my sensibilities as an artist and a human being. I encourage my viewers to go beyond the titles and experience my art at a personal level on their own terms. The painting "In the Thick" was inspired by the lush surroundings and my experience at a property while on a family vacation.

An Exercise in Teeth

after Charles Baudelaire

Taking the world to bed, to the grey-stone wall—this is a game of ghosts, of dressing in the dead man's clothes and calling ourselves strong, unafraid, parading the bruised jaw, the bloody tooth, the orange legs behind the paper lamp. Scrapping the scabs and letting all of the boils bleed. The script shifts by the letter but the language remains the same. The same veil draped over a sickly morning. Every night I become your wife —as if I hadn't forgotten your name, as if I spun it into silver. Smoke sticking to a carpet tongue—the fibers slick against my thighs. This is how we reward ourselves: letting names rot in our hands. How could we know them anyway, trapped beneath the blue light and plastic? I could never stagger the glow of skin, unearth the spider trapped in the amber of your eyes. Your hand is the only invitation. There isn't a hidden design. We play the game. Drinking in the red light, tapping the bare shoulder, departing from the body as we crawl beneath the sheets and pretend I can wind the broken jaw shut —that I could forgive the day by searching for the sun in your gut.

Reimagining Eden

The garden glistening through the lake
is nothing short
of green miracle. The days are reinventing
themselves.
The birds are becoming wary of what
they are yet to become—
silent & searching for fulfillment. I believe
everything needs saving.
Isn't that why I'm here? Can you see my
contentment, the shape of bones
hidden under my flesh? The angels are singing
my praise from heaven.
The doubt between us hangs low
& waiting to be plucked.
Nothing is more certain than uncertainty itself.
I believe everything needs saving.
Isn't that why I'm here?
I have ached to be so beautiful.
It doesn't take much to love anything that
knows nothing of impermanence.
I know nothing of grief yet—not the banishment,
not the endless walking.
The crickets are burning their sullen songs
into the night.
There's a serpent coiled around a trunk.
Eve is stretching her hand again. I trust completely
whatever is in it.

AFTERCRASH IN THE GARDEN

It's not like we had enough room, anyway, your words so full they spill
out of my mouth, greedy as an empty vase, wishing for violence
just to feel full. In the living room, the burgundy rug we forgot to throw out
absorbs the spilled water like a bloodstain, the glass shards like mirrors
too ashamed to be windows. When I look at you, I can't tell if it's your body
or its too-large reflection through the shattered glass. When I look
at myself, I know it's a reflection, because all reflections are lies.
On the rug, strewn tulips lay like shards of plastic, unremarkable, so I tell myself:
this is not a tragic scene—just a replica of one. In other words,
I am not sure if I was ever alive, so you can't call us *dead,* surely.

                                                   Still, I am not sure
who I am talking to anymore, what I am supposed to call *mine—*
the burgundy rug, these glass pieces that forget their shape the harder
I try to kick them together, your cross-armed stock-image stance as still
and buried as a good, good mine.   Ticking. Waiting.
It's been three years and still you haven't fixed the leak in our bedroom ceiling,
citing *the drought* and money issues, but you didn't have to try very hard—
it takes two to keep a dead thing moving. The next morning,
you'll claim your side of the bed is wet because you cried after
you hurled the tulip vase at me. Cried all night long.

                                             But it rained yesterday.
The first time in months. There's wet trails not down your face
but blossoming darkly on the wallpaper, the same way
a paintbrush pressed too hard crushes every image into
the same oversaturated bloodstain, even the most beautiful,
especially the most beautiful. Everyone was going crazy about the end
of the drought—if only you'd looked outside, or up from your own body
so dry it must be cracking. I would know. I was there, sprawled in the dirt,
mouth as open as it was empty, letting the water fill my nose and ears and palms
and thinking: *is this what it's like, being watered as a plastic flower?*
                                                   Really?

Three years ago, I'd made fun of the vase for its absurd shape
when you first got it for our garden's extra tulips. I had spent
the afternoon pulling weeds to delay talking to you about moving in together—
which is why you probably bought the vase, too. *What a pity,* I remember thinking,
the earth rupturing between my fingers, roots grown long for survival
choking themselves into knots. *They could be beautiful if only they stopped multiplying.*
When I came back inside, tired from killing the unkillable, my first instinct
was to laugh at the florid, garish thing. *What's the point of the huge stomach*
if the neck is so thin? How much space is wasted?
But what I didn't understand
was that nothing here would ever become pregnant, just hollow,
as if swallowing more and more space could thin us into existence.
What I always believed, and so could never know, was that
you could teeter a vase on the edge of a bed and I'd spend three years
thinking: *if I can keep it from falling to the bruised floor long enough, it'll stay*
when I let go, that physics will forgive us, as if physics had anything to do
with attraction or the tears running through our walls.
That the ensuing crash is just because I needed to hold you still
for one, or three, or twenty years more. You could ask me what we *really*
look like and I'd shatter every full wineglass against our mirror
until I realize how we all love the same, which is to say love the same
types of pain. And even then, I'd replant the tulips, over and over,
until the weeds swallow the soil itself.

Zé, Outside

Zé thought he'd never get laid again. A decade spent trying to write a faithful screen adaptation for *The Palm-Wine Drinkard* had left him more drained than inspired. By his fourth attempt, his body began to mount tiny revolts—imperceptible at first, subtle enough to let him go about his daily routine undisturbed. A year later, he noticed less blood flowing to his penis when he was excited and that his bussy had shrunk to the size of his pinkie. The men he usually scheduled to visit him on Sundays between 5 am and 7 am became redundant—each attempt at pleasure felt like relearning how to walk. One Sunday, after a disastrous hookup where, throughout the session, he felt himself lose control of his body— a feeling similar to a puppeteer watching a puppet grow sentient, its limbs independent of its strings, each fluid movement tugging back at the puppeteer's fingers—he deleted all dating and hookup apps. *More time to dedicate to my art,* he thought. And he went on with his life—sitting at his desk after work to type, print, and stack pages onto a pile already occupying half his rented room; waiting for the Concerta to wear off so he could catch a few hours of sleep.

Mzi's love handles suggested intelligent design: perfectly symmetrical, perfectly parallel; they gently sloped downwards and pointed towards his navel like a cat's whiskers. When Zé first saw them in a headless profile picture on Grindr, they had a vertical straight line of hair running along the middle of his abdomen and a rectangular fuzz across his chest, like the letter 'T'. Zé wondered what it would feel like to put his finger inside one of those folds, push it deeper until it hit a ribcage, and run it around to his back, where it shallows and disappears. The thought resurrected a lust long dormant. Suddenly it made sense to him why the writing had gone awry in the previous weeks; why the Red-men of Red-town disrobed the minute they left his mind and entered the page; and why with every attempt he made to clothe them again, every backspace, they behaved even more petulantly: disrobing again, whipping their red dicks out, swinging them around as though telling him, Just because you choose to live like a eunuch doesn't mean we should too. We are going to ejaculate all over this page, and ruin whatever it is that you are trying to do here. With no other choice, he paused the writing until he could make sense of it all, then he reinstalled every dating and hookup app.

In these parts of the city, the wastelands. Grimy and crumbling art deco buildings with walls stained by mould and water streaks; windows shattered and patched with plastic and adhesive tape; barbed-wire-fortified balconies. Here, everyone is stacked on top of everyone and barely tolerating one another. It's a lover's desert—if you're not keen on getting fucked in a secluded passageway while suffocating from the foul stench of piss and decaying refuse seeping through accumulated trash bags, or in the remains of a building that went up in flames decades ago, then searching for dick is like running an ultra-marathon that has no prize money. Three-fifths of the men you chat with are dead-ends—they can't host. The other fifth flake when it's time to meet. And the fifth Mzi eventually hooks up with reingests their self-loathing and turns into Martin Ssempa the minute they cum. He couldn't figure out which category Zé fell into. On the one hand, in the several weeks since they started chatting—even though he lived by himself only a fifteen-minute walk away from where Mzi lived with his two brothers and cousin—Zé was always cagey when it came time to meet. On the other hand, at random moments throughout the day, Zé requested pictures of Mzi's midriff, and at night, when they were video chatting, he would ask Mzi to redirect the camera to his stomach and move around a bit so he could watch his tummy jiggle.

One morning, Zé awoke to a text—an ultimatum: *I can't keep chatting with you if we're never going to meet. I'll be around the mall tomorrow at around ten, it would be nice to see you face to face.* But a few hours before ten, a message changed hands from Mzi's brother's girlfriend's brother to Mzi's brother's girlfriend, then Mzi's brother, then Mzi: *Christmas, which hardly ever comes for us, has arrived ahead of schedule. Head on over to your favourite store and have a respite from a life of perpetual lack.* Mzi ran to the mall with his brothers and cousin instead.

The streets were littered with rocks, bricks, and debris; black-patched with burnt tyres; white-streaked from the pavement where concrete curb-ends and curb-ramps were uprooted and left lying across the breadth of the road. Intersections were blocked with tyres aflame. In winter, power often goes out and never comes back for weeks on end. And people riot. Zé wondered whether this was one of those times. He had no way of being sure, having shut himself in his room for days trying to sort through ten years' worth of pages, figuring out which corner to hide all those failed attempts in, all those many revisions he had done throughout the years. He wanted only the current iteration of his script to remain so his room could look presentable when he finally invites a lover over. The only time the outside world existed was when he paused his tidying up to text Mzi, and even then, the only topic discussed was their bodies, not an imprisoned ex-president.

Now, standing at the mall entrance, Zé felt the full weight of what he had ignored. Before him, a crowd restless and impatient like water knocking on a dam wall after a deluge; a handful of cops, hesitant and helpless; and a news broadcast crew, motionless like a stalking predator. As he was texting Mzi and asking him what was happening, the wall broke and the river galloped forth, unruly and vengeful, flinging back rocks for each rubber bullet. He watched the cameraman try to keep pace with his anchor as she ran towards the cops caught in a loop of advance and retreat.

When Mzi replied and said he was by the mattress store, Zé dove into the river and let it carry him through. It swallowed him, rendering him indistinguishable from its raging current. Inside the mall, the river branched in multiple directions, blasting through shatterproof glass, upending roller doors, and toppling mannequins. When he couldn't find Mzi at the mattress store, the river whisked him to the pharmacy. Curving past metal shelves set askew and a floor slick with spilt cosmetics, he ran to the dispensary at the back of the store. There, the floor was littered with capsules and button pills, and nothing remained but a few scattered pill bottles. Among them were four bottles of 54mg Concerta that he desperately needed. He grabbed it just as the cops stormed into the mall and the current reversed, skipping over sprawled bodies and carrying off its prized loot: clothes, food, furniture, appliances, and electronics.

Having evaded the now sizeable police contingent and out of breath, he tried to ring Mzi a few times, but his calls went unanswered. On his way home, he tried again, and it went straight to voicemail.

In the following days, as the rest of the country burned, and his texts undelivered, Zé assumed Mzi had gone ghost. Their regular conversations had widened the tunnels inside his heart and moulded them into Mzi's silhouette, but now, the abrupt silence had left caverns no one else could fit through. How long before they shrank back to their original shape and size? Resigned to the fact that his frustrations wouldn't be allayed, Zé took out his phone, jerked off to a photo of Mzi's midriff, then sat in front of his laptop and started typing away. The Red-men of Red-town remained fully clothed on the page.

S U S I E   O H

Folklore-2

Mixed Media and Digital
10x10 inches, 2024
(Next Page)

According to the local lore of rural Korea, every lake, glade, and grove is a grave. The women in white who haunt each site aren't just the ghastly threats in cautionary tales that keep children hurrying home before dark; they are the embodiments of our collective grief and guilt.

Homework: Lessons in Forgetting

1. Fill in the blank

Choose the correct word to complete the sentence.

<table>
<tr><td>secret</td><td>gaze</td><td>shadow</td><td>pillow</td></tr>
<tr><td>void</td><td>robin's egg</td><td>mouth</td><td>tea kettle</td></tr>
</table>

1. You'll never attract a man if you keep your ______________ closed.

2. It is much more dangerous to be a ______________.

3. You can tell if a woman is a witch by looking at her ______________.

4. Men will only hit (on) a woman if they see a ______________.

5. The secret of success lies in your ______________.

6. No Godly woman would ever allow her ______________ to be sullied by a ______________.

7. A woman must learn to control her ______________.

2. Sort

Things you forgot	Things you never knew	Things you will never forget

- The names of the made-for-TV movies you watched in the middle of the night during your years long bout of childhood insomnia.

- The scene from one of those movies where the panic of avalanche victims caused the death of their rescuers.

- The combination to your first high school locker.

- The lyrics to Audio Adrenaline's album Underdog that got stuck for eight months in the CD player of your first car.

- The color of your first car—a Crown Vic that people sometimes mistook for an undercover cop car.

- The number of times your mother found you asleep in the beanbag in your walk-in closet so that you could read late at night without anyone knowing.

- The feel of cold metal pressed against your lips as you blew into your flute to warm up your instrument.

- The first seven measures of "O Come all Ye Faithful"—the duet you played with your friend's father, a cop, for the Christmas service and rehearsed alone together in the sanctuary for two months.

- How your posture shifted when your friend's father put his hands on your pelvis and lower back to teach you how to breathe and coax out a stronger sound.

- The reason why you never agreed to spend the night at your friend's house.

- The taste of red fruit punch from a Styrofoam cup.

- The look on your high school history teacher's face when he found out that your boyfriend from church was older than him.

- The number of men over the age of twenty from your church who asked your father to date you while you were still a teenager.

- The pattern the frosted windows painted in light on the carpet of the sanctuary floor.

- Whether you spent more time in your bed at night or in various other locations in your house from the ages of ten to 16

3. Arrange

Put the clauses below in the correct order.

1. Through your strong discipline, remind them of your infinite mercy and grace.
2. In your name we pray
3. We bring before you those possessed by this sinful earth.
4. We seek your wisdom Father.
5. Amen
6. Convict the hearts of your wayward sons and daughters so that they return to the path of righteousness.
7. Dear Heavenly Father
8. Remind all of us of the joy that comes from submitting to you completely.
9. God, we know you are in control and you will not give us more than we can handle.
10. Strengthen our will and protect us from the temptations we are assailed with every day.

4. Match

Draw a line between the word on the left that corresponds with the word on the right. The first one has been done for you.

Masturbation   Sin

Joy[1]   Sin

Wanting[2]   Sin

Sex[3]   Sin

Self-esteem[4]   Sin

Anger[5]   Sin

Pleasure[6]   Sin

Thoughts[7]   Sin

---

[1] In anything other than worshiping and celebrating the glory of God.
[2] God has provided you with everything you need.
[3] Except in a godly marriage.
[4] Or the belief that you, as a fallen human could accomplish anything good without God working through you.
[5] At your parents, at your church, at anyone that God has placed in authority over you. And, of course, God.
[6] In the sun on your skin, the taste of chocolate melting on your tongue.
[7] "Everyone who hates his brother is a murderer;" (1 John 3:15) and "...everyone who looks at a woman with lust for her has already committed adultery with her in his heart." (Matt. 5:28)

the summer of the cicadas

it was the summer of the cicadas, which meant bodies
everywhere – molted to the barn doors, petals,
windowpanes, spat and stuck like outgrown bubblegum
to the sidewalk. each cloud was an avalanche of antennae,
thoraxes against thoraxes. each song on the radio:
the whirring of wings.
       i drank a beer downtown
and plucked little legs from its foam. stuck in my teeth.
a bitch, aren't they? said a girl three stools down,
and i said *i guess so*, 'cause they were, and i don't disagree
with pretty girls in sundresses. she bought me another.
outside,
   abdomens eclipsed the windows. shuttered the sun.
when we walked to her car they crunched beneath us
like carpet-pretzels, like split spilt chips. her bed smelled
of sap and summer sweat and lavender.
         thank god i found
you, i said, and sundress wilted to floor. her skin unzipped
and her face peeled off like a hood. she kissed like they do
in movies, blossoming bugs through my throat.
        these days,
i cough black bile and crave twigs, twin wings sprouting
from my shoulder blades. each night i sit in the garden
and listen to them sing, and i wake in the dirt to that
strange, cicada sun.

Chicago Winter 1994

My first real winter, niña fresh out of México. Face pressed against the window; I feel the cool air against the glass. Our apartment sits on the third floor, hidden from the street view as it faces the parking lot. The building itself is squeezed between two other buildings, a staple of our neighborhood. The alley is dark, but I keep my eyes peeled for headlights. My Uncle Tony still isn't home from work. I get as excited about him arriving home, as I used to whenever I heard the phone ring, thinking it was my dad. It never was, though. At least Uncle Tony is here, and that's why I wait in front of the window. I wait for my uncle who takes care of his two sisters, mom, and me, his niece. A contradiction to my dad.

Inside our one-bedroom apartment that fits six of us, my mom has the television on in the living room that doubles as our bedroom. She's in the kitchen with her sister, my Aunt Luisa, and grandma, making something that smells like cinnamon.

"July," my mom calls me, pronouncing my name the Spanish way, Yu-lee, instead of like the month. "Vas a querer comer?"

"Later."

"Later?" she repeats. "Later, later, later." Soy mula, and my mom doesn't appreciate it.

"Ya ni se lo que voy a hacer. Esa niña ya no quiere hablar español," my mom says to my grandma and aunt. I turn away from the window to try and overhear.

"Pues, no la dejes que se le olvide como hablar español," my grandma says, and I roll my eyes.

"Eso es difícil," my mom says.

"Que no se le olvide de donde viene," my grandma responds.

"Dile que *aquí* se habla español," my aunt adds.

I wonder if American families talk about their kids close enough for them to hear or if it's just part of our culture. "No se me va a olvidar el español," I mumble. I turn back to the window. "Look at the snow," I say to myself and grin at the double o sound in *look*. "Wow, guau, wow, guau," I say switching between both porque soy mula. My mom doesn't understand that I like hearing myself speak in English, hearing the roughness of the sounds.

The window fogs up from my breath. I draw a smiley face on the glass. A bright light shines through the alleyway. Headlights! Soon a car slides into the parking lot below. It's a green 1993 Mustang, my uncle's car! I smile with my mouth open and squeal softly. I trace my index finger along the window mapping out the car's trail to its parking spot. As my uncle adjusts the car to get into the spot, I place my hand out to guide it as if it were a Hot Wheels car in my snowy town's miniature parking lot. He's parked, but the engine is still running. I take a step back and put my arms in front of me as if there is a steering wheel in front of me. I grip the steering wheel and move it side to side. "Vroom, vroom," I whisper and make a sharp turn before recovering control of my Mustang again and then I hit the brakes hard. I'm spinning! I'm spinning! My Mustang comes to a stop and the soft purring of its engine fills my ears. I smile a toothy grin only brought back to reality by the sound of the car's door closing below. I peek out the window again.

My uncle walks up to the building. I wave from the window, but he doesn't see me.

"Ya están listos los buñuelos. ¿Que vas a tomar?"

"Milk, please," I say.

"July, a mí me hablas en español," she scolds.

I roll my eyes and respond with, "Leche."

I run to our apartment's door and push my ear against it. My uncle's footsteps have an even rhythm to them as he climbs the stairs. He's barely at the first floor where Doña Rebecca, our landlady and my grandma's chisme compañera, lives. There's a soft break indicating he's made it to the second floor where Marilu and her cat, Michi, live. Imagine, Michi the michi. My uncle's footsteps continue up the stairs and soon he will be on the third floor right outside our apartment door. I've been waiting all afternoon for him, but I run off to the kitchen just as his keys jingle.

I grab a buñuelo from the kitchen table and climb onto a seat across from my mom and aunt.

"Parece que ya llego Toño," my grandma says. She stands over the stove and turns it on as my uncle opens the apartment door. I take a bite of my buñuelo because I'm too cool to have been waiting for him. My aunt stands up to wash the dishes while my mom helps my grandma. When my uncle returns to the kitchen, he sits across from me, and I give him my big toothy grin.

The adults talk about adult things like "Como están cosas en el trabajo?" and "tendremos que hablar con el abogado" while I sit quietly and eat my buñuelo. Snow flurries peek in through the small kitchen window.

Soon, my mom ushers me to bed. Bits of sugar and cinnamon still linger around my lips. I lied to her about brushing my teeth porque soy mula, don't forget it.

The next day, I wake up at six o'clock in the morning to a loud gurgling noise outside. I run to the window and see the Mustang choking with snow. My mom and uncle are pushing the back of the car, while my aunt attempts to steer. My grandma and I both watch for a bit before she tells me to get changed. We bundle up and go outside.

I leave my grandma's side and run over to the Mustang. Standing in between my mom and uncle, I begin to push. I'm the missing piece to help my uncle get to work. The Mustang roars and spits snow while my grandma talks to Doña Rebecca. I overhear snippets of their conversation. The snow "es mucho mas que el año pasado." My uncle needs a new car because "ese carro no es para la nieve." I wrinkle my nose at the thought. No, no, the Mustang is perfect, I whisper to myself. "Encontraron a un muerto el otro dia." A dead man? I'm sweating, but I think it's from pushing the car. I ignore the Mustang and glance up at the women who say "que lastima" porque el era "el hijo de alguien" and I wonder if my uncle is safe coming home late in the evening.

A few weeks later my uncle still drives a Mustang that slips and slide in the snow, Doña Rebecca will fall on the ice in the parking lot after picking me up from school, and I will laugh porque soy mula, una niña mula, sin saber el futuro.

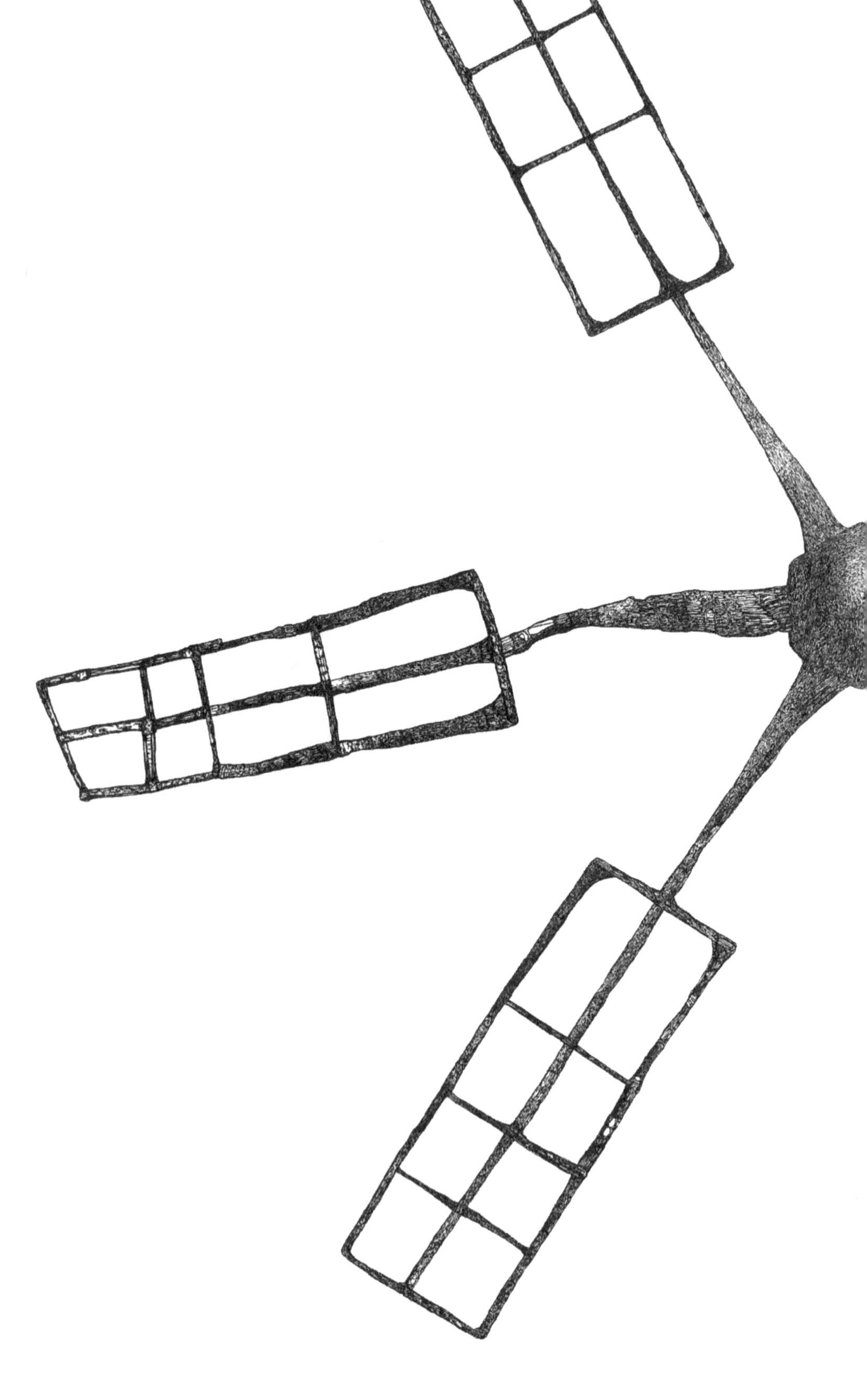

windcatcher

Ink on paper
9x12 inches, 2024

I wanted to do a windmill that had cyberpunk free-form assembly feel, like it was created from found materials, but also something that looked natural and was a net good for the earth.

Wedding Night

I)
I watch in the mirror of my new bedroom
his hands unclasping the safety pins
from the back of my sari jacket. At my feet,
the pins collect

          one by one, their pointed ends
glistening with metallic foreshadow. I imagine
only misstep—the prick, the bead of red,
the small

        and forever stain. When the last pin
falls and the pallu unravels, revealing
my stomach and its sun-concealed tenderness,
I am pulled

        through the mirror into the backyard
of my father's house, where under the nelli tree
I had watched one evening a Ceylon paradise
-flycatcher

        dive into a puddle of rainwater.
Under the spread saffron-wings, its stomach
white like an impenetrable gauze. In the water,
the reflection

        of its tail feathers, a pleated pallu
and I, untailed bird in a strange palm.

II)
I wait for the certainty of his snoring,
then, gathering the safety pins from the floor,
I re-pleat in the dark the sari borrowed
from my mother. Moving

         in circles, I drape
myself in its folds. Beside him in his bed again,

I retreat into myself, my pallu, a womb wall
covering
            my face. The sound of his breath fills
my chest with the thunder of then. In my father's
house as a girl, forehead pressed against window
glass cobwebbed
                    with rain, tasting the rust
of iron rails spiraling into empty space, the search
for the splendor of the gone bird. How, after
parting
            the waters, it had risen flame-feathered
to shake the wetness off in beads and then,
disappeared. How my body, drenched
with its flight,
                    tightened like a millipede
curling at the touch of a flycatcher's beak.

The Birth, Kentucky, 2005

Hands far into my entrance, he
pulls on my insides

                      as though
                      I'm a fish's mouth

inside of which he's lost
a good hook. I wince on the table.
Wordless as a worm. I want
a capacity I don't have. Belly up,
I am skimmed

                      from the surface.

There was blood on his hands,
on the floor,

                      until I tremored,
I winced from the inside out.

There was a full, wet child
outside of me, moving
as it did inside. Still,
I left blood where I moved. The days
were growing longer, but still
short; still the blizzard moved
outside the window and left itself
piled up on the sill.

The lakes had frozen. The piss
collected under the seal of the cleanest of toilets.
A body may heal, though it may change
in its healing. There were things I had made
within me that moved. Uncontrollable and desperate.

The doctor called me back to him,
considered me like a caught fish held out by the mouth.

You need to stop having children. He laughs.
You have had enough. He tells me
what I am allowed to do. I am a dumb girl
from a dumb girl from a dumb girl.
I will always remember his name.

He will forget mine as soon as the meeting is over.
I'm the blemish that would take down the whole lake.

CONTRIBUTORS

Trinity Catlin (they/she) is a queer writer and poet from Los Angeles, California. Their poems have been featured in *Bicoastal Review, Beyond Words Magazine,* and *Sunstroke Magazine,* among other places. Their chapbook of poems, *Bone Hunting,* was published by Cathexis Northwest Press in 2024. They are currently an MA candidate at Loyola Marymount University and residing in Venice, CA with their cats, Skitty and Ruthy.

Maya Cheav is a Cambodian-American writer and artist from Southern California, as well as the author of the poetry chapbook, *LYKAIA* (Bottlecap Press, 2023). Her poems and flash fiction have been featured in *Stone of Madness, ALOCASIA, Scapegoat Review, The Weaver, Across the Margin,* and elsewhere. Her work has received a Best Small Fictions Nomination. She was a top 10 finalist for the 2023 *Palette Poetry* Chapbook Prize, guest judged by Danez Smith, as well as a 2024 Tin House Workshop alum, under the faculty mentorship of Roy G. Guzmán. She is currently a 2024-2025 poet in residence with Collections of Transience. Read more at mayacheavwriter.myportfolio.com

Ava Chen is a writer and editor from Massachusetts. Her work has appeared in or is forthcoming with *The Rumpus, Salt Hill, Gigantic Sequins,* and elsewhere. She hopes you have a wonderful day.

Angelica Julia Dávila is author of poetry chapbook, *Bilingual Bitch* (Abode Press 2025). She is a multidisciplinary artist that focused on writing, comedy, and performance. She received her PhD from the Program for Writers at University of Illinois Chicago. Her literary work has been published in a variety of magazines, and she was an invited poet for 2024's Poesía en Abril (International Festival of Spanish Poetry in Chicago). She was also a featured poet in "Pop-up Gallery Readings with Contratiempo" as part of ECOS: A Chicago Latine Poetry Festival by the Poetry Foundation. Her work is an exploration of the Latinx and bilingual identity, autistic self-expression, and mental borderlands.

Ridwan Fasasi: Swan I, is a Nigerian poet of Yoruba descent. He is the winner of the 2024 Labari Prize for Poetry. A Pushcart Prize Nominee whose works have appeared/ are forthcoming on *ANMLY Lit*, *Akpata Magazine*, *Euonia Review*, *Lucent Dreaming*, *Strange Horizon*, *Hindsight creative* and elsewhere. He tweets @Ibn_Yushau44.

Bad futa is a self-taught lgbtq artist residing in the United States. She has been published in *Blood Orange Review*, *Grim & Gilded*, *Paper Dragon*, *Tint Journal*, *Red Noise Collective*, *Quible.Lit*, *Months to Years*, *Assignment Literary Magazine*, *God's Cruel Joke*, *Vermillion*, and *Flyway Journal*. https://@badfuta.bsky.social, https://www.instagram.com/badfuta_artlabs

Alexander Gast, 21, lives and writes in Chapel Hill and attends UNC as the 2022 Thomas Wolfe Scholar. More of his work can be found in *Shooter Literary Magazine*, *Ghost City Review*, and *Oyster River Pages*.

Ranudi Gunawardena is a Sri Lankan poet whose work explores the wombscape, childhood in rural landscapes, and the uncanny in nature, among others. Her work has appeared in literary magazines such as *Action*, *Spectacle*, *Equatorial*, *Magma*, *Samfiftyfour*, and *Shō*. She studies at Williams College.

Patricia Joynes is a nature photographer whose photos are on book covers, in annual Blue Ridge Parkway calendars, a National Geographic online story, and in literary journals including two covers for *County Lines* (2015-2024), *Evening Paper* (cover) *Camas*, *THE SUN* (March 2021 cover), *Oracle Fine Arts Review*, *Sunlight Press*, *DASH*, *RiverSedge*, *San Pedro River Review*, *Blue Mesa Review*, *Proud to Be: Writing by American Warriors*, *Brushfire*, *Talking Writing*, *Leaping Clear*, and *Woods Reader* (cover). Visit her photography blog at https://patriciajoynes.wordpress.com/about.

Katie Kemple's poems are published in or forthcoming from *Beloit Poetry Journal*, *Ploughshares*, and *The South Carolina Review*. More of her work can be found at katiekemplepoetry.com. *Big Man* is her debut collection.

Mai Mageed is a writer from Texas. She holds an MFA in Creative Writing from Cornell University, where she worked as an editor for *EPOCH Magazine*. As a writer, she is inspired by Wikipedia deep dives, public fights, and '80s Europop music.

Madelaine Hunter Millar was born and raised in Missoula, Montana, and spent five years in Boston, Massachusetts studying journalism. She rediscovered her love of visual art during the pandemic and began to identify her unique voice when an overlapping bad breakup, mental health diagnosis, unexpected move, major job change, and serious surgical procedure made for a deeply strange 2022. She is now a digital nomad, painter, and freelance writer. Her work can be found at soupin-thewoods.com or at @soup.in.the.woods.art on Instagram.

Andi Myles (she/her) is a Washington DC area science writer by day, poet in the in between times. Her favorite space is the fine line between essay and poetry. She is the author of the chapbook *Fractured Symphony* (Cathexis Northwest Press) and her work has appeared in *Fourth Genre, Rattle,* and *Tahoma Literary Review,* among others. You can find her at www.andimyles.com.

Nzeru Aquilar Nsaí (she/he/they) lives in Johannesburg. *No Poison No Paradise,* their novel manuscript, was longlisted for the 2022/23 The Island Prize.

Susie Oh is a Korean-born, Brooklyn-based artist, illustrator, and author of picture books. She studied illustration at Pratt Institute, and her debut picture book, *Soomi's Sweater,* was a silver medal winner of the 2020 Key Colors Illustrators Competition. She wrote and illustrated *Odd Duck Out* and *A Book for Pio* and is represented by Astound Illustration Agency.

Mary Tina Shamli Pillay is an abstract artist and writer based in India. Her art, poems, and fiction have featured on BBC Radio, *Kitaab, The Mean Journal, Blink-Ink, Borderless Journal, The Chakkar, Madras Courier, The Pine Cone Review, The Literary Times Magazine, The Punch Magazine, Shooter Magazine, Artist Talk magazine, The Penn Review, Inscape Journal,* and A*nother Chicago Magazine* among others. Her art has been showcased in exhibitions, and collected in many parts of the world. She is passionate about painting, writing, cats and food. Find her on Instagram @marytinashamlipillay and www.tinapillay.com

Caroline Plasket's work has been published or is forthcoming in *Gulf*

Coast, Lunch Ticket, Pithead Chapel, Sycamore Review, Pleiades, Copper Nickel, Threadcount Magazine, and elsewhere. She was previously a mentee in the AWP Writer to Writer Program.

Hunter Prichard is a writer of prose and drama from Portland, Maine.

January Santoso (she/her) is a writer & sex worker from Fresno, CA. She is currently pursuing an MFA in Poetry at the University of Maryland. Her work has been featured or is forthcoming in *The Champagne Room, SHIFT & Pine Hills Review*. She also reads prose submissions for *The Paris Review* & poetry for *The Adroit Journal*. You can e-stalk her most places @januarysantoso.

Chestnut Review

EDITOR-IN-CHIEF
James Rawlings

MANAGING EDITOR
Maria S. Picone

POETRY EDITOR
B. Luke Wilson

PROSE EDITOR
Brooke Randel

ASSOC. POETRY EDITORS
Michael Imossan, Mohammed U. Yusuf

ASSOC. PROSE EDITORS
Praise Osawaru, Annie Schoonover

EDITORIAL ASSISTANT
Courtney Heidorn

COMMUNICATIONS
Semilore Kilaso,
Roseline Mgbodichinma,
Samira Shakib-Bregeth

ART/LAYOUT EDITOR
Teresa Snow

WEBSITE EDITORS
Kieran Galloway, Julia Walton

POETRY READERS

Adamu Yahuza Abdulahi, Arowolo Abdulroqeeb, Samuel Adeyemi, Addhaya Anil, Alexis Barton, Paul Bluestein, Zaynab Iliyasu Bobi, Shitta Faruq, Reina Garcia, Prosper Ifeanyi, Ayesha Jamal, Nwenna Kai, Autumn Koors-Foltz S.G. Mallett, Corey Martin, Emma McCoy, Trevor Moffa, Saty Mukherjee, Brian O'Sullivan, Maddison Sellers, Cosima Smith, Saheed Sunday, Jong Won

PROSE READERS

Shedrack Akanbi, Ellis Breunig, Keeley Burmeister, Erin Challenor, Carlos Contreras, Subhravanu Das, Ejiro Edward, Bronwyn Galloway, Jacob Ginsberg, Kyle Givens, Lana Hall, D.E. Hardy, Noon Herd, Steven Hopkins, Dynamic Rahma Jimoh, Charlotte Kidd, Emmie Kline, Rick Krizman, Rebecca Nakaba, Kortney Nash, Andrew Nickerson, Nicholas Leon, Saty Mukherjee, Rachel Murray, Lee Paehler, Michelle Panik, Shella Parcarey, Max Pasakorn, Hemmy So, Sharon Thomas, Colby Vargas, Julia Walton, Joel Worford, Xueyi Zhou

INTERNS

Michelle Mangione, Andrew Pilet, Natalie Whitehair, Claire Zhou

www.ingramcontent.com/pod-product-compliance
Lightning Source LLC
Chambersburg PA
CBHW071349300726
48976CB00006B/1817